Internet Law

Internet Law

A Concise Guide to Regulation Around the World

Edward J. Swan

Wolters Kluwer

Published by:
Kluwer Law International B.V.
PO Box 316
2400 AH Alphen aan den Rijn
The Netherlands
E-mail: international-sales@wolterskluwer.com
Website: www.wolterskluwer.com/en/solutions/kluwerlawinternational

Sold and distributed by:
Wolters Kluwer Legal & Regulatory U.S.
7201 McKinney Circle
Frederick, MD 21704
United States of America
E-mail: customer.service@wolterskluwer.com

ISBN 978-94-035-4294-2

e-Book: ISBN 978-94-035-4295-9
web-PDF: ISBN 978-94-035-4300-0

This book is dedicated to my daughters, Molly and Mary.

About the Author

Dr. Swan has been one of the world's leading lawyers advising major international financial businesses, international organizations, national governments, banks, exchanges, clearinghouses, markets, and tech companies.

He was Partner and Consultant in major international law firms, including Skadden Arps, Brown Rudnick, Cameron McKenna and Simmons and Simmons.

Professor Swan has been Visiting Professor of Law at University College London and the Catholic University in Lille and Paris, France, and the IESEG School of Management in Lille and Paris. He has been Member of the Board of the Institute of Advanced Legal Studies at the University of London.

Dr. Swan has published many law books and dozens of articles, including law books for Oxford University Press and Kluwer Law International.

Dr. Swan attended Rocky Mountain College and Harvard University and has a Juris Doctor degree from New York University and a PhD in Law from the University of London.

Table of Contents

Preface

The "Internet" is an international network of interconnected computers. It developed from what began in 1969 as a military program called "ARPANET," which was designed to enable computers operated by military defense contractors and universities involved in defense-related research to communicate by redundant channels even if some portions of the network were damaged by war or other causes. ARPANET no longer exists, but it provided a model for the development of civilian networks that now enable millions of people to communicate and access huge amounts of information around the world. The Internet is a unique, new medium of worldwide human communication.[1]

The regulation of the Internet throughout the world consists of a complex and frequently changing collection of international agreements, national legislation, local laws, and regulations. The purpose of this book is to provide the reader with an overview of the development and scope of regulation of the Internet around the world.

However, the material provided in this book is not legal advice. The Internet and its regulation are changing too rapidly to be able to comprehend all the details of how one must behave responsibly and legally when using the Internet. To obtain an understanding of that or legal advice about specific issues relating to the Internet, it is necessary to consult local legal and technical experts familiar with the laws and regulations of the relevant jurisdictions.

This is an unusual book. I have written other law books, but this one presented an entirely new situation. With most law books, the law that is being described is already largely in place and has been for some time. A difficulty here is that the Internet is so new that the creators of Internet law are only beginning to establish rules and regulations for its permitted operation. A major problem for regulators is that the Internet is rapidly evolving, and changing, both technically and in usage, literally every day. As a result, Internet law, and its application, demands constant reexamination. As

1. Justice Stevens, giving the Opinion of the Court in, *Janet Reno, Attorney General of the United States, et al., Appellants v. American Civil Liberties Union, et al.*, 521 U.S. 844 (1997).

a few examples of the issues developing as these pages are being written in the autumn of 2021 are:

- Quantum computing development, by Google, IBM and others, promises exponentially more powerful computers that will analyze data and provide solutions in seconds that would take computers currently in use a week, months or years.[2] The implications of this for privacy and security are huge.
- The founder of the world's most powerful online social media group, Mark Zuckerberg, was accused, by a former employee, testifying before a United States (US) Senate committee, of allowing Facebook's platforms to "harm children, stoke division, and weaken our democracy" for the sake of profit. This is bound to intensify increasing demand for expanded social media regulation.[3]
- Dangerous and expensive hacking and ransomware attacks, where hackers break into computer systems, encrypt their data, and demand payment for unencrypting the data, increased by 92% in the first half of 2021.[4]

These are just a few of the problems the Internet regulators are being asked to deal with and solve now and in the future.

Another difficult characteristic of the Internet is that its use is a rapidly expanding worldwide phenomenon. It is not restricted to any particular jurisdiction or region. Users of the Internet can reach out electronically to billions of people across the globe. Response to this in the world's countries has been uneven. Some jurisdictions have already established laws and regulations to control the use and operation of the Internet and related electronic devices. Others have only begun to decide how they wish to deal with the Internet, and some jurisdictions have made little progress in dealing with the complexities and problems created by the World Wide Web.

Consequently, unlike other books I have written on international law, the law of the Internet has been evolving as the book was being written. I was required to continuously adapt and modify the text of this book while writing it. More devices are being created to use or communicate with the Internet. Each of these raises new issues about communication and regulation.

The necessity for legal modification and change has become particularly acute with the rapid and dangerous growth of online crime and online attacks, some of which may be sponsored by the governments of countries. These issues make up the new and particularly worrying areas of "cybercrime" and "cyberwar." These things are increasing.

As time goes on, the purpose of most cybercrime seems to be to extract money or "ransom" from individuals, organizations and even nations that are connected to the

2. "What Is Quantum Computing," *IBM*, online, https://www.ibm.com/quantum-computing/, accessed October 7, 2021.
3. Ryan Mac and Cecilia Kang, "Whistle-Blower Says, 'Facebook Chooses Profits over Safety'," *The New York Times*, online, October 3, 2021.
4. Sebastian Klovig Skelton, "Ransomware Attacks Increase Dramatically During 2021," *Computer-Weekly.com*, online, August 3, 2021, accessed October 7, 2021.

Internet and use it as an important part of their daily activities or businesses. A number of these criminal groups, known as hacking groups, may be private organizations acting for their own account, but others are allegedly sponsored by nation-states. These latter groups are used to prosecute attacks on the assets of other nations that can be characterized as "cyber warfare." One of their purposes may be to extract large payments, but another purpose can be to bring about disruption to important infrastructure that relies for its operation on the Internet, and another could be to steal information that will allow the attacker to know best how to injure those that it considers opponents.

These worrying developments have caused those responsible for creating laws and regulations to continually make efforts to prevent these from damaging things important to their ways of life.

This legal evolution is occurring throughout the world and will continue to do so for the foreseeable future. No country or region will be immune from the effects of the Internet and the vulnerabilities it may create. Regulatory steps to protect those connected to the Internet must change and grow continuously for the foreseeable future.

In this volume, I have tried to cover the key issues that affect the Internet, its use and regulation throughout the world. Most of the text is devoted to some of the world's most important market areas, and to those areas where efforts have been made to provide the most detailed and comprehensive regulation of the Internet. However, attention has been paid to developing areas as well.

It is my intention that this book provides the readers with a concise overview of how the law and regulation of the Internet has evolved and where it is heading. Although, as stated above, this book does not provide legal advice about the laws and regulations of any particular jurisdiction, its intention is to help the readers increase their understanding of the framework that is developing to regulate the Internet around the world and to provide some understanding of where that framework is heading.

Professor Edward (Ned) Swan
BA, JD, PhD
Catholic University (Lille and Paris)
IESEG School of Management (Lille and Paris)
Attorney admitted to New York, and US federal courts
nedswan@gmail.com

Acknowledgments

I thank all the friends, colleagues, clients, opponents, judges and acquaintances, who, over many years, taught me how to be a thoughtful and effective analyst and problem solver.

I must also thank my dear friend Vanna Fadda. Without her support and meticulous editing, my books would not have been possible.

CHAPTER 1

The Internet

A PRELIMINARY AND CAUTION

It should be noted that the regulation of the Internet throughout the world consists of a complex and rapidly changing collection of international agreements, national legislation, local laws, regulations, and commercial customs. The purpose of this book is to provide the reader with an overview of the development of the regulation of the Internet.

However, the reader must understand that the material provided below is not legal advice. The Internet and its regulation are changing too rapidly to be able to comprehend all the details of how one must behave responsibly and legally when using the Internet. To obtain a detailed understanding of that, or legal advice about specific issues relating to the Internet, it will be necessary to consult local legal and technical experts, familiar with the laws and regulations of the relevant jurisdictions.

Internet law consists of the law, regulations, policy, agreements, and customs that regulate and govern all types of Internet use.

However, the Internet has become a part of so many activities, both commercial and private, that it is not possible to consider Internet law as consisting of one well-defined area of law. It includes significant parts of intellectual property law, data protection law, competition law, privacy law, criminal law, contract law, and other areas of law.

For example, the United Nations (UN) has tried to extend internationally recognized human rights onto the Internet. In June 2012, it proposed a resolution on human rights on the Internet.

Another transformative aspect of the Internet is that it has fundamentally changed business forever. Until the arrival of the Internet, and its subsequent dramatic growth, physical and face-to-face business was much more important. Commerce, to a large extent, relied on attracting people to specific physical locations (such as stores, shops, showrooms, warehouses, and offices) for the execution of many transactions.

The Internet has changed that dramatically. The locations of customers, merchants, business contacts and colleagues have become much less important. Indeed, they have become irrelevant for many transactions relating to the acquisition of goods, food, clothing, tools, and the transaction of business, etc. In many cases these can be completed online.

And increasingly, this is not true only for sales of small, personal items with the growth in sophistication and size of 3-D printers. We are rapidly approaching situations where major purchases, such as cars, trucks, ships, houses, and buildings, can be designed far from the site of delivery, and computerized instructions for the printing of their components, or perhaps for the "printing" of the entire object, can be sent over the Internet to a distant 3-D printer for printing and, perhaps assembly, by robotic assemblers. These developments are rapidly moving from conception to reality, and it is impossible to foresee how extensive the changes to our lives and our persons triggered by the development of the Internet will be. However, there is little doubt that our lives are being and will continue to be utterly transformed by the Internet.

Certainly, those parts of our lives that involve shopping, communication, social interaction, work, and information gathering have already been completely changed by the appearance in growth of major tech companies such as Amazon, Facebook, Google, Apple and Microsoft, to name just the biggest and best known, but these changes are just the tip of the iceberg.

Of the ten most valuable companies in the world, eight are Internet-dependent computer tech companies. Interestingly enough, and unlike the huge international companies of the past (Exxon, General Motors, etc.), the value of many of the world's most valuable companies is not based on the ownership of physical assets, but on their methods of interacting with the Internet. Their most valuable asset is their skill in managing electronic information. And consequently, the ability to scale their businesses is theoretically infinite. Even if Facebook, Google, Amazon, etc., reached the stage of having recruited every person on earth as an active customer, they always have the option of offering them more and different services over the Internet. In other words, there is really no limit to the possible take-up of the services offered by the Internet tech giants. To expand into new areas, it is not necessarily required that they acquire additional physical assets, such as factories and transportation vehicles. They just need to add to their electronic configurations:

> You can't lay a finger on the primary assets of Facebook and Google—it's all information fizzing at the speed of light through electrons, which, in summary interpretations of physics, don't really exist anyway. We live in the new capitalism's floating world ... .[5]

A name that is given to this new type of economy by some commentators is the "exponential economy." One commentator, Azeem Azhar, writes that these exponential tech companies:

5. Bryan Appleyard, "Exponential by Azeem Azhar Review: Can We Stop the Tech Giants?," *The Sunday Times*, online, August 29, 2021.

> Know that if they stopped growing, they would soon cascade into irrelevance ... .[6]

More recently, the importance of the Internet has changed from something affecting private individuals, commercial institutions, and educational institutions to something of critical importance to nations for communications, surveillance, defense and even, war.

All these developments are startling, amazing, and in many cases unforeseen. But there is absolutely no doubt that the changes triggered by the Internet will continue to become more complex, and take place at increasing speed.

The next computer revolution, the move to "quantum computing," will increase the speed at which computers perform their functions by factors it is difficult to imagine. For example, a calculation that it is estimated would take the fastest of today's supercomputers about 10,000 years to complete was completed by Google's experimental Sycamore quantum computing operating system in 200 seconds in October 2020. Now China claims a machine a million times more powerful than other quantum systems. It is impossible to say when quantum computers will become generally available, but it is also impossible to know the limits of how transformative their power will be on computing, the Internet and life.

The study of Internet law requires understanding the Internet, understanding how the Internet is used, and understanding how the Internet is governed.

Internet-related government policies cover wide areas of trade, govern website creation, regulate Internet service providers (ISPs), determine protection of copyrights, trademarks and other intellectual property, and prescribe methods of conflict resolution. All these and more affect Internet usage.

The Internet is global and complex. It is not covered by one country, one jurisdiction or one set of laws and regulations. The Internet itself is constantly evolving and changing. It is constantly expanding its reach in relation to different aspects of life. Consequently, Internet law must be flexible enough to accommodate this endless change.

The Italian physicist, Carlo Rovelli, tells us that the only certain thing in the universe is change. In that sense, the Internet reflects life better than many other human creations. Governing it requires adjustment to new problems either constantly arising or having the potential to arise.

The British novelist L.P. Hartley wrote: "The past is another country. They do things differently there."

Because of its global and intellectual scope and its constantly changing nature, the same may be said of the Internet. Therefore, Internet lawyers must attune themselves to thinking and acting flexibly and creatively. The Internet is a world of its own, independent of any country.

---

6. *Id.*

CHAPTER 2
Internet Regulation

A WHAT IS INTERNET REGULATION?

Because of its worldwide expansion and growing international usage, it is appropriate to begin a discussion of Internet law with some of the basic developments affecting across the globe.

A question to begin with is, "What does Internet regulation mean?" The Internet is regulated in several ways by several factors.

Structure

The Internet is first regulated by its structure. That is, what is found on the Internet is that which the state of technology makes possible and efficient.

Commerce

One step beyond that, the Internet is regulated by the commercial market in which it operates. At its most basic, things that users buy and use shape the market. Things that users reject disappear and have little or no impact.

Custom

In addition, the Internet is regulated by customs: those things that users reasonably expect and believe as determined by past practice and experience.

Policy

Next, the Internet is regulated by government policies. These are political philosophies and positions that determine how governments respond to activities relating to the Internet.

Laws and Regulations

On a more formal level, governments also regulate the Internet by legislated laws and regulations. These are statements and declarations that reflect what a nation believes should be available via the Internet, what should not be available, how transactions should be conducted, how disputes are resolved and how violations of laws and regulations should be treated. In many cases, these help users understand what they may do through the Internet. However, government regulations sometimes take the form of repressive censorship or restriction such as alleged to be a practice in countries such as China, Iran, Russia, Saudi Arabia and some others.

Treaties and Conventions

Beyond national government regulation, behavior on the Internet is also shaped and restricted by international treaties and conventions.

B INTERNATIONAL IMPACT OF THE INTERNET

The rapid growth of the Internet and the huge number of people that have access to it means that its influence throughout the world increases day by day. The Internet is changing the world in two important ways. First, it allows more people more connections and greater communication with people from all over the world. The opportunities for people to connect with each other have reached a point where there is no parallel in history with the variety of possibilities that individuals now have to communicate with other individuals no matter who they are or where they are. Second, there is a parallel expansion of the opportunities for access to information now available to a significant percentage of the world population that have never existed before.

These two things not only represent an expansion of education for the population of the world but also represent a dramatic shift in power from a few people who previously had access to important, relevant information to a very large number of people that now have opportunities to be influenced themselves and to influence others that, before the Internet, were available only to a few.

C RESTRICTING INTERNET ACCESS

Although there are many positive elements to these dramatic developments, they also threaten small groups of politically powerful people that have controlled society in several countries or regions. For purposes of simplicity, we can refer to these politically controlling groups as "Power Groups." There is no doubt that these Power Groups now often feel threatened by this expansion of communication and information. This can lead to exchanges of ideas that clash with the philosophies that the Power Groups impose on their societies. Consequently, in several places, Power Groups are seeking to limit and restrict access to the Internet to reduce the threats to their control.

For several years, *The New York Times* has reported that Internet restrictions are becoming more common around the world:

> Governments around the world, claiming they want to protect children, thwart terrorists and silence racists and hate mongers, are rushing to eradicate freedom of expression on the Internet, the international "network of networks," touted as the Information Superhighway.[7]

Fifteen years later, it appears that nothing much has changed. Increasingly, political leaders in some countries are seeking to restrict access to the Internet and to control what their citizens can do and say on the Internet. Sometimes the Internet itself is completely shut down, or access to specific sites is blocked, or the Internet is monitored and those that post material or messages that offend the government are punished or criminally prosecuted. Such Internet policies not only cause inconvenience but are also intimidating, which is apparently one of the goals of Power Groups. Following are some examples.

Florida, US

In Florida, in the United States (US), the governor signed a bill threatening to fine social media companies that permanently bar political candidates or figures from their platforms within the state of Florida. This is seen as a naked political response to the decisions of Facebook and Twitter to ban President Donald Trump from expressing his views on their platforms in January 2021 when Trump was strenuously arguing that the presidential election of 2020 had been stolen from him by Democrats committing electoral fraud. No significant evidence of electoral fraud has been found, either by Republican or by Democratic officials despite numerous claims and related lawsuits by Trump and his supporters. It was considered by many that Trump's claims which he expressed on public media platforms, particularly Twitter, were injuring the democratic process within the US.

7. Human Rights Watch, "Silencing the Net: The Threat to Freedom of Expression On-Line," *The New York Times*, online, May 1996, https://archive.nytimes.com/www.nytimes.com/library/cyber/week/0910hrw.html, accessed April 8, 2021.

China

The most onerous restrictions of Internet communication are in countries that have dictatorial systems of government. China is one that is often cited, especially after its crackdowns on democratic processes, the rule of law and peaceful protest in Hong Kong. Because of the size of China and the importance of the Chinese market, Chapter 8 below gives a more detailed review of Internet law and regulation in China. However, here are a few preliminary examples of China's Internet restrictions.

Most social networks are forbidden to operate in China. LinkedIn, principally a network of business contracts, is permitted to operate but has been punished for failing to prevent posts the government finds objectionable.[8] In Hong Kong, the Internet provider Hong Kong Broadband Network has blocked websites giving information concerning pro-democracy protests.[9]

There is much concern that actions like this are just the beginning of an expanding policy of Internet control, in conjunction with restriction of freedom of expression.

China is not the only country that sees this as a good policy. Several countries around the world are following China's example and using Internet control as a way of blocking anti-government communication and demands for democratic reform.

The government of China is also flexing its muscles to control the influence of successful Internet entrepreneurs. Several governments, not only that of China, are concerned that the number of people that certain entrepreneurs interact with and the amount of money they earn from it is so extensive that it can translate into political influence and power. Several countries are taking steps to moderate that power. In China, Jack Ma who became a billionaire from his success in founding and running Alibaba has become a target of the Chinese government. In 2021 he disappeared for a period. When he reemerged, he was required to leave his position as President of the business school that he founded. This has been seen as part of the continuing effort to reduce the influence that his success with Alibaba has given to him.[10]

India

India has passed laws that came into effect at the end of May 2021, which are called as "mass surveillance laws" by social media companies. WhatsApp has sued the Indian government claiming that the new laws will substantially damage the privacy of Internet users. Basically, the laws are intended to overcome the end-to-end encryption offered to users of communications apps like WhatsApp that allow users to have private conversations which are impenetrable to third parties. The new regulations require that Internet communications will have to be preserved in a database

8. Paul Mozur, Raymond Zhong and Steve Lohr, "China Punishes Microsoft's LinkedIn over Lax Censorship," *The New York Times*, online, March 18, 2021, accessed April 7, 2021.
9. Jessie Pang, "Hong Kong Censorship Debate Grows as Internet Firm Says It Can Block 'Illegal Acts'," *Reuters*, online, January 15, 2021, accessed April 7, 2021.
10. "Beijing Turns the Screws on Billionaire Who Crossed Party," *The Times*, online, May 25, 2021.

which allows the government to discover who the authors of the communications are. WhatsApp, which has over four hundred million users in India, filed suit alleging that the laws violate India's constitution and rights to privacy.[11]

India, despite priding itself on its democratic political system, also uses Internet shutdowns as a way of hobbling dissent. India cuts the Internet more frequently than any other nation.[12] In Kashmir, the control of which is disputed with Pakistan, India has not provided Internet service for a year. India's courts have declared that unlimited Internet shutdowns are unconstitutional, but that has not deterred the government manipulation of the Internet for political purposes, particularly in Kashmir.[13]

Pakistan

Pakistan has used its "electronic crimes" law to prosecute journalist for criticizing the military.[14]

Myanmar

Following a military coup, the ruling junta of Myanmar shut off the Internet several times to cut protesters access to information.[15] Countries that are controlled by dictatorial rulers often reenforce their control through Internet shutdowns, slowdowns, and censorship.

In January 2021, it was reported that governments in Africa "regularly shut down Internet access or online conversations to control dissent."[16]

Uganda

The government of Uganda had done both during a recent presidential vote.

Ethiopia

Ethiopia was also reported to have cut off Internet and other communications "during its military campaign in the Tigray region."

---

11. Hannah Ellis-Petersen, "WhatsApp Sues Indian Government over 'Mass Surveillance' Internet Laws," *The Guardian*, online, May 26, 2021, accessed May 27, 2021.
12. DW (*Deutsche Welle*), February 15, 2021, accessed April 7, 2021.
13. *Id.*
14. DW (*Deutsche Welle*), January 1, 2021, https://www.dw.com/en/internet-freedom/t-55547767, accessed April 7, 2021.
15. DW (*Deutsche Welle*), February 15, 2021, accessed April 7, 2021.
16. Shira Ovide, "What Internet Censorship Looks Like," *The New York Times*, online, January 21, 2021, accessed April 8, 2021.

Somalia

In Somalia, people who are critical of the government on Facebook and Twitter can be subject to government harassment.[17]

Zambia

In Zambia, a new Cyber Security and Cyber Crimes bill became law in March 2021. Apparently, it was made law in anticipation of elections scheduled for a few months later. It was claimed that the purpose of the law is to protect adults and children from cyberbullying. However, those opposed to the bill point out that it would allow the government to listen to private conversations. There is also concern that it would allow the government to shut off the Internet on election day—a tactic that has been used by the governments of several countries.[18]

Russia

Russia has long been known for making strenuous efforts to control both the Internet and Internet users. Over the past few years, they have adopted new laws and regulations to increase their ability to control Internet content and block content the government disapproves of. In 2019, the government introduced something called the "Sovereign Internet Law" which requires Internet providers to install software that allows the government to automatically block Internet traffic or reroute it to government reviewers.

This government enthusiasm for knowing what is going on the Internet also extends to private data. There are laws in Russia that require Internet companies that collect the private data of citizens to store the data and be prepared to hand it over to the security services on request. The security services have an automatic right to get access to company information systems without the need to apply to any court for permission. There are also several government agencies that have the power to block Internet content, and the number of these empowered agencies has been increasing since 2017. Obviously, these laws are intended to restrict freedom of expression on the Internet.

The Russian government wants to restrict discussion of anything that it considers a threat to its power or its policies. As a result, topics such as sexual identity, LGBT rights, democratic freedoms, and even health issues like the COVID-19 virus are severely restricted.[19]

---

17. *Id.*
18. "Zambia Passes Sweeping Cyberlaws Ahead of Elections," *TryWorld*, online, March 9, 2021, accessed April 8, 2021.
19. "Russia: Growing Internet Isolation, Control, Censorship," *Human Rights Watch*, online, June 18, 2020, accessed April 19, 2021, https://www.hrw.org/news/2020/06/18/russia-growing-internet-isolation-control-censorship.

Middle East

The Middle East is a region where several countries restrict or block Internet information that is contrary to government policies and that could cause internal dissent. Most countries in the region engage in blocking content from other countries that they believe oppose their interests.

This list includes Saudi Arabia, Bahrain, Egypt, the UAE, Qatar, Jordan, Iran, Yemen-Houthis, Syria, and Turkey.

Saudi Arabia, the United Arab Republic, Bahrain, and Egypt all block Iranian websites that convey Iran's official policies, particularly those that oppose the policies of other Middle Eastern countries, including those mentioned.

In response, Iran also blocks Internet posts from those countries which are critical of Iran.

Saudi Arabia seems to be the most enthusiastic blocker of Internet content. It filters content from at least nine other countries or regional nation groups. Iran and Egypt are not far behind, with Iran filtering content from at least seven other countries, and Egypt filtering at least six.[20]

Restrictions like those in the countries mentioned above put limitations on those trying to use the Internet as a way of increasing information and the spread of ideas. The only thing good that can be said about such policies is that they do demonstrate the power of the Internet. Those leaders that wish to prevent their citizens from knowing what is going on in the world and in their own countries fear this power.

D EXPANDING INTERNET ACCESS

European Union

There are moves in the European Union (EU) to make it possible for EU citizens to use the Internet regardless of where they are within the EU.

In February 2021, the European Commission proposed a new Roaming Regulation. This will enable citizens traveling within the EU to enjoy the same quality of mobile Internet access that they enjoy in their home country. This is intended to correct the current situation where surveys of EU citizens have concluded that the citizens believe they have lower quality mobile Internet when traveling abroad than they have in their home country. The new regulation will also provide traveling EU citizens with accurate information about what possible service charges they may encounter when using mobile services in other EU countries. The previous regulation on roaming services and charges was introduced in June 2017 and was scheduled to expire in 2022. The new regulation replaces this and was intended to provide even better service and more complete information than the Regulation of 2017.

20. Helmi Noman, "Internet Censorship and the Intraregional Geopolitical Conflicts in the Middle East and North Africa," Berkman Klein Center for Internet & Society at Harvard University, January 16, 2019, *see* Table 1: Summary of Test Results, online, accessed April 12, 2021.

United States

In the US, there are positive efforts to make Internet service available to as many people as possible. In January 2021, proposals were introduced in New York State, making it mandatory for Internet providers to extend $15 per month Internet access plans to low-income families. This would involve a price limit on high-speed Internet service. Governor Cuomo said:

> I propose that we pass the first in the nation mandate, ... for $15 per month high speed Internet service to all low-income households.

This is substantially below the current cost of Internet service in New York State. The State of New York has now passed a law which mandates the provision of that service. In his budget presentation, Governor Cuomo said:

> To these Internet companies I say to you again, you do not operate in the State of New York by an act of God. You operate by the will of the people. If you do not do this, you will lose your franchise in the State of New York, and that's a promise.[21]

Once again this shows the growing power of the Internet. It is no longer considered a hobby or an exotic activity of technological nerds. It is increasingly considered a basic right that should be available to all citizens to permit them to improve their access to information and communication.

E INTERNET AS ESSENTIAL UTILITY

Obviously, not every country takes this attitude but within the EU and certainly some parts of the US this is becoming a matter of not only policy but also positive law. New York has indicated that it is the first state to adopt this kind of legislation, but it cannot be long before others will see the importance of following suit.

If politicians fail to see the importance of affordable Internet access, it seems likely that a significant portion of citizens will demand it. From a legal point of view, it will be necessary for Internet companies and their legal advisors to keep abreast of evolving access laws and regulations of the type introduced in New York.

The Internet is no longer considered a luxury; it is now widely considered an essential utility that must be provided to the general population.

21. CBS 6 Albany, https://www.wktv.com/content/news/2021-State-of-the-State-Cuomo-introduces-affordable-internet-proposal-for-low-income-families-573578861.html.

CHAPTER 3

International Internet Law

The following constitute important international treaties and conventions, regulations and legal instruments that affect the governance of the Internet.[22]

A UNITED NATIONS DECLARATION ON HUMAN RIGHTS

The Universal Declaration of Human Rights promulgated by the UN in 1948 asserts the fundamental rights that all human beings are entitled to simply by being human.[23]

Particularly relevant for Internet law is the second paragraph of the Preamble which states that "... human beings shall enjoy the freedom of speech and belief ... ." Also, the statement in the third paragraph that "... human rights should be protected by the rule of law ... ." Furthermore:

> Member States have pledged themselves to achieve, in cooperation with the United Nations, the promotion of universal respect for and observance of human rights and fundamental freedoms.

There is also Article 12 that asserts protection of privacy, stating:

> No one shall be subjected to arbitrary interference with his privacy, family, home or correspondence nor to attacks upon his honor and reputation. Everyone has the right to the protection of the law against such interference or attacks.

Article 19 is particularly relevant to Internet usage, stating:

> Everyone has the right to freedom of opinion and expression; this right includes freedom to hold opinions without interference and to seek, receive and impart information and ideas through any media and regardless of the frontiers.

22. UNESCO, Internet Governance Glossary, sections 7, 7.1, 7.2, 7.3, https://en.unesco.org/glossaries/igg/groups/7.4%20Conventions%20and%20treaties%2C%20regulations%20and%20legal%20instruments, retrieved August 11, 2020.
23. *Id.*, section 7.4.1.

It is certainly true that the Internet has the potential to fulfill and enhance the right to cultural life asserted in Article (1), which states:

> 1. Everyone has the right to participate in the cultural life of the community, to enjoy the arts and to share in scientific advancement and its benefits.

Although this Universal Declaration of Human Rights is not legally binding, all 192 members of the UN have agreed to it because it is an intrinsic document for membership to the UN. In addition, 150 countries have ratified and signed the International Bill of Human Rights, which consists of the Universal Declaration of Human Rights and two other international treaties:

(1) The International Covenant on Civil and Political Rights (ICCPR, 1966); and
(2) The International Covenant on Economic, Social and Cultural Rights (ICESR, 1966).

Internet Communication as a Human Right

The UN has tried to extend internationally recognized human rights onto the Internet.

In June 2012, it proposed a resolution on human rights on the Internet. The resolution sought to promote the protection and exercise of human rights on the Internet through Article 19 of the Universal Declaration of Human Rights.

However, it is not certain that this resolution (which remains in draft) has any significant legal impact because several countries have reservations about it, and it has not yet been approved.

Resistance to the UDHR

Over 150 countries have ratified the UN conventions protecting human rights discussed above but there is a significant group of countries that are opposed to some of their protections.

Saudi Arabia has not signed United Nations Declaration on Human Rights (UDHR), claiming that violates Islamic law and fails to account for the religious and cultural backgrounds of non-Western countries. All Saudi citizens are required to be Muslims, and there are restrictions on women's rights. An Iranian representative to the UN has also said that it is impossible to comply with the UDHR without violating Islamic law.[24]

In response to the concerns of Muslim countries, forty-five countries belonging to the Organisation of the Islamic Conference agreed to adopt the Cairo Declaration of Human Rights in Islam (CDHRI) in 1990, which does not conform to the UDHR and

24. Dania Akkad, "The Universal Declaration vs. The Cairo Declaration," *blogs.lse.ac.uk*, online, December 10, 2012, accessed November 13, 2021.

"undermines many of the rights the UDHR is supposed to guarantee." For example, it allows for the establishment of different rights for men and women.[25]

The CDHRI has the effect of restricting freedom of expression in a number of ways that would limit using the Internet to express certain ideas. Article 22 of the CDHRI says that "Everyone shall have the right to express his opinion freely in such manner as would not be contrary to the principles of the Shari'ah."[26]

Since 1990, there have been several proposals to expand interpretations of human rights under Islamic law, but so far, they have not met with significant success.[27]

It is likely that, although many countries respect the breath of human rights guaranteed under the UDHR, and their application in relation to the Internet, there will be a group of countries that for religious and political reasons will be unwilling to extend those rights to all their citizens.

B INTERNATIONAL TELECOMMUNICATION REGULATIONS

The International Telecommunication Regulations (ITR) came into force in 1998 through the International Telecommunication Union (ITU). Its purpose was to promote international liberalization of pricing and Internet services and to permit new functions of basic services with respect to the Internet. This involved such things as leased lines and helped the rapid growth of the Internet by the 1990s. The principal international organizations responsible for the international regulation of telecommunications are the World Trade Organization (WTO) and the ITU.[28]

C BASIC TELECOMMUNICATION AGREEMENT

The formal name of this agreement is the Fourth Protocol to the General Agreement on Trade in Services. This came into force in 1998. Under this agreement, over hundred countries have opened their telecommunication markets to promote the development of new communication services, including Internet services.[29]

25. *Id.*
26. Alan Sears, "Protecting Freedom of Expression over the Internet: An International Approach," *Notre Dame Journal of International & Comparative Law,* Volume 5 (2015), online, accessed November 13, 2021.
27. *See,* Konstantinos Magliveras and Gino Nardi, "The Arab Court of Human Rights: A Study in Impotence," *The Quebec Journal of International Law*, Volume 29 (2016) 1-342, online, accessed November 13, 2021.
28. UNESCO Glossary 7.4.2.
29. UNESCO Glossary 7.4.3.

D UNCITRAL MODEL LAW ON ELECTRONIC COMMERCE

This was issued by United Nations Commission on International Trade Law (UNCITRAL) in 1996. It is not a legally binding instrument, but it provides a model for legislation and also assists Internet users in drafting their contracts.[30]

E BERNE CONVENTION FOR THE PROTECTION OF LITERARY AND ARTISTIC WORKS (BERNE CONVENTION)

This is an international convention with a long history. It was first adopted in 1886. The signers of this agreement are required to recognize the copyright of authors from other signing countries in the same way that they recognize the copyrights of their own citizens. Signatories to this agreement are known as the Bern Union.

The agreement also requires signatories to provide minimum standards in their copyright law.[31]

F WIPO COPYRIGHT TREATY

This treaty was agreed by the Member States of the World Intellectual Property Organization (WIPO) in 1996. It was created as an enhancement to existing copyright treaties because of advances in digital information and Internet technology.[32]

G AGREEMENT ON TRADE-RELATED ASPECTS OF INTELLECTUAL PROPERTY RIGHTS

The Trade-Related Aspects of Intellectual Property Rights (TRIPS) is an international intellectual property agreement administered by the WTO. It establishes standards for applying intellectual property regulations to nationals of other countries that also happen to be WTO members.[33]

H BUDAPEST CONVENTION ON CYBERCRIME (BUDAPEST CONVENTION)

The Budapest Convention was entered into in July 2004. It was the first treaty trying to deal with Internet and other computer crimes. The goals of the treaty are to align the Internet laws and regulations of the signatory countries, to update and improve their

30. UNESCO Glossary 7.4.4.
31. UNESCO Glossary 7.4.5.
32. UNESCO Glossary 7.4.6.
33. UNESCO Glossary 7.4.7. For additional information about these and other agreements regulating intellectual property on the Internet, please *see* Chapter 14 on Intellectual Property Law and the Internet.

methods of investigation, and to get them to cooperate more in preventing international cybercrime.[34]

I CONVENTION ON THE RECOGNITION AND ENFORCEMENT OF FOREIGN ARBITRAL AWARDS (NEW YORK CONVENTION)

This is a convention that has been in existence for some time. It was created in 1958, long before the Internet rose to prominence. Its purpose has been and remains the regulation of the terms under which the national courts of signatories are obliged to enforce arbitration awards regardless of where the arbitration awards are made. It is commonly called "the New York Convention." About twenty-four countries are signatories that allow their national courts to enforce the arbitration awards of other signatories under the terms of the Convention.[35]

J UNCITRAL MODEL LAW ON INTERNATIONAL COMMERCIAL ARBITRATION

This is a template that nations can use to create their own commercial arbitration law. The Model Law itself is not legally binding, but it is something that countries can make part of their own national law if they wish. It was introduced in 2006.[36]

K W3C WEB ACCESSIBILITY INITIATIVE WEB CONTENT ACCESSIBILITY GUIDELINES

The World Wide Web Consortium (W3C) has issued a series of guidelines on web accessibility that were published by the Web Accessibility Initiative (WAI) of W3C. They are a collection of ways to make the web accessible for users who may be disabled, or who are using mobile devices such as phones. The latest version was published in 2008, and a related standard from the International Organization for Standardization was issued in 2012.[37]

L UNITED NATIONS CONVENTION ON THE USE OF ELECTRONIC COMMUNICATIONS IN INTERNATIONAL CONTRACTS (ELECTRONIC COMMUNICATIONS CONVENTION)

The United Nations Convention on the use of Electronic Communications in International Contracts (Electronic Communications Convention) was initially adopted in 2005.[38] However, since then it has been adopted by only eighteen countries. The only

34. UNESCO, Internet Governance Glossary, 7.4.8.
35. UNESCO Glossary 7.4.9.
36. UNESCO Glossary 7.4.10.
37. UNESCO Glossary 7.4.11.
38. Vienna Convention, Introduction, 2, online at uncitral.org, accessed August 18, 2020.

major country being the Russian Federation. It only entered into force for those signatories in 2013. However, the importance of this convention goes beyond those countries. A number of countries have adopted parts of this convention as provisions in their own national legislation. Others have indicated any interest in adopting the Convention or preparing legislation to include provisions like those of the Convention. That interest has been expressed by several major countries including the US.

In fact, the Convention was based on the already existing laws of the US (*American Uniform Electronic Transactions Act*) and Canada (*Canadian Uniform Electronic Transactions Act*).[39]

The purpose of this convention is to provide a treaty which removes the formal obstacles that separate electronic from written contracts. It is aimed at providing an opportunity for countries involved in international commerce, whether signatories or not, to adopt similar legislation governing the creation of contracts in electronic commerce. This would make international trade easier by harmonizing the different national regulations that govern electronic commerce.[40]

If this convention is more widely adopted, by major legal jurisdictions such as the US, the EU, China, India and the EU, it is thought that its provisions could have a significant impact on trading areas such as energy, shipping, technology and financial services.[41]

President Obama sent the Convention to the US Senate along with a recommendation of ratification on February 10, 2016.[42] However, the US Senate has not yet agreed to ratify the Convention. In the Senate, issues have been raised that may delay or prevent ratification of the Convention. The first is that provisions of the Convention are like provisions already existing in US law, such as the Uniform Commercial Code (UCC). It is the thought that many US legal practitioners would prefer to operate under established law rather than a new treaty that may make small variations to the law that may be confusing. The second is that the Convention is not self-executing and would therefore require further legislation implement provisions into US law. Consequently, there does not seem to be a strong likelihood that the Convention will be ratified by the US any time soon.

M INTERNET CORPORATION FOR ASSIGNED NAMES AND NUMBERS

Internet Corporation for Assigned Names and Numbers (ICANN) was established in 1998. It is an international organization, overseen by the US government.[43] ICANN is responsible for the administration of three kinds of Internet identifier systems. These

39. J. Benjamin Lambert, "The U.N. Convention on Electronic Contracting: Back from the Dead?," *Michigan State International Law Review*, Volume 25, 32-75, online at Digital Commons Network, accessed August 18, 2020.
40. UN Commission on International Trade Law, online, accessed at uncitral.un.org, August 18, 2020.
41. Lambert, *supra*, p. 34.
42. *Id.*
43. *See* the discussion of US domain name regulation in Chapter 4.

are: domain names, numerical Internet protocol (IP) addresses, and a code that identifies port and parameter numbers. The Internet community can participate in determining the policy of ICANN through the Non-commercial Users Constituency[44] and/or the At-Large Advisory Committee.[45]

N INTERNET ASSIGNED NAMES AND NUMBERS AUTHORITY

The Internet Assigned Names and Numbers Authority (IANA) is the department of ICANN. It was established in 1988 to execute policy with respect to IP number allocations and some administrative functions for the Internet Engineering Task Force and ICANN.[46]

O NUMBER RESOURCE ORGANIZATION

This is an unincorporated group formed in 2003 to coordinate the Regional Internet Registries (RIRs), of which there are five RIRs around the world. Those five RIRs are:

(1) APNIC, covering India, the Far East, and the Antipodes;
(2) ARIN, covering North America;
(3) LACNIC, covering Latin America;
(4) RIPE NCC, covering Europe, the Middle East, and the Russian Federation; and
(5) AFRNIC, covering Africa.

The Number Resource Organization's (NRO's) goal is to provide a coordinating body for the registrations of domain names through the RIRs.[47]

The NRO does not do domain name registration. Rather it functions as a central registry and communication point for the RIRs with respect to such things as statistical reports, Internet governance efforts and coordination of policy. To help do that, it supports coordinating groups on common issues such as communications, registration services, engineering, and administrative leadership. The aim of these groups is to help promote security, stability, and cooperation in global domain name registration.

44. http://ncdnhc.org/.
45. http://www.allarge.icann.org/.
46. *Id.*
47. NRO website, nro.net, retrieved September 7, 2020.

CHAPTER 4

US Internet Law

In the US, the regulation of activities on the Internet is divided between federal laws and the laws of the fifty states. This is not unusual under the US legal system. Many areas of commercial activity such as banking, insurance, and investment business are subject to both US federal and state laws.

A FEDERAL TRADE COMMISSION

The federal regulation of Internet began as the regulation of common activities that were migrating from the physical world to the digital world of the Internet. Many of these were commercial activities and, at an early stage of the Internet's development, came under the jurisdiction of the US Federal Trade Commission (FTC). The FTC is a US federal government agency, the mission of which is defined as:

> protecting consumers and competition by preventing anticompetitive, deceptive, and unfair business practices through law enforcement, advocacy, and education without unduly burdening legitimate business activity.[48]

Their stated goals are:

(1) to protect consumers from unfair and deceptive practices in the marketplace;
(2) maintaining competition and promoting a marketplace free from anticompetitive mergers, business practices, or public policy; and
(3) performing these tasks well by managing their resources, people and information technology.[49]

48. FTC, "About the FTC, Our Mission," https://www.ftc.gov/about-ftc, retrieved August 5, 2020.
49. FTC, "About the FTC, Our Strategic Goals," https://www.ftc.gov/about-ftc retrieved August 5, 2020.

As can be seen, the FTC considers "information technology" as an important tool for its own activities and it clearly recognizes its importance in US commerce.

The first interactions of the FTC with the Internet were in the context of enforcing general anti-crime and misconduct policies. As the Internet expanded, some activities on the Internet violated established laws and policies. This was true of laws and policies against fraud, misrepresentation, and theft.

Most of these activities were not confined to the boundaries of a particular US state. Electronic communications frequently crossed state and even international boundaries. Consequently, these activities came within the jurisdiction of the US federal government which is responsible for regulating interstate and foreign commerce. This got the FTC involved.

Initially, the FTC's involvement with the Internet was in the context of investigating, and sometimes prosecuting and imposing fines for, unfair and deceptive marketing and unfair competition. These are among the duties imposed on the FTC by US federal laws, such as the Federal Trade Commission Act ("Act").

Under section 5 of the Act, unfair or deceptive practices in or affecting commerce are prohibited. These prohibitions apply to all persons engaged in commerce, that is anyone or any entity engaged in any activity for profit. The FTC is given the power to investigate and prevent such acts to protect competition and consumers.

The importance of controlling the Internet through the FTC was brought home in June 2021 by President Biden's appointment of Lina Khan as chairperson of the FTC. This seemed to be a signal from the administration that the FTC will increasingly focus on the power of the big tech companies. It was noted that Ms. Khan, a 32-year-old professor at Columbia University Law School, has been a vocal critic of the big tech companies. In the past, she has advocated the breakup of big companies such as Amazon, Facebook and Google. There seems a little doubt that with her as the head of the FTC there will be increasing scrutiny of the behavior of Internet companies and robust action against instances where they misuse their power.[50]

Private Rights of Action

Under section 5, consumers can file a complaint with the FTC but consumers may not bring a private legal action under section 5.

This is where state law comes in. Most, if not all, US states have laws prohibiting unfair and deceptive trade practices and unfair competition. Unlike section 5 of the Federal Trade Commission Act, these state laws usually permit private rights of action. This allows injured parties themselves to bring lawsuits seeking damages or injunctive relief for Internet misconduct that they allege has harmed or is harming them.

For example, New York state antitrust law (the Donnelly Act) prohibits "unfair competition" and allows parties claiming injury to bring lawsuits seeking remedies for

50. Simon Duke, "Lina Khan, Biden's Choice to Lead Federal Trade Commission Is a Warning to Big Tech," *The Times,* online, June 17, 2021.

any bad faith misappropriation of material value via the Internet. This covers any bad faith misappropriation of the labors or expenditures of another.[51]

B COMPUTER FRAUD AND ABUSE ACT OF 1986

In 1986, becoming increasingly aware of the importance and uses of computers, the US Congress passed the Computer Fraud and Abuse Act of 1986 (CFAA). This makes it a crime to obtain information to which a person is not entitled by accessing a computer without permission.

The intention of this law was to criminalize hacking, fraud, and other computer crimes.

However, in a June 2021 decision, the US Supreme Court apparently narrowed the application of this law in a case in which a policeman in the state of Georgia was prosecuted for using his patrol car computer to obtain automobile license plate information in exchange for payment.[52] In a 6 to 3 decision, the court said that the officer did not violate the specific provisions of the computer crime law because it did not apply to people who have "improper motives for obtaining information that he is otherwise available to them." The majority's view was that although the law penalizes a person who "exceeds authorized access," this does not apply to someone who improperly uses their authorized access. This case was particularly complicated by the fact that the police officer in question used his access to the license plate database in connection with working with the US Federal Bureau of Investigation (FBI) on an investigation being conducted by the FBI. The three members of the Supreme Court in the minority argued that the law did apply in this case because the correct interpretation was that a person was not entitled to get information that he is not entitled to even using a computer system which he is authorized to access.[53]

C CHILD PROTECTION

When it comes to the privacy of children, there is a federal law that limits information that can be collected by ISPs about children that are using their services, such as YouTube. Such activity is governed by the US Children's Online Privacy Protection Act of 1998 (COPPA). This prohibits Internet users from collecting data on children under 13 years of age without their parents' express consent.

In 2019, YouTube was found to be collecting data on children under the age of 13 without obtaining the consent of their parents. The FTC fined YouTube $170 million for this violation of COPPA.[54]

51. Case of *Jeffrey Milstein, Inc. v. Greger, Lawlor, Roth, Inc.*, 58 F.3d 27, 34 (2d Cir. 1995). Note that the case cited is a federal court case, in New York, enforcing New York law, rather than federal law.
52. Melissa Quinn, "Supreme Court Narrows Scope of Computer Fraud Law with Ruling in Cybercrime Case," *CBS News*, online, June 4, 2021.
53. *Id.*
54. *The Sunday Times*, online, May 10, 2020.

There are also strict federal and state laws against providing child pornography on the Internet. Just how strictly they can be interpreted was demonstrated in a case before the Maryland Court of Appeals which upheld a lower court finding that a 16-year-old girl had violated criminal pornography laws by sending a "sext" of herself to friends as a joke. Under such an interpretation, even the minor subjects of revenge porn could be treated as child-pornographers if they forwarded such postings to others. Consequently, rather than sending copies of such postings to friends, or even adults, child victims of pornography should immediately inform adults and/or the law enforcement authorities of such postings.

If an Internet operator creates videos for children, they are required to label those videos as being created for kids. No personal data about the children viewing those videos can be collected from the views, and no child-targeted ads can accompany the videos. If providers of such videos do not comply, they can be subject to lawsuits and fines.

In 2021, US Representative Kathy Castor of Florida proposed new legislation to expand the protections of the COPPA. The additional protections that she proposed were set out in a bill called the Protecting the Information of Our Vulnerable Children and Youth Act. This would extend the protections of existing law to all persons under 18 years of age and would apply to all sites used by those under 18 years of age. It proposes forbidding advertising targeted at people under 18 and requires obtaining the consent of teenagers before storing their personal data. This is a significant extension of COPPA which only applies to children under the age of 13.

The new bill would also apply to sites that are aimed at children under 13. However, there is a wide recognition that children under 13 often gain access to sites aimed at older audiences by lying about their age. It has been shown that COPPA did not provide adequate protection to children under 13 with respect to collection of their personal data, as found in the FTC investigation of the activities of the Google-owned website YouTube. Representative Castor's bill is intended to cover gaps in the COPPA, which was originally passed in 1998 and is considered to be outdated because of all the changes in the Internet and its use that have taken place since then.[55]

It is reported that the big tech companies have for some time been attempting to deal with child protection laws by developing apps and sites specifically aimed at children under 13 and teenagers under 18. However, these have been subject to a number of criticisms that they do not effectively protect children from inappropriate material. For example, there is wide recognition of the fact that children under 13 often gain access to adult sites by lying about their age. Some lawmakers want to see stricter Child Protection requirements imposed.[56]

55. Rachel Lerman, "New Bill Would Update Decades-Old Law Governing Children's Privacy," *The Washington Post*, online, July 29, 2021.

56. *Id.*

D US ADOPTION OF DIGITAL MILLENNIUM COPYRIGHT ACT

In 1998, the US also passed the Digital Millennium Copyright Act (DMCA). The purpose of this Act was to implement most of the provisions of the WIPO Copyright Treaty (WCT) that protect intellectual property.

One year prior to that, in 1997, the US enacted the No Electronic Theft Act, which established criminal prosecution for those who violate copyright using the Internet or other electronic means.

E COMPETITION LAW

Another important US act which has significant impact on Internet use is the Sherman Antitrust Act of 1890.

The Sherman Act prohibits two things. Section 1 prohibits agreements and restraint of trade. This includes such things as price-fixing, refuses to deal, bid rigging and other attempts by conspiring partners to control prices and markets for their own benefit. Section 2 prohibits attempts to monopolize markets. Both these issues have arisen with respect to the behavior of certain companies or parties using the Internet and will undoubtedly continue to arise in the future.

Uniform Commercial Code

In addition to federal law, there are a number of other state laws that affect Internet transactions. For example, there is section 5 of the UCC.

Because of different state laws, there have been several difficulties in doing transactions across state lines in the US. As a result, an effort was made to create a uniform set of laws for commercial transactions. The result is called the UCC. The UCC was originally drafted as a joint project of the National Conference of Commissioners of Uniform State Laws and the American Law Institute. They began drafting their first version in 1942 and the original complete version was published ten years later in 1952. Several top legal scholars in the US participated in the project.

The UCC was developed as a private project. It is not, of itself, law, and is not legally binding. Basically, it represents detailed suggestions to the states to adopt uniform commercial laws. When a state adopts all or part of the UCC, those provisions become part of the state commercial law. Over the years, there have been several modifications or changes to the original draft of the UCC.

Most states have adopted the UCC, although there may be some variations from state to state. The only significant US jurisdictions that have not adopted most of the UCC are Louisiana and Puerto Rico. This is because, prior to acquisition by the US, the fundamental laws of these jurisdictions were not based on English common law, but rather on the Napoleonic Code.

It is important to keep in mind that the provisions of the UCC can be interpreted differently by different state courts, which unlike the federal court system do not function within a single jurisdictional framework, but operate differently in different states.

The UCC covers many different aspects of commercial relations and, therefore, if dealing with private commercial transactions that involve US states, it would be useful to review sections of the UCC to determine whether it might be relevant for that particular transaction. The articles of the UCC deal with the following topics:

- General Provisions.
- Sales and (2A) Leases.
- Negotiable Instruments.
- Bank Deposits and Collections, (4A) Funds Transfer.
- Letters of Credit.
- Bulk Transfers and Bulk Sales.
- Documents of Title.
- Investment Securities.
- Secured Transactions.

As can be seen from the titles of these articles, they can have a significant impact on international transactions that involve persons in US states. For example, Article 5 (Letters of Credit) regulates a variety of financial instruments that are often used and international banking transactions. An extensive revision of Article 5 was undertaken in 1995 to take account of many changes in international transactions, including the fact that significant parts of the agreements relating to them had become "non-documentary" because of the growth of electronic commercial transactions on the Internet.[57]

A copy of the full UCC can be found online from the Legal Information Institute (LII) of Cornell University.[58]

Federal and State Concern about "Big Tech"

US federal concern about the power of major tech companies such as Google, Amazon, Apple and Facebook has been growing.

In response to these concerns, the US Justice Department, the FTC, and a number of state attorney generals have begun investigations aimed at bringing competition lawsuits against these companies in an effort to limit their powers and/or punish perceived abuses of their market power.

A major step in that direction was taken when the FTC and a coalition of forty-eight US state attorney generals filed antitrust cases against Facebook in 2020. However, these cases suffered an embarrassing setback in June 2021 when a federal court dismissed those cases on the grounds that the FTC had failed to define the market

57. James G. Barnes, "Internationalization of Revised UCC Article 5: Letters of Credit," *Northwestern Journal of International Law and Business*, Volume 16 (Winter 1996).
58. Legal Information Institute, Cornell University, https://www.law.cornell.edu/ucc.

in which Facebook operated and that the states waited too long to act against Facebook.

US District Judge, James Boasberg, wrote that the FTC had not provided sufficient detail to support its allegations that Facebook was monopolizing the online social media market. The FTC was given until August 19, 2021, to file a new and better complaint.[59]

These dismissals raise questions as to what will happen in the many cases filed by the Justice Department and state attorney generals against Google in the autumn of 2020 and with respect to cases that it is believed may be filed against Amazon in the near future.[60]

However, the FTC was not discouraged by the dismissal they suffered in June 2021. On August 19, 2021, the FTC refiled their antitrust suit against Facebook with a new complaint alleging that Facebook violated competition laws when it bought Instagram and WhatsApp.[61] The complaint alleges that they were purchased to eliminate them as competitors.

This new filing does have political aspects. There are five Commissioners at the FTC—two Republicans and three Democrats. The Commissioners voted 3 to 2 to refile a complaint with Democrats voting in favor and Republicans voting against the filing.

This case is representative of the efforts being made by different government branches in the US to control the powers of the big tech companies such as Facebook, Amazon, and Google.

Senator, Amy Klobuchar of Minnesota, the chairperson of the antitrust panel of the US Senate, issued a statement supporting the FTC suit against Facebook, saying:

> Facebook's long history of anti-competitive behavior is no secret ... The company's acquisitions of Instagram and WhatsApp have made the digital landscape less competitive ultimately harming consumers.

Both US Justice Department and several states have also filed lawsuits against Google.

In Congress, legislators are presenting bills to control the expanding business of the big tech companies.

It seems that for some time, big tech companies, and those that seek to imitate their market dominance, will be under US governmental scrutiny and pressure aimed at controlling what are perceived as the anticompetitive effects of their market power.

59. David McLaughlin, "Facebook Hit by New U.S. Antitrust Case as FTC Seeks Do-Over," *Bloomberg*, online, August 19, 2021.
60. Sheelah, Kalhatkar, "What's Next for the Campaign to Break up Big Tech," *The New Yorker*, online, July 6, 2021.
61. David McLaughlin, "Facebook Hit by New U.S. Antitrust Case as FTC Seeks Do-Over," *Bloomberg*, online, August 19, 2021.

F US LAW ON DOMAIN NAMES

Another important issue that has arisen from Internet use is the issue of who owns and who can use "domain names," or registries of "internet protocol identifiers," such as domain names and IP addresses.

Domain Name History

Domain name registration was originally performed by a man named Jon Postel. Dr. Postel was a UCLA and USC computer scientist who worked on early computer networks such as ARPANET. He is famous for a number of contributions to computing development, such as "Postel's Law" for computer software design, "Be conservative in what you do. Be liberal in what you accept from others." While he was working for ARPANET, he did domain name registration as a "side interest."

In 1983, the Domain Name System (DNS) was first introduced by ARPANET. Today it is managed by the ICANN. ICANN is a US not-for-profit corporation headquartered in Los Angeles, California.

Domain names are electronic addresses which are posted on the Internet to allow users to connect with the owner of the name.

Consequently, it has been important for businesses to acquire domain names that indicate association with them or their products. However, who can acquire certain domain names has not always been subject to strict rules about who will be allowed to purchase a particular domain name.

There are also multiple domain name groups, beginning with ".com" and progressing to name groups associated with countries (uk, fr, ..., etc.), cities or other affiliations. As a result, there are numerous affiliation groups within which one can register a domain name of one's choice.

Very early in the development of the Internet this became a problem for major companies that had a valuable brand name they wished to protect. Domain name registrants, known as "cyber-squatters," began registering domain names that indicated affiliation with major companies and then demanded payment from those brand-owning companies in order to give up the "squatted" domain names.

It was not long before there were complaints about the fact that such a practice was seen to cross the line to fraud, extortion and even blackmail. Consequently, efforts were made to be more restrictive in granting domain name registrations.

One can see that for companies like Coca-Cola, Apple and Microsoft, this can be a major headache. The argument of companies wishing to protect their brands is that cyber-squatting was a form of fraud on consumers that were being enticed to click on those domain names hoping to find information about the brand owners.

It did not take much for these major companies to bring this problem to the attention of the US Congress. In response, Congress passed the Anti-Cybersquatting Consumer Products Act of 1999[62] (ACPA).

62. 15 U.S.C. section 1125(d).

The ACPA permits a lawsuit to be brought for registering, using, or trafficking in a domain name that is confusingly like a trademark or a personal name. The purpose of this statute is to discourage those who plan to sell domain names to the legitimate owners of the name or trademark. The owner of the name or trademark can be successful if they show that use of the domain name in question was done in bad faith with the intent to profit from its misuse, and the complainant can show that the domain name in question is the same or confusingly like a well-known trademark or personal name.

Domain names are also protected by the more general, but still applicable, Federal Trademark Dilution Act enacted prior to the ACPA in 1995. This protects trademarks against the registration of domain names similar or remarkably like the trademarks. This act also permits actions against those who are using trademark-affiliated domain names for deceptive purposes.

There is also another identifier called a "hostname." These are the labels that are given to DNSs. This is a component of the Uniform Resource Locators, which are commonly known as "URLs." These are the digital addresses of Internet resources such as websites. Their purpose is to identify Internet resources such as computers, networks, and websites.

Domain Name Dispute Resolution

There are a colossal number of domain names in use in the Internet world.

At first, there was not much conflict over who could register a domain name. Originally, there was not a requirement that the registrant be someone who has a natural or commercial interest in a particular domain name. As a result, people who thought they were being clever registered the domain names that appeared to be related to major commercial companies in the hope that these companies would pay them to take over the domain name.

As shown above, there are now laws to protect brand owners from deceptive domain name registration and formal lawsuits can be filed. However, the use of domain names is so extensive that it became necessary to try to set up more efficient and less costly ways to resolve disputes between parties that contested rights to particular domain names.

The first formal effort undertaking to create a system for resolving domain name registration disputes was undertaken by ICANN. In 1999 ICANN set up the Uniform Domain Name Dispute Resolution Policy (UDRP).

The purpose of the UDRP is to resolve disputes regarding the registration of Internet domain names.

It was set up to solve the problem of the registration of trademarks as domain names by people who did not have the permission of the trademark owner. The UDRP came about because of a report prepared at the request of ICANN and published in 1999. The report recommended a mandatory administrative procedure for solving the problem of abusive registration of the main names. Consequently, ICANN introduced a mandatory agreement in every domain name application which requires a party to submit to the UDRP procedure if a claim is against it by a third party.

UDRP Cases

The UDRP was launched in 1999, and the WIPO Arbitration and Mediation Center offered dispute resolution under the UDRP.

The first case using this procedure was entitled *World Wrestling Federation Entertainment Inc. v. Michael Bosman*. The *Bosman* case was over the use of the domain name of WWF. Bosman was found to have registered a domain name identical or confusingly similar to the trademark and service mark in which the WWF has rights.

It was alleged that Bosman was using the domain name (worldwrestilingfederation.com) in bad faith. The WIPO Panel's decision agreed with that allegation and ruled that the domain name be transferred to WWF.[63]

There are a couple of other interesting high-profile cases which have arisen in the entertainment industry.

The first is *Madonna Ciccone, p/k/a Madonna v. Dan Parisi and Maddona.com.*[64] Again, the WIPO Panel decided that the domain name registration by Mr. Parisi was identical or confusing with or similar to the trademark in which Madonna had rights. Mr. Parisi, on the other hand, was found to have no rights or legitimate interests in the domain name and so it was ordered to be transferred to Madonna.

Here is another domain name dispute involving a famous entertainment figure: *Tribeca Film Center, Inc. v. Lorenzo Brusasco-Mackenzie* that was also decided by WIPO.[65] In that case, Robert De Niro, the famous actor, complained that Mr. Lorenzo Brusasco-Mackenzie (Respondent) registered a domain name of "tribecafilmcenter-.com." De Niro complained that the domain name was identical or confusingly similar to a trademark in which De Niro had acquired common law rights. Despite recognizing that the name "Tribeca Film Center" had become famous because of its association with Robert De Niro and his films, the WIPO Panel decided that De Niro had failed to meet the burden of proving that the Respondent had registered and used the domain name in "bad faith." Therefore, even though the Panel recognized that the Respondent had registered a domain name identical to a trademark in which De Niro had rights, the domain name should continue to belong to the Respondent.

The key point about the *De Niro* case is that WIPO's decision emphasized the fact that proving "bad faith" was more important than proving legal rights to a confusingly similar or identical trademark.

There, the Respondent's arguments against the charge of "bad faith" included his assertions that he believed he had a legitimate interest in the domain name because he

63. WIPO Arbitration and Mediation Center, Administrative Panel Decision, Case No. D99-0001, January 14, 2000, www.wipo.int, retrieved August 25, 2020.
64. WIPO Arbitration and Mediation Center, Administrative Panel Decision, Case No. D2000-0847, October 12, 2000, www.wipo.int, retrieved August 26, 2020.
65. WIPO Arbitration and Mediation Center, Administrative Panel Decision, Case No. D2000-1772, April 10, 2001, www.wipo.int, retrieved August 28, 2020.

lived close to Tribeca in New York City and chose the name in good faith to create a fan site dealing with film and film-related interests, including films in which Mr. De Niro was involved.

After reviewing the allegations in the case, the Panel concluded that although it was a "close decision" on the issue of bad faith, the burden of showing bad faith had not been met.

Despite this unfavorable decision, Mr. De Niro remains aggressive in disputing the ownership of domain names that include the geographic designation "Tribeca." It has also been reported that he is disputing ownership of the website "http://tribica.net with the owner of that domain name."[66] De Niro's claims have caused considerable controversy among other residents and businesses in that Manhattan neighborhood south of Greenwich Village, but De Niro and his representatives remain adamant that use of the name Tribeca by other businesses causes confusion with De Niro's businesses in the area.[67]

G SOME US INTERNET CASES

Free Speech

The first important case that raised the issue of what kind of information can be allowed to be put on the Internet was *Reno v. The American Civil Liberties Union* (1997). That case was filed as a response to the Communications Decency Act passed by Congress in 1996. That law allowed for criminal prosecution of anyone that knowingly directed anyone under 18 to Internet content that showed "any comment, request, suggestion, proposal, image or other communication that in context, depicts or describes, in terms offensive as measured by contemporary community standards, sexual or excretory activities or organs."

In the *Reno* case, that law was struck down by US federal courts including the Supreme Court because, as written by Supreme Court Justice John Paul Stevens:

> We are persuaded that the CDA lacks the precision the First Amendment requires when a statute regulates the content of speech. In order to deny minors access to potentially harmful speech, the CDA effectively suppresses a large amount of speech that adults have a constitutional right to receive and to address to one another. ... It is true that we have repeatedly recognized the governmental interest in protecting children from harmful materials. But that interest does not justify an unnecessarily broad suppression of speech addressed to adults.[68]

66. Richard Johnson, "I Am Tirbeca, De Niro Claims," *New York Post*, online, December 31, 2006, retrieved August 28, 2020.
67. *Id.*
68. *Reno v. American Civil Liberties Union*, 521 U.S. 844 (1997).

The Internet as a Public Utility

The Trump Social Media Case

In June 2021, Former President Donald Trump filed a lawsuit against major tech companies including Facebook, Twitter and YouTube claiming that they violated his First Amendment rights by barring him from posting on those social media platforms. The essence of his claim is that these social media platforms should no longer be entitled to the immunities granted by private companies because they had become virtually public utilities in the position of "state actors" that are required to comply with the standards of the First Amendment which restrict the rights of public bodies, as opposed to private companies, to limit speech.

The First Amendment to the US Constitution says that "Congress ... (not private businesses that operate social media platforms) ... shall make no law abridging the freedom of speech or of the press."

What the real status of social media platforms is has become a political issue because the social media platforms have taken action to block certain controversial ideas and statements of politicians, including Mr. Trump, whose use of the platforms they have considered to be violations of law or dangerous to the public, because of Trump's claims about the "theft" of the US 2020 presidential election and what some have interpreted as his calls for overthrow of the government to help him retain his position as President, despite having lost the election.

Certain Republican politicians and government officials have tried to introduce laws to prevent private social media platforms such as Facebook from banning politicians from posting their ideas on those platforms. For example, Ron DeSantis, Governor of Florida, approved a Stop Social Media Censorship Act for the State of Florida in May 2021. However, enforcement of that Act was blocked by federal courts in several cases.[69]

Manhattan Community Access Case

Whether the US federal courts will ultimately decide that social media platforms are, in effect, functioning as state actors remains to be seen, but there is another case that has come before the Supreme Court which will undoubtedly shed some light on this issue. That is the case of *Manhattan Community Access Corporation v. Halleck*. In New York, a nonprofit public access cable television station is operated by the Manhattan Neighborhood Network (MNN).

This station was operating under an agreement with the city of New York. There was an incident in which the station sought to restrict the access of two contributors to the programming because the station claimed that these contributors were urging violence against employees of the station. Those contributors sued, claiming that MNN was restricting their rights of free speech in violation of the First Amendment. Although this case was dismissed by a federal court, the US Court of Appeals for the Second

69. Kara Swisher, "Donald Trump Just Can't Quit Zuckerberg and Dorsey," Opinion, *The New York Times*, online, July 8, 2021.

Circuit ruled that the station could be considered a state actor because the operator had been directed by New York City to provide the station.

The US Supreme Court agreed to hear the case in October 2020. If they issue a decision in this case, it will undoubtedly explore what characteristics determine whether or not a nongovernment entity is, for purposes of the First Amendment, acting as a state entity.

Protection of Websites Regarding Illegal Content Posted by Others

Zeran v. America Online, Inc.[70]

In this case the plaintiff, Zeran, sued America Online (AOL) because an advertisement posted on an AOL site offered T-shirts with offensive messages that identified the plaintiff as a retailer and gave his phone number.

Zeran claimed he was not involved in selling the T-shirts but nevertheless received a huge number of objectionable phone calls including some that threatened him with death.

AOL removed the offensive advertisement. Zeran sued in federal court because AOL had not posted a retraction.

The lower court dismissed Zeran's suit ruling that section 230 of the Communications Decency Act of 1996, which protects providers or user of interactive computer services from being treated as the publishers or speakers of information provided by third parties.

In other words, ISPs, such as AOL, cannot be held liable for information posted by third parties even if that posting contains defamatory or otherwise offensive material.

Zeran appealed, but the Fourth Circuit Court of Appeals confirmed the District Court decision also rejecting the additional argument that, even if AOL could not be treated as publisher of the defamatory material, it could be regarded as a distributor, stating that Zeran's argument could not transform AOL, "to a distributor in the eyes of the law."

The US Supreme Court declined to consider Zeran's case.

Since the Fourth Circuit's decision in Zeran, other federal courts have dismissed defamation claims on similar grounds.[71]

Section 230

Perhaps the most prominent and most controversial section of US Internet law is section 230 of the Communications Decency Act, cited above. This provision has a large impact on the business of major communications service providers such as Facebook, Twitter, and Google. Section 230 defines legal responsibility for content that appears on those sites posted by third parties.

70. 129 F.3rd 327 (4th Cir. 1997).
71. Including, *Blumenthal v. Drudge* (D.D.C. 1998); *Green v. America Online* (3rd Cir. 2003); and *Batzel v. Smith* (9th Cir. 2003).

Section 230 says that "No provider or user of an interactive computer service shall be treated as a publisher or speaker of any information provided by another information content provider."[72]

Essentially this protects Internet service companies from liability for the information published on their websites by others.

This relieves them from the responsibility of having to police the accuracy or legality of third-party information contributed to their platforms.

This is a significant relief for social media companies and search engines because the amount of data that can be accessed through their platforms is enormous. Facebook has almost 3 billion users, and YouTube has over 700,000 hours of videos uploaded to it every day.[73]

The protection of this section is very broad. It applies not only to the well-known Internet intermediaries such as those named above but also to any Internet service that publishes content provided by others. Some of the better-known beneficiaries include Craigslist, Amazon, Yelp, YouTube, Facebook, Twitter, and Trip Advisor. Considering the extent to which the Internet is used by a wide spectrum of parties these days, this section has come to be regarded as a significant pillar supporting free speech.[74]

However, in June 2021, the Texas Supreme Court ruled that Facebook could be sued by minors who became sex trafficking victims of people who used Facebook to entice them into illegal sexual activity. The court said that the immunity provided by section 230 does not apply in such situations.[75]

Some regard section 230 as an unjustified protection for big tech companies against legitimate complaints that inappropriate and harmful material is being posted on their websites.

In July 2021, some Republican members of Congress have drafted legislation to nullify the protections of section 230 with respect to big tech companies. Their objection to section 230 is largely political. Some Republicans claim that social media companies are using the protection of section 230 to "silence conservatives."

The proposed bill is aimed at amending section 230 in significant ways. First, certain platform providers would be exempt from the project protection of section 230. Presumably, this is aimed at companies like Twitter, Instagram and Facebook which in the recent past have banned President Trump from posting statements that they believe to be false and harmful. Secondly, Internet platforms would be required to have reasonable appeal procedures available to permit review of bans on certain content or proposed content.[76]

However, section 230 still remains in effect as of this writing.

---

72. 47 U.S.C section 230.
73. Written on March 26, 2021.
74. *See*, Ïnternet Law. Communications Decency Act. Texas District Court Extends Section 230 Immunity to Social Networking Sites. *Doe v. MySpace, Inc.*, 474 F. Supp. 2d 843 (W.D. Tex. 2007), *Harvard Law Review*, Volume 121 (January 2008), 930-937.
75. Heidi Johnson, "Texas Supreme Court Rules Facebook Can Be Sued for Sex Trafficking," *Jurist*, online, June 28, 2021.
76. Brooke Singman, "House Republicans Introduce Draft Bill to Strip Big Tech Companies of Section 230 Protections," *Fox Business*, online, July 28, 2021.

Establishing Standards of Personal Jurisdiction in Internet Cases

Zippo Manufacturing Co. v. Zippo Dot Com, Inc.[77]

Zippo Manufacturing is a Pennsylvania company that makes the iconic metal Zippo cigarette lighters. Zippo Dot Com was a California Internet company operating the site that offered access to various newsgroups. Any services that Dot Com offered to Pennsylvanians were offered online. Zippo Manufacturing filed a trademark infringement suit in the Federal District Court for the Western District of Pennsylvania. Dot Com filed a motion to dismiss the case based on lack of personal jurisdiction. The court denied that motion to dismiss ruling that personal jurisdiction in Pennsylvania was established by the nature of Dot Com's website activity, on the grounds that:

> In these cases, the exercise of jurisdiction is determined by examining the level of interactivity and commercial nature of the exchange of information that occurs on the website.[78]

The court ruled that the proper test for personal jurisdiction is:

> If the defendant enters into contracts with residents of a foreign jurisdiction that involve knowing and repeated transmission of computer files over the Internet, then personal jurisdiction is proper.[79]

In this case, the court found that:

> Dot Com had contracted with approximately 3,000 individuals and seven internet access providers in Pennsylvania. The intended object of the transactions had been the downloading of electronic messages that formed the basis of a suit in Pennsylvania.[80]

Therefore, the court concluded, sufficient grounds for personal jurisdiction existed.

Clicking to Agree Establishes Contract

ProCD v. Zeidenberg (1996)[81]

A graduate student purchased a CD-ROM of a telephone directory database. The student, Mr. Zeidenberg, used the directory to create an online telephone directory where he charged customers a lower fee for usage than the original creator of the CD-ROM, ProCD, charged its commercial customers. This was a use prohibited by the license included on the CD-ROM. When Zeidenberg installed his CD-ROM, he simply

77. 952 F. Supp. 1119 (WD Pa. 1997).
78. *Id.*, at 1124.
79. *Id.*
80. 952 F. Supp. 1126 (WD Pa. 1997).
81. 86 F.3d 1447 (7th Cir. 1996). The lower court case, decided in favor of Zeidenberg, was before the US District Court for the Western District of Wisconsin. 908 F. Supp 640 (W.D. Wis 1966). The Seventh Circuit reversed and remanded.

clicked agreement to the license without bothering to read it. The question before the court was whether this type of license, referred to as a "click-through license," was valid and enforceable.

The court held that Zeidenberg had agreed to the terms of the license by clicking his agreement. He had the opportunity to refuse to agree and return the CD-ROM. However, by clicking his acceptance of the license terms and installing the software, Zeidenberg had entered into a valid contract under Article 2 of the UCC, section 2-204, 2-206 and 2-606.[82]

Linking to Author Site Is Not Stealing Content

Religious Technology Center v. Netcom.[83]

The plaintiff, Religious Technology Center (RTC), owns the copyrights to the writings of the creator of Scientology, L. Ron Hubbard. A critic of Scientology, Dennis Erlich, gained access to these writings through a bulletin board linked to Internet through Netcom's platform, and used part of them in postings critical of Scientology.

RTC sued Netcom for violating RTC's copyrights by facilitating display of portions of Hubbard's writings.

The court held that Netcom was not liable for infringing copyright because it did not play any part in copying the writings and realized no direct financial gain from any third-party copyright infringement.

Image Search Technology Does Not Violate Copyright

Perfect 10, Inc. v. Amazon.com, Inc[84]

The plaintiff in this case claimed ownership of copyrighted nude model photographs. The plaintiff claimed that by allowing computer searches to locate the plaintiff's site and display results which may include text, videos and/or photos, the defendant Google violated the plaintiff's copyrights.

Google's affirmative defense was that displaying search results linked to the plaintiff's website was a permitted "fair use," which allows use of copyrighted work under particular circumstances.

In considering Google's defense, the court found that:

- search engines are of significant value to the public;
- the thumbnail images resulting from Google's search were significantly "transformative" of the originals—that is, that they presented a significantly different visual experience;

82. *See*, Bradon L. Grusd, "Contracting Beyond Copyright: *ProCD, Inc. v. Zeidenberg*," *Harvard Journal of Law & Technology*, Volume 10 (Winter 1997).
83. *Religious Technology Center v. Netcom On-Line Communication Services, Inc.*, 907 F.Supp. 1361 (N.D. CA, 1995).
84. 487 F.3d 701 (9th Cir. 2007).

- the amount and substantiality of Google's use of the original material was not a significant factor; and
- it was not proved that Google's search results would harm the plaintiff's market for the original photographs, and such harm could not be presumed.

The court's conclusion was that Google's search results constituted a permitted "fair use" of the plaintiff's copyrighted material, and Google was not liable for copyright infringement.

New Mexico Internet Censorship Law

ACLU v. Johnson, US Ct. Appeals, 10th Cir., November 2, 1999

In 1998, New Mexico enacted a statute that criminalized the dissemination of computer material that is harmful to minors (N.M. Stat. Ann. section 30-37-3.2(A)). The American Civil Liberties Union (ACLU) and other organizations brought suit in the Federal District Court, claiming that the New Mexico statute violated the First Amendment and the Commerce Clause of the United States Constitution.

After examining the evidence, the District Court found:

- Plaintiffs are various organizations and individuals who maintain or use computer systems to provide access to a range of information through a variety of media which is accessible by residents of the state of New Mexico on the Internet.
- Plaintiff's speech includes discussions of women's health and interests, literary works, fine art, gay and lesbian issues, prison rape, and censorship and civil liberties issues.

The Tenth Circuit Court upheld the District Court's grant to the plaintiffs of a preliminary injunction preventing the statute from taking affect because in accordance with criteria outlined by the US Supreme Court, plaintiffs have standing when an alleged injury is in pending.

In this case, if the statute were allowed to take affect and the material the plaintiffs post on the Internet was deemed "harmful to minors," they would face the risk of being arrested for a crime, publicly shamed, and required to pay for a defense only to have a court find that the newly enacted statue is unconstitutional.

As the 10th Circuit said, this issue should be determined before the injury occurs.

Although the court notes that the plaintiffs are certainly successful on their First Amendment objections, there are commerce clause issues raised by the statute. The commerce clause prohibits state regulation that discriminates against or unduly burdens interstate commerce. The court found that the statute is an attempt to regulate interstate commerce and therefore violates the commerce clause in three ways:

(1) it regulates conduct occurring holy outside the state of New Mexico;

(2) it constitutes an unreasonable and undue burden on interstate and foreign commerce; and
(3) it subjects use of the Internet to inconsistent state regulation.

The court notes that under the language of the statute, the State of New Mexico would be entitled to bring prosecution against parties who are outside the state and whose only contact with the state is through the Internet.

The court notes that interstate flight, rail, and highway traffic requires a cohesive national scheme of regulation so that users are reasonably able to determine their obligations. Statutes like the New Mexico statute would potentially create inconsistencies with other state statutes that frustrate this necessity for cohesive regulation.

Therefore, the 10th Circuit affirmed the injunction against enforcement of the New Mexico Internet censorship statute.

High-Speed Internet Fraud

At the end of 2018, Charter Communications, an ISP, agreed to pay a total of $174.2 million to settle consumer fraud charges brought by the New York State Attorney General, including $62.5 million in direct consumer refunds.[85] At the time, this was believed to be the largest payout ever by an ISP to consumers.

The ISP was accused of failing to provide consumers with the high-speed Internet service it had promised. There were 700,000 customers who would receive refunds of up to $150 each plus additional payments relating to streaming services and premium channels.

Charter was criticized for a number of failings, including:

- leasing inadequate modems and routers;
- aggressively marketing high download speeds that they could not deliver;
- guaranteeing seamless access to programs while engaging in "hard ball" tactics with Netflix and other service providers that interfered with consumer reception of service; and
- claiming both cable and Wi-Fi access speed would be the same, which they knew not to be true.

Website Accessibility for the Disabled

In 2010, the US Congress passed the Americans with Disabilities Act (ADA).

Title III of the ADA requires that:

> No individual shall be discriminated against on the basis of disability in the full and equal enjoyment of the goods, services, facilities, privileges, advantages, or

85. Office of the NYS Attorney General, Press Release, December 18, 2018, online, accessed April 17, 2021.

> accommodations of any place of public accommodation or by any person who owns, leases (or leases two) or operates a place of public accommodation.[86]

Several recent law cases have made it clear that this prohibition of discrimination also applies to websites. If one operates a website that is not ADA compliant, one can be sued or fined or be subject to other penalties.[87]

The *Domino's Pizza* Case

A key case on this issue is the US Supreme Court's decision in June 2019 that it would not consider reversing the decision of the US Ninth Circuit Court of Appeals that Domino's Pizza LLC had failed to design, construct, maintain and operate its website and mobile application to be fully accessible to a blind man named Guillermo Robles.[88]

In that case, Domino's was sued because Mr. Robles was unable to use his screen reading software to order pizza from Domino's website. He sought damages and injunctive relief, requiring Domino's to comply with the requirements of the ADA. The lower court dismissed Mr. Robles' suit on grounds that there were insufficient guidelines to allow specifying the level of compliance that Domino's would need to comply with.

The Ninth Circuit held that the ADA clearly applies to Domino's website and app because:

> The ADA expressly provides that a place of public accommodation, like Domino's, engages in unlawful discrimination if it fails to "take such steps as may be necessary to ensure that no individual with a disability is excluded, denied services, segregated or otherwise treated differently than other individuals because of the absence of auxiliary aids and services."[89]

The Ninth Circuit disagreed with the lower court finding that the lack of specific regulations does not eliminate Domino's statutory duty to comply with the ADA. They reversed the decision of the District Court and remanded the case back to the District Court for decision holding:

> We expressed no opinion about whether Domino's website or app comply with the ADA. We leave it to the district court, after discovery, to decide in the first instance whether Domino's website and app provide the blind with effective communication in full and equal enjoyment of its products and services as the ADA mandates.

Domino's applied to the Supreme Court to review the Ninth Circuit's decision, but the Supreme Court declined to do so.

86. 42 U.S. Code section 12182.
87. *See*, Amanda Robert, "How to Make a Website Accessible," *ABA Journal*, online, July 1, 2019, accessed April 19, 2021.
88. *Robles v. Domino's Pizza, LLC*, 913 F.3d 898 (9th Cir. 2019).
89. *Id.*

After *Domino's*

Website access for disabled people particularly, for the blind, has become an important issue in the US. The number of lawsuits on this issue has increased dramatically. One indication is that the number of lawsuits on this issue filed in federal courts in 2018 was approximately three times the number of such suits filed in 2017.[90] Most of these suits relate to problems like that in the *Domino's* case experienced by disabled people trying to use "screen reader" software to speak the words on the website.[91]

Navigating the Internet can be a frustrating experience for the visually impaired. Joseph DiNero, an enabling technology specialist with Helen Keller Services for the Blind, says when he tries to use websites and mobile apps, it sometimes feels like "I am penalized because I am blind":

> On an inaccessible site, screen readers can't properly translate the content. They get stuck, simply saying "image" instead of describing it, or not saying which information should be typed into blank fields on an ordering page.[92]

Web Content Accessibility Guidelines

Since the mid-1990s, there have been efforts to create and adopt web accessibility guidelines to enable disabled people to have equal access to the Internet. This effort has largely been led by the W3C which is an international organization created to set international standards for the operation and use of the World Wide Web. W3C is led by Tim Berners-Lee who is credited with inventing the World Wide Web.

Berners-Lee highlighted the issue of web access for the disabled in a speech he gave in Chicago in 1994 at the Second International Conference on the World Wide Web.

In 1995, the first accessibility guidelines were drafted and released by Greg Vanderheiden. After that, various authors suggested additional guidelines.

In 1998, the University of Wisconsin undertook to organize these guidelines into a publication entitled, *Unified Web Site Accessibility Guidelines* (Version 8).

Using those University of Wisconsin guidelines as a starting point, W3C published a version of web accessibility guidelines in 1999 known as (Web Content Accessibility Guidelines) WCAG 1.0 consisting of fourteen guidelines setting out basic principles for website accessibility. Each of the guidelines referred to "checkpoints" detailing how to make web pages effective in satisfying the requirements of the guidelines. These "checkpoints" were assigned priority numbers 1, 2 or 3 depending on how important they were thought to be in facilitating web access.

Over several years additions and corrections were suggested to WCGA, which evolved into WCAG 2.0 that was formally recommended by W3C in December 2008.

---

90. Sara Randazzo, "Lawsuits Surge over Websites' Access for the Blind," *The Wall Street Journal* (February 17, 2019), online, accessed April 20, 2021.
91. *Id.*
92. *Id.*

Since then, a version 2.1 has been developed and was formally recommended by W3C in 2018. As of late 2020, a version WCAG 2.2 was being worked on.

The WCAG versions were originally created by developers not working directly for government, but over time several nations and groups of nations have adopted their principles as having the force of law. These include the US, the EU, and the United Kingdom (UK).

The issue of website accessibility for disabled people has become such a serious matter in the US that it has affected even the most sophisticated and liberal providers of online websites. An important example of this is a detailed settlement reached by the US Department of Justice (DOJ) in April 2015 with edX, which is a nonprofit online educational program created by Harvard and Massachusetts Institute of Technology (MIT) in 2012 to allow top universities and educational institutions to offer thousands of courses online.[93] The other universities subscribing to the program include Georgetown, Dartmouth, Caltech, the Sorbonne, and Peking University, in addition to Harvard and MIT. By 2015, there were more than sixty institutions of higher learning using the platform to provide around five hundred courses to thousands of online students.

The significance of these goals and their importance to providing higher education to those who for several reasons, including physical disability, would find it too difficult or too expensive to seek these educational experiences through regular university attendance make it worthwhile to repeat some of the key details of this settlement here. At the very least, this matter provides a good summary of the attitude of the US government to issues relating to website accessibility, and what the DOJ may expect of online website operators.

The agreement with the DOJ requires edX to make significant modifications to its website, platform, and mobile applications to conform to the WCAG 2.0 AA, which the DOJ recognizes as industry guidelines for making web content accessible to users with disabilities. edX is also required to provide guidance and tools to the organizations that create and/or post courses on the website to assist them in creating accessible course content. The settlement includes a four-year agreement which requires edX to:

(1) make the edX website, its mobile applications and learning management system software, through which online courses are offered, fully accessible within eighteen months;
(2) ensure that its content management system, called Studio, which edX makes available to entities creating online courses, is fully accessible and supports authoring and publishing of accessible content within an additional eighteen months;
(3) provide guidance to course creators and its member universities and other institutions on best practices for making online courses fully accessible;

93. Department of Justice, Office of Public Affairs, *Justice News*, Thursday, April 2, 2015, "Justice Department Reaches Settlement with edX Inc., Provider of Massive Open Online Courses, to Make its Website, Online Platform and Mobile Applications Accessible Under the Americans with Disabilities Act," online, accessed April 21, 2021.

(4) appoint a Web Accessibility Coordinator;
(5) adopt a Web Accessibility Policy:
   - solicit feedback from learners on the accessibility of the courses.
(6) conduct web accessibility training for employees responsible for the website, platform, and mobile applications; and
(7) retain a consultant to evaluate conformance of the website, platform, and mobile applications.

The Acting Attorney General stated that the Justice Department attitude toward this kind of enterprise is that:

> Massive open online courses have the potential to increase access to high-quality education for people facing income, distance and other barriers, but only if they are truly open to everyone. This landmark agreement is far reaching and ensuring that individuals with disabilities will have equal opportunity to independently access quality higher education online. edX is to be commended for working with the Justice Department to take such steps.[94]

Confusion from Winn-Dixie

However, as a Florida case showed in 2021, there is still a considerable lack of clarity in establishing what services the ADA applies to.

In April 2021, the US Court of Appeals for the 11th Circuit issued a decision holding that websites are not "places of public accommodation" within Title III of the ADA.[95] The court held that:

> Winn Dixie's website does not constitute an "intangible barrier" to the plaintiff's ability to access and enjoy fully and equally the goods, services, facilities, privileges, advantages or accommodations of a place of public accommodation.

The plaintiff, Juan Carlos Gil, is a visually disabled customer of the defendant who found he was not able to access the defendant's website using his screen reading software.[96]

The 11th Circuit did not follow the holding of the *Domino's Pizza v. Robles* case discussed above. Following the decisions of other US courts of appeals such as those of the 3rd, 6th and 9th Circuits, the 11th Circuit concluded that "places of public accommodation" are limited to physical locations, and do not include websites on the Internet.

However, the court points out that the ADA's antidiscrimination provisions apply "not just to physical barriers but also to 'intangible barriers'." Nevertheless, the court held that:

> Winn-Dixie's limited use website, although inaccessible by individuals who are visually disabled, does not function as an intangible barrier to an individual with

94. *Id.*
95. *Gil v. Winn-Dixie Stores, Inc.*, No. 17-13467 (11th Cir. 2021).
96. *Gil* Opinion, p. 2.

> a visual disability accessing the goods, services, privileges, or advantages of Winn-Dixie's physical stores (the operative place of public accommodation). Specifically, Winn-Dixie's website has only limited functionality. More importantly, it is not a point of sale, all purchases must occur at the store.[97]

Therefore:

> Accordingly, we hold that Winn Dixie's website does not constitute an "intangible barrier" to Gil's ability to access and enjoy fully and equally "the goods, services, facilities, privileges, advantages or accommodations of" a place of public accommodation (hear a physical Winn-Dixie store). Consequently, Gil's inability to access the website does not violate Title III of the ADA in this way.[98]

The *Gil* court's view of the language of the statute was that the statutory language was ambiguous and unclear in defining "places of public accommodation" as tangible physical places. Consequently, the definition does not include websites.[99]

The 11th Circuit distinguished the *Gil* case from *Domino's* decision by focusing on the "point of sale" issue:

> In contrast, in this case, Winn-Dixie's website does not provide any direct sales of goods or services or impede access to the goods and services offered in the physical stores.[100]

There was a strong dissent from 11th Circuit Judge, Jill Pryor, who wrote:

> Winn-Dixie does not dispute that it failed to provide an auxiliary aid when it refused to make its website compatible with screen-reading technology. As a result, visually-impaired individuals could not access the website. And Winn-Dixie provided no alternative way for them to request express prescription refills or digitally link coupons to their rewards cards so that discounts could be applied seamlessly at checkout—privileges and advantages that sighted customers enjoyed. That amounted to discrimination under [the ADA] and was therefore prohibited ... .

Consequently, it now appears that there will need to be either clarifying legislation from the US Congress or a ruling from the US Supreme Court to settle this apparent conflict between the decisions of different Circuit Courts of Appeal.

Privacy of Digital Records

Fourth Amendment Protection

The purpose of the Fourth Amendment to the US Constitution is to protect persons against unreasonable searches and seizures by the government. The Fourth Amendment says:

97. *Id.*, p. 22.
98. *Id.*, p. 23.
99. *Id.*, pp. 17-18.
100. *Id.*, p. 31.

> The right of the people to be secure in their persons, houses, papers, and effects, against unreasonable searches and seizures, shall not be violated, and no warrants shall issue, but upon probable cause, supported by oath or affirmation, and particularly describing the place to be searched, and the persons or things to be seized.

Riley v. California[101]

Petitioner Riley was stopped for a traffic violation and was found to have a weapon which led to his arrest on a weapons charge.

During the arrest Riley's cell phone was seized. When examining the information on the phone, indications were found that Riley was a member of a street gang. The phone was turned over to an officer specializing in street gangs who examined the phone's digital contents. In the phone's contacts, photographs, and videos, there was material that led the State of California to charge Riley in connection with a shooting that had occurred a few weeks earlier.

Riley's attorney moved to suppress all evidence the police obtained from his cell phone. The trial court denied the motion and this decision was affirmed by the California Court of Appeals. In reviewing this conviction and a companion case from the First Circuit Court of Appeals, the US Supreme Court held that the police generally may not, without a warrant, search digital information on a cell phone seized from an individual who has been arrested.

After quoting the language of the Fourth Amendment, the court said that the Fourth Amendment made it clear that the ultimate test for searches and seizures was "reasonableness," and that reasonableness generally required the obtaining of a judicial warrant.

Consequently, regarding searches of data from mobile phones, the key question is whether the hey search of mobile phone data without a warrant could fall within an exception to the requirement of a warrant.[102] One such exception previously established by the court is where an arrest is made; it is reasonable for an arresting officer to search the person arrested in order to make sure they do not have any weapons they could use to resist arrest or make their escape.[103]

The court pointed out that the adoption of cell phones and other stores of digital data required a rethinking of when a warrantless search could be considered reasonable.[104] The court concluded that cell phones can contain a huge amount of digital data which may be related to all aspects of the owner's life. The data itself cannot be used to harm an arresting officer or to allow a prisoner to escape. Therefore, it would not be reasonable to allow searches of that data without first obtaining a warrant.[105]

Although there is an argument that an arrested person may wish to destroy evidence stored on his cell phone, they cannot do that once the cell phone has been

101. *Riley v. California*, 573 U.S. 373 (2014).
102. *Riley v. California*, p. 5.
103. *Chimel v. California*, 395 U.S. 752 (1969).
104. *Riley v. California*, p. 9.
105. *Id.*, p. 10.

seized. Once a cell phone is in the possession of law enforcement authorities, it is not unreasonable to require the government to obtain a warrant upon probable cause to allow them to search the data on that cell phone.[106] Fourth Amendment protections are not limited to physical items only but can extend to any possessions which a person has a reasonable expectation will remain private, including stored digital records.[107]

Carpenter v. United States (US Supreme Court, 2018)

Whenever cell phones connect to communications masts, known as "cell sites," they create a time-stamped digital record called "cell site location information" (CSLI). This information is stored by the wireless carriers and used for their own business purposes.

Timothy Carpenter was a robbery suspect. The FBI had his cell phone number, and prosecutors were able to get court orders to obtain his cell phone records under the Stored Communications Act (SCA). Carpenter's wireless carrier produced CSLI for the government, and prosecutors were able to obtain 12,898 location points which identified Carpenter's movements over 127 days. In other words, the government had approximately 101 data points showing his location per day.

Carpenter's attorneys moved to have these records suppressed arguing that the government did not have sufficient probable cause when seeking these records, and therefore their acquisition of these records was in violation of the protections of the Fourth Amendment. The lower court denied this motion and Carpenter was convicted at trial. The Court of Appeals for the Sixth Circuit ruled that Carpenter lacked a reasonable expectation of privacy with respect to the location information because he had shared that information with his wireless carriers.

The Supreme Court[108] held that the acquisition of these location records did constitute an improper Fourth Amendment search. The court said the Fourth Amendment protects not only property interests but also certain expectations of privacy. If that expectation of privacy exists, the government requires probable cause to obtain information covered by that reasonable expectation.

The Supreme Court had previously recognized individuals have a reasonable expectation of privacy with respect to their physical movements. The court held in order to acquire such records, the government had to show "reasonable grounds for believing that they were relevant and material to an ongoing investigation."

Therefore, the Carpenter search fell short of probable cause. Consequently, it was not a permitted way to get cell-site records.

As a result of these holdings, it should be noted that a warrant is required in any case where the suspect has a legitimate privacy interest in records held by a third party. Consequently, the government will usually need a warrant to access cell-site records. However, it is recognized that there may be some specific cases, such as those where there is urgency, which may support a search of those records without a warrant.

106. *Id.*, pp. 12-15.
107. *Id.*, pp. 19-20.
108. *Carpenter v. United States*, No. 16-402, 585 U.S. XX (2018).

Data Privacy Law Battles

$5 Billion Fine Against Facebook

In July 2019, the US FTC imposed a $5 billion penalty on Facebook and required Facebook to submit to new and modified corporate structure requirements that are intended to make the company more responsible for the way it treats the privacy of its users.

Facebook agreed to these requirements to settle charges brought by the FTC that Facebook had violated a 2012 FTC order by deceiving Facebook users about Facebook's ability to protect the privacy of the users' personal information.[109]

This was the largest penalty ever imposed by the FTC for violating consumers privacy and was almost twenty times larger than the largest data security penalty ever imposed in the world. It was one of the largest penalties ever imposed by the US government for any regulatory violation. The penalties imposed by the FTC centered around the issue that:

> Despite repeated promises to billions of its users worldwide that they could control how their personal information is shared, Facebook undermined consumers choices.

The FTC went on to say:

> The magnitude of the $5 billion penalty and sweeping conduct relief are unprecedented in the history of the FTC. The relief is designed not only to punish future violations but more importantly, to change Facebook's entire privacy culture to decrease the likelihood of continued violations. The Commission takes consumer privacy seriously and will enforce FTC orders to the fullest extent of the law.[110]

Stored Communications Act

One area of data protection that has been particularly troubling is the SCA. This is a statute that large tech companies have repeatedly used to justify their failure to comply with court case subpoenas, particularly in criminal cases where the defendant's life may be at stake.

Supposedly a protection for data privacy, this law is used to bar criminal defendants from obtaining the contents of a third person's Internet communications by means of subpoenas.

Apparently, courts are interpreting the law in a way that defines it as a privilege that prevents defendants from obtaining online communications from the tech companies that have stored copies of these electronic messages.

109. Federal Trade Commission, "FTC Imposes $5 Billion Penalty and Sweeping New Privacy Restrictions on Facebook," online, July 24, 2019, accessed May 4, 2021.
110. *Id.*

Rebeca Wexler, an assistant law professor at the Berkley School of Law of the University of California, has argued that this interpretation is incorrect and in violation of basic criminal justice principles of search for truth and fairness.[111]

Cases that have been particularly troubling to Professor Wexler include the following:

- A California case in which a defendant was hampered in arguing self-defense because he was unable to obtain records of online death threats and other harassing conduct that had made him fear for his own life.
- A district of Columbia defendant was unable to get copies of an important prosecution witnesses' social media postings which the defendant claimed would have allowed him a more effective cross-examination of that witness.
- A refugee from Iraq who was denied the right to get Facebook and Twitter posts which could have prevented his extradition by providing evidence that he could face torture and death if he were extradited back to Iraq.

Professor Wexler's principal complaint is that judicial interpretations of the SCA give tech companies special entitlements not to comply with judicially ordered compulsory process, and that those entitlements are more important than the life and liberty of the criminally accused. Indeed, Facebook and Twitter recently argued to the Supreme Court that it is wrong to "prioritize a criminal defendants desire to obtain relevant, exculpatory evidence over 'trust in the privacy of electronic communications,' because doing so 'threatens to discourage the use and development of innovative technologies'." To date, courts have agreed.

The interpretation to which Professor Wexler objects has not been limited to federal courts; it has been endorsed by both federal and state courts.

Although the SCA lists several exemptions to disclosure requirements, it does not mention criminal defense subpoenas. Nevertheless, the courts have relied on the SCA as a reason for suppressing relevant and exculpatory evidence subpoenas.

In Professor Wexler's view, judicial decisions recognizing the SCA as creating a privilege violates "A binding rule of privilege law: courts must not interpret an ambiguous silence in statutory text as impliedly creating a privilege because privileges are 'in derogation of the search for truth'."

This issue has yet to be resolved. At some point, the US Supreme Court will need to define the issue of exactly what legislative language is required before a court can legitimately decide that a statute has created an exemption from accepted judicial practice.

Compelled Decryption

In 2020, the New Jersey Supreme Court ruled, in the case of *State v. Andrews*, that compelling a defendant to disclose his iPhone passcodes was not protected by Fifth

111. Rebecca Wexler, "Privacy as Privilege: The Stored Communications Act and Internet Evidence," *Harvard Law Review*, Volume 134 (June 2021), online.

Amendment privilege.[112] A subsequent article in the *Harvard Law Review* argues that this was a mistake.[113] The article said:

> In stretching the so-called "act of production" doctrine to cover the compelled provision of iPhone pass codes, a step beyond the compelled unlocking of the device, the Andrews Court inappropriately narrowed the privilege against self in incrimination, contravening judicial precedent and constitutional history alike.

In this case, the defendant Andrews, a suspected drug trafficker, was required to surrender two of his iPhones to the police. However, without his passcodes they could not read the text messages contained in the phones. The prosecution moved to compel disclosure of the passcodes. In opposition, the defendant argued that the Fifth Amendment clause against self-incrimination and parallel New Jersey statutory and common law privileges prohibited compelling Andrews to reveal his passcodes.[114]

The *Harvard Law Review* article argues that some acts of production, although not compelled statements, may have testimonial aspects that would be subject to Fifth Amendment protection as described in the US Supreme Court case of *Fisher v. The United States*[115] where the court held that the production of information may not be oral testimony in itself but can still be protected by the Fifth Amendment privilege against self-incrimination because "the act of production itself may implicitly communicate incriminatory statements." The article argues that the New Jersey Supreme Court was wrong in holding that production of Andrews' passcodes was not protected by the Fifth Amendment because under rulings by the US Supreme Court and other US federal courts, Fifth Amendment privilege has been held to cover physical acts with "communicative aspect(s)."[116] For example, the *Fisher* Court pointed out that responding to a subpoena for documents included within it "tacit averments" of "the existence of the papers demanded and their possession or control by the defendant" could be potentially incriminating and may be within Fifth Amendment protection.[117]

The article says that the New Jersey Supreme Court in *Andrews* should have seen the passcode production as compound testimony protected by the Fifth Amendment.[118] The article sees the production of these iPhone passcodes as protected because they "may lead to incriminating evidence"[119] even if the disclosed information itself is not incriminating.[120]

Any new issues introduced using new technologies should not be excuses to weaken the Fifth Amendment protection against self-incrimination.[121]

---

112. *State v. Andrews*, 234 A.3rd 1254 (N.J. 2020).
113. "Fifth Amendment, *State v. Andrews*, Supreme Court of New Jersey Holds that Compelling Disclosure of Defendant's iPhone Passcodes Does Not Violate the Self-Incrimination Clause, Recent Case: 234 A.3rd 1254 (N.J. 2020)" 134 Harvard Law Review 2267, April 12, 2021.
114. 134 HLR 2267.
115. 425 U.S. 391 (1976).
116. *United States v. Hubbell*, 530 U.S. 27, 44 (2000).
117. *Fisher*, 425 U.S. at 410.
118. 134 HLR 2272.
119. 134 HLR 2273.
120. Citing, *United States v. Hubbell*, 530 U.S. 27, 38 (2000).
121. 134 HLR 2274.

It seems likely that the issue raised by the New Jersey Supreme Court in *Andrews* will come before other state courts, US federal courts and possibly, the US Supreme Court. So, it is fair to say that although the *Andrews* case may have taken a too narrow view of Fifth Amendment protection, this issue has not been finally resolved. So, it would make sense to consult any post-2020 cases in the state or federal courts that refer to the *Andrews* ruling to see whether those other cases reach different conclusions about the application of Fifth Amendment protection to instances of compelled disclosure, particularly those relating to passwords, access numbers, etc., and new technology.

More US Internet Cases

US Internet case law is extensive. There are well over a hundred significant Internet cases that have been reported during the "Internet era" which began sometime before 1990. It is not possible, within the scope of this book, to describe, analyze and comment on all the cases that have been brought in US federal and state courts. However, searches on the Internet should reveal many more cases on the issues discussed above and other Internet issues that this book does not have the space to analyze.

H PRIVACY AND DATA PROTECTION

Data privacy and protection in the US is established by a combination of federal and state statutes and regulations.

Recently, there has been some private efforts in the tech sector to provide greater data privacy for Internet users.

Apple Transparency Feature

In April 2021, Apple introduced some modifications to its operating software that permits users to refuse to allow apps to collect data about their usage. This is the new App Tracking Transparency feature included in iOS 14.5. This requires apps to ask users whether the app is permitted to use something called Identifier for Advertisers (IDFA) that allows the app to collect data about an Internet user's activities on the Internet that can be helpful in allowing Internet advertisers to develop targeted ads aimed at users.[122]

This is apparently in line with the attitude of Apple founder Steve Jobs who is reported to have said back in 2010 that Internet users should always be asked whether they want their data used by others.[123]

It was reported that:

122. Jane Wakefield, "Facebook v. Apple: The Ad Tracking Row Heats Up," *BBC News*, online, April 29, 2021.
123. *Id.*

> Privacy campaigners have applauded the new safeguards, which they believe will make it harder for private companies to snoop on our digital lives and reap profit from our personal data by selling targeted adverts.[124]

It is believed that most users will decline to allow IDFA to be used on their systems.

The introduction of this new feature on Apple devices was a matter of openly expressed public concern for Facebook.

Facebook said that this new Apple feature could diminish Facebook advertising revenue by as much as 50%. Facebook is heavily dependent on user data to be able to allow its advertisers to create ads targeted at the interests of particular Internet users.

However, Facebook's opposition to this Apple feature has not proved very popular. So, Facebook did change its public stance about this and conceded that Internet advertisers will have to change the way they use data gathered from Internet use so that in the future they need to use less collected data in their advertising.

Although the step by Apple is a positive way of giving Internet users a way of having greater privacy about their Internet use, not all big tech companies agree with this proconsumer attitude.

For example, it is reported that Google has come up with something called Federated Learning of Cohorts (FloCs). This is a tool that allows tech companies to gather information about consumer use of browsers that will allow even more focused advertising campaigns directed at Internet users.[125]

FloC collects information about the browser use of individuals that enables a browser company, such as Google, to group users together with those of similar usage histories (FloCs). This allows advertisers to more easily be able to target large groups of users with similar interests.

Whether this FloC idea will be widely employed is hard to say. Reportedly, other browser companies, such as Mozilla and Firefox, are not enthusiastic about Google's idea. The Electronic Frontiers Foundation, a nonprofit organization that supports data privacy on the Internet, strongly opposes Google's plan, calling FloC "a Terrible Idea," and is committing to fighting it.[126]

Apple v. FBI[127]

In December 2015, the FBI began investigation of a mass shooting in San Bernardino, California, in which fourteen people were killed and twenty-two injured.

As part of that investigation, the FBI wanted access to the information contained on the iPhone of one of the shooters. The information was encrypted, and the FBI

124. Simon Duke, "Apple's Bid for Moral High Ground Privacy Is Good for Business," *The Times*, online, April 29, 2021.
125. *Id.*
126. EFF, "Google's FloC Is a Terrible Idea," online, March 3, 2021, accessed April 29, 2021.
127. *In the Matter of the Search of an Apple iPhone Seized during the Execution of a Search Warrant on a Black Lexus 1S300, California License Plate 35KGD203* in the U.S. District Court for the Central District of California.

sought court orders under the All-Writs Act, 28 USC section 1651, requiring Apple to bypass the security of the phone and assist the FBI in obtaining the encrypted data. Apple challenged the order on the grounds that it was unconstitutional to compel them to do as the FBI asked.

Eventually, the FBI withdrew its request because it said it found a third party who helped them unlock the phone, and there was no information relevant to the crimes on the phone.[128]

Nevertheless, the desire of law enforcement agencies to be able to compel tech companies to provide assistance in decrypting data from smartphones and other digital devices has remained an issue of contention.

In April 2016, two US senators published draft legislation that would permit state and federal judges to order "any person who provides a product or method to facilitate communication or the processing or storage of data" to provide the data in readable form or to provide the technical assistance necessary to unlock encrypted data. The legislation also would require any person who provides software or devices that hold data to be capable of complying with any such court orders.[129]

The bill has been amended and was still being debated in Congress as of October 2020.[130]

US Data Protection Regulations Overview

There is no overall constitutional right to privacy within the US. However, US federal courts, including the Supreme Court, have found that the bill of rights creates certain areas of personal privacy which are constitutionally protected.[131] Also, some state constitutions contain specific prohibitions against government intrusions into private matters.[132]

Certain limited specific rights of privacy are affected and/or protected by Amendments to the US Constitution. The First Amendment does guarantee freedom of speech but places some restrictions on certain kinds of speech. For example, for a public official to be successful in a suit for defamation, the official must show that the statement complained about was made with malice. This constitutes kind of a guarantee of privacy to certain aspects of the thought process which someone accused of defamation may have undergone in deciding to make a statement that a public official considers to be offensive.

---

128. Joseph Tanfani, "Race to Unlock San Bernardino Shooter's iPhone Was Delayed by Poor FBI Communication, Report Finds," *Los Angeles Times*, March 27, 2018.
129. Dustin Volz and Mark Hoseball, "Leak of Senate Encryption Bill Prompts Swift Backlash," *Reuters*, April 8, 2016; and Dustin Volz and Mark Hoseball, "U.S. Senate Panel Releases Draft of Controversial Encryption Bill," *Reuters*, April 13, 2016.
130. Bob Swanson, "In Response to the Lawful Access to Encrypted Data Act," *Nextgov*, online, October 15, 2020, accessed June 25, 2021.
131. *Roe v. Wade*, 410 U.S. 113 (1973), right to privacy of a woman's decision to have an abortion; *Griswold v. Connecticut*, 381 U.S. 479, rights to marital privacy; *Paul v. Davis*, 424 U.S. 643 (1976), constitutional right to protection against government intrusion into private family matters such as having children, etc.
132. For example, Illinois, California and Arizona.

The Fourth Amendment protects people against unreasonable searches and seizures by the government. This does provide some level of protection of privacy with respect to the property, papers, and personal effects of US citizens. The Supreme Court has held that this not only applies to "physical invasions" but can also extend to other kinds of government intrusion such as telephone tapping.[133]

However, this protection is not complete.

Other than these somewhat narrow protections, there is no overall US law which protects the privacy of personal information, although some federal statutes provide some protection in specific limited areas. For example, there is the US Electronic Communications Privacy Act (ECPA). This was passed in 1998 to protect personal information on the Internet. The ECPA applies to all forms of communication on the Internet, whether oral, text or pictorial.[134] However, there are gaps in this protection. System operators are allowed to store and review any messages that are communicated over their digital systems, although it is usually illegal for them to reveal any of that information to third parties. Also, system operators are permitted to reveal such information to government agents if they reasonably believe that the communicator is engaging in illegal activity.[135]

I BROADBAND ACCESS IMPROVEMENT

In August 2021, US Senate passed a $1.2 trillion infrastructure bill to improve roads, bridges, transit systems, electricity distribution, water systems and broadband. The bill earmarked $42 billion to expand broadband access and maintain the Internet. Over $14 billion was focused on making the Internet more affordable, including expanding an emergency broadband benefit program to provide subsidies for Internet service to less affluent households. Another $2.7 billion was to be focused on providing people of all ages and abilities with training in how to use the high-speed Internet. These improvements were intended to improve broadband service throughout the US. According to one report, 15% of people older than 50 do not have any Internet service and 60% of people over 50 feel that the cost of Internet is too high. Broadband-related provisions in the infrastructure bill are intended to help solve these problems.[136]

That bill, pared down to $1 trillion, was passed by Congress and signed into law by President Biden in November 2021.

In the final bill, $65 billion is earmarked to provide grants to states to bring or improve broadband service in rural areas, to low-income families and Native American tribal communities.[137]

133. *Katz v. United States*, 389 U.S. 347, 363 (1967).
134. 18 U.S.C. sections 2510-2521 and 2701-2711.
135. Domingo R. Tan, "Personal Privacy in the Information Age: Comparison of Internet Data Protection Regulations in the United States and European Union," Digital Commons at Loyola Marymount University and Loyola Marymount Law School, *International and Comparative Law Journal*, Volume 21, 660-681, 672.
136. Dena Bunis, "Senate Passes Infrastructure Bill That Makes Broadband More Affordable," *AARP*, online, August 10, 2021.
137. Mary Clark Jalonick, *AP News*, online, November 6, 2021.

CHAPTER 5

EU Internet Law

In those twenty-seven nations[138] that are members of the EU, access to the Internet is governed by EU law promulgated by the European Parliament and implemented by the legal and regulatory authorities of the Member States.

A FUNDAMENTAL RIGHTS

The fundamental principle that supports this access is the EU's founding principle of Freedom of Speech contained in Articles 10, 11 and 14 of the European Convention of Human Rights.[139]

Article 10 states that everyone has the right to freedom of expression, including the freedom to hold opinions and to receive and impart information and ideas without interference by the government, although governments retain the right to license broadcasts and exhibitions and to limit this freedom with the legal restrictions "necessary in a democratic society."[140]

Article 11 guarantees a right of freedom of assembly and association, including the right to join trade unions. Again, any restrictions on these rights must be those that "are necessary in a democratic society in the interest of national security or public safety … ."[141]

Article 14 prohibits discrimination in the enjoyment of the rights and freedoms set forth in Articles 10 and 11. It states that those rights "shall be secured without discrimination on any ground such as sex, race, color, language, religion, political or

138. Austria, Belgium, Bulgaria, Croatia, Cyprus, Czechia, Denmark, Estonia, Finland, France, Germany, Greece, Hungary, Ireland, Italy, Latvia, Lithuania, Luxembourg, Malta, the Netherlands, Poland, Portugal, Romania, Slovakia, Slovenia, Spain, and Sweden.
139. European Union, Convention for the Protection of Human Rights and Fundamental Freedoms (Rome, 1950).
140. European Union, Convention for the Protection of Human Rights and Fundamental Freedoms, Article 10.
141. *Id.*, Article 11.

other opinion, national or social origin, association with a national minority, property, birth or other status."[142]

Implied by this right to receive and distribute information is the right to access to and use of the Internet. However, not content to leave the regulation of Internet access and use to be implied by more general rights, the EU, through the European Parliament and the European Council, promulgated several directives and regulations that address the Internet directly.

The *Telegram App* Case

Although freedom of speech is generally accepted to be an important right in the EU, it is accepted that some limitations on that right are justifiable.

In Germany, in June 2021, the German Ministry of Justice launched proceedings against the Telegram Messenger app because they had violated German laws by failing to have a contact person in Germany and failing to provide a channel for making complaints.

The Ministry of Justice wrote to the Telegram operators in the UAE informing them of the proceeding in Germany, informing them that if they fail to comply with German requirements, they could be fined as much as €5.5 million.

The Telegram app was founded by two Russian brothers and claimed that it operates with encryption that prevents government investigators from reading the users' messages.

Telegram has been very popular with right-wing groups, including groups opposed to governments, against coronavirus lockdowns, for promoting various right-wing causes.[143]

Ironically, despite being founded by Russians, Telegram app was fined 4 million rubles by Russian authorities in November 2021 for failing to remove illegal content.[144]

B TFEU OPEN INTERNET ACCESS

The key EU agreement that underpins open access to the Internet is the Treaty on the Functioning of the European Union (TFEU) of 1957. Article 101 of the TFEU prohibits any things that restrict or distort competition within the EU, including any actions that "(d) apply dissimilar conditions to equivalent transactions with other trading parties thereby placing them at a competitive disadvantage."

The detail of enforcing that level Internet playing field is set out in the Open Internet Access Regulation.

142. *Id.*, Article 14.
143. Euronews, online, June 14, 2021.
144. Deutsche Welle, online, November 8, 2021.

C OPEN INTERNET ACCESS REGULATION

In November 2015, the EU adopted the Open Internet Access Regulation (Regulation)[145] that provided for individual enforceable rights to end-users in the EU to access and distribute Internet content and services. It also reinforced nondiscriminatory Internet traffic management to ensure that the same provisions of open Internet access applied across all Member States.

The Regulation came into effect on April 30, 2016. Under the Regulation, ISPs are not allowed to block, throttle, or discriminate against Internet traffic within the EU.

The only exceptions to this general rule are:

- compliance with legal requirements; preserving the integrity of the network; and
- managing congestion in exceptional, temporary situations.

All traffic must be treated equally. The prioritization of traffic in Internet service is not permitted. Traffic management must be conducted in accordance with objective technical requirements, independent of the origin or destination of the traffic or of commercial considerations.

Member State regulatory authorities are required to monitor the Internet within their jurisdiction. They can set minimum quality requirements on ISPs and require measures to ensure all end-users have good quality Internet service.

D BODY OF EUROPEAN REGULATORS FOR ELECTRONIC COMMUNICATIONS

In December 2018, to promote and protect the EU electronic market, the EU adopted a regulation establishing the Body of European Regulators for Electronic Communications (BEREC).[146] BEREC was established with three objectives:

(1) promoting competition and investment;
(2) promoting the EU internal market; and
(3) empowering and protecting end-users of the electronic market.[147]

To make certain that all Member State National Regulatory Authorities (NRAs) understood how to enforce open Internet access regulations, a set of guidelines on the Implementation of the Open Internet Access Regulation was promulgated.[148]

145. European Parliament and Council, Regulation on Open Internet Access, EU 2015/2120, November 25, 2015.
146. Regulation (EU) 2019/1971, December 11, 2018.
147. https://berec.europa.eu/eng/about_berec/what_is_berec/.
148. https://ec.europa.eu/digital-single-market/en/policies/open-internet.

On June 16, 2020, BEREC updated its guidelines on implementing the Regulation.[149]

BEREC defines the Internet as a global system of interconnected networks that enable connected end-users to connect to one another.

The purpose of the Regulation is to establish common rules to protect equal and nondiscriminatory treatment of traffic in Internet access and to protect the rights of end-users. Its aim is to protect end-users and simultaneously to guarantee the functioning of the Internet system as an engine of innovation.[150]

The Regulation requires "technological neutrality" in that there should be no discrimination in favor of a particular type of technology.[151]

One concern is that a significant number of end-users are affected by traffic management practices to block or slow specific applications or services. The Regulation supports common rules within the EU to ensure openness of the Internet and to avoid fragmentation of the internal market resulting from the Internet regulations of individual Member States.[152]

BEREC identifies an "end user" as a natural person or "legal entity" who is using or requesting a publicly available electronic communications service. It does not include those providing public communications networks or publicly available electronic communication services.[153]

There are certain networks that, for purposes of the Regulation, are not considered networks being made publicly available such as:

- networks providing access to the Internet in cafés or restaurants;
- internal corporate networks; and
- private networks such as those sometimes found in factories and ports.[154]

The Regulation defines an "internet access service" as a publicly available electronic communication service that provides access to the Internet and connectivity to virtually all the endpoints of the Internet, regardless of the network technology or computer equipment used.[155]

Article 3 of the BEREC Guidelines deals with Regulation provisions protecting open access to the Internet. Article 3(2) of the Regulation limits the contractual conditions that Internet providers may use to restrict end user rights. Article 3(3) requires that Internet providers must treat all data traffic equally except for certain specified conditions.[156]

End-users' rights are covered by Article 3(1) of the Regulation. They include key things such as the right to give and receive information, the right to choose computer

149. BEREC, Guidelines on the Implementation of the Open Internet Regulation, BoR (20) 112, June 16, 2020.
150. EU Regulation on Open Internet Access, Recital 1.
151. *Id.*, Recital 2.
152. *Id.*, Recital 3.
153. BEREC, Guidelines, Article 1.
154. *Id.*, Article 2, 12.
155. *Id.*, Articles 2, 13.
156. *Id.*, Article 3(1), 19-21.

equipment, the right to use and provide applications and services.[157] The choice of computer equipment should be limited only by technological necessity.[158]

Article 3(1) also deals with the legality of content, applications, and services on the Internet. Service providers are required to comply with EU law and national law that conforms to EU law.[159]

Article 3(2) requires that agreements between service providers and end-users, although they should deal with such things as price, services, and speed, should not limit to the basic rights of end-users specified by the Regulation and other EU law.[160]

The Regulation deals with equal treatment of traffic in Article 3(3). The basic principle is that service providers are required to treat all traffic equally.

To be sure that traffic is being treated equally, as required by the Regulation, Member State authorities are provided with assessment guidelines to ensure that service providers are treating traffic without discrimination, restriction or interference without regard to the sender or receiver, or to content and services being provided or the equipment being used.[161]

E DUTIES OF SERVICE PROVIDERS

Detailed guidelines are also provided as to what constitutes reasonable traffic management by ISPs.[162]

There is a broad spectrum of laws, regulations, and orders that service providers must be prepared to comply with. These include Union law, Member State law that complies with EU law, as well as orders by courts and relevant public authorities.[163]

Network Integrity Protection

One of the important duties of ISPs is protecting the integrity of the network. To that end, service providers are required to adopt integrity and security measures to protect against cyberattacks, the spread of malicious software and the use of spyware to steal the identities of end-users. It is also the responsibility of NRAs to assess whether the measures employed by service providers constitute a reasonable level of protection.[164]

157. *Id.*, Article 3(1), 22-26.
158. *Id.*, Article 3(1), 27.
159. *Id.*, Article 3(1), 28-29.
160. *Id.*, Article 3(2), 30-48.
161. *Id.*, Article 3(3), 51-56.
162. *Id.*, Article 3(3), 57-80.
163. *Id.*, Article 3(3), 81-82.
164. *Id.*, Article 3(3)(b), 83-87.

Traffic Management

Reasonable traffic management measures should be employed by service providers to prevent network congestion.[165]

Geographic Verification

In June 2021, BEREC published Guidelines on the Geographic Verification of Information. The purpose of the guidelines is to assist the NRAs in the consistent application of geographical surveys of work deployment. Basically, these guidelines are to assist in analyzing the current reach and quality of service of broadband networks as described by the operators.

It is important to know the accuracy of the operators' representations of the area covered by fast broadband. The goal of these regulations is to encourage national authorities to publish their verification methodologies and to present the verification results in a way that is transparent and comprehensible by market participants.

BEREC has published a handbook setting out the guidelines to make them conveniently accessible and to provide easy reference.[166]

F DATA PROTECTION

The principal regulation setting out the EU rules on data protection is the General Data Protection Regulation (GDPR). This sets up the requirements that apply to the collection, storage and managing of personal data. The GDPR applies to both European organizations that process the personal data of individuals in the EU and organizations outside the EU that target people living in the EU.[167]

The GDPR will apply to an organization in the following circumstances:

- your organization is based in the EU and processes personal data. This applies even if the actual data processing takes place elsewhere;
- your organization is based outside the EU but processes personal data relating to offering goods or services to persons in the EU; or
- your organization monitors the behavior of persons in the EU.

Representative in EU

Please note that if your organization is based outside the EU, but it processes data of EU citizens, you are required to appoint a representative in the EU.

165. *Id.*, Article 3(3)(c), 88-93.
166. Handbook of BEREC Guidelines on geographical surveys of network departments, online at BEREC.europa.eu.
167. "Data protection under GDPR," *Your Europe*, https://europa.eu/youreurope/business/dealing-with-customers/data-protection/data-protection-gdpr/index_en.htm.

GDPR Exemptions

There are certain specific circumstances where the GDPR will not apply to an organization. These include situations where:

- the individual who is the subject of the data is no longer living;
- the data subject is not an individual but is a legal entity such as a limited company or a corporation;
- the data processing is done by a person who is doing the processing outside the purposes of his trade, business or profession.

Personal Data and Data Subjects

Under the GDPR, personal data consists of any information about an identified or identifiable person ("data subject"). Personal data includes the following information about a data subject:

- Name.
- Address.
- ID card or passport number.
- Income.
- Cultural profile.
- IP address.
- Data held by a hospital or medical professional that identifies a person for health purposes.

Under the GDPR, there are certain categories of data that one is not allowed to process. This includes personal data about a person's:

(1) race or ethnic origin;
(2) sexual orientation;
(3) political opinions;
(4) religious or philosophic beliefs;
(5) trade union membership;
(6) genetic, biometric or health data, except:
   - when you have explicit consent to do so;
   - when such processing is needed for substantial public interest reasons, as established under EU or national law.
(7) data relating to a person's criminal convictions or offenses unless the processing is authorized under EU or national law.

The processing of personal data can occur through several companies or organizations and their subsidiaries or affiliates. Within this process, there are two main operators that are considered to be the key persons responsible for data processing for purposes of the GDPR:

(1) the "data controller," defined as the one who decides the purposes for which data is processed and the methods used to effect the processing; and
(2) the "data processor" who holds and processes data for the data controller.

Data Protection Officer

Within any organization that processes data subject to the GDPR, the person responsible for monitoring data processing is the Data Protection Officer (DPO). The DPO is responsible for informing and advising other persons within an organization what their obligations are with respect to data processing.

One is required to appoint a DPO if:

- one systematically monitors persons or processes special categories of data;
- the data processing is a central business activity;
- one does large-scale data processing.

Examples of when a DPO is needed can include using data to construct targeted advertising campaigns based on information about the online activities of people or processing genetic or health information about a lot of people for a hospital or insurance organization.

However, if one's activities are much more limited such as by being a doctor who maintains health information about patients or by being an organization that sends clients promotional material once a year, a DPO is not needed.

A DPO can be a member of internal staff, or someone contracted to perform that function in an outside entity. A DPO can either be an individual person or part of an organization.

Data Processor Restrictions

There are restrictions as to what type of data processor a data controller is permitted to use. A data controller can only use a data processor that provides written contractual guarantees, with mandatory clauses promising only to process personal data when and as instructed to do so by the data controller.

Transfer of Data Outside EU

The transfer of personal data outside the EU is a sensitive and highly controversial subject because it involves the transfer of personal information of persons subject to EU legal protections to jurisdictions that have different legal systems and different regulations about the collection, holding and use of data.

The principal concern of the EU is that when personal data is transferred outside the EU, it should continue to have the same level of data protection granted by the

GDPR. This requirement means that anyone transferring personal data outside the EU must make sure that:

- the non-EU jurisdiction's data protections are adequate with reference to EU law;
- the transferring person or organization is undertaking adequate safeguards to make certain that a non-EU data importer is adequately protecting the transferred data, including specific contract clauses mandating adequate data protections;
- the transferring person or organization has adequate authority under EU law to transfer the data to a non-EU jurisdiction, such as express consent of the individual subject of the data.

Making certain that one has obtained adequate legal consent of the subject of the processed data is an important fundamental issue for a number of reasons. In the first place, personal data is only allowed to be processed if the processing proceeds in a fair and lawful manner for a particular legitimate purpose and the data processed is limited to data that fulfills that limited purpose. The key conditions that give a data processing project legitimacy are one of the following:

- That adequate consent of the data subject has been obtained.
- That the personal data obtained is to fulfill a contractual obligation with the data subject.
- That the obtaining of the personal data satisfies a legal obligation.
- That the data is needed to protect the vital interests of the data subject.
- That the data processing satisfies a public interest.
- That the data processing does not seriously impact the rights and freedoms of the data subject. If the rights and freedoms of the data subject are seriously impacted, one cannot proceed with the data processing.

The US Tech Companies Issue

One of the more difficult issues that has arisen under European law with respect to data protection and data privacy is that many of the major tech companies are American. This means that they may have obligations under American law with respect to the information they collect about their users.

This raises the question of what happens to the data they collect? Do they send it to the US for technical or legal reasons? If data collected by these companies is sent outside of Europe, what happens to it? Most importantly, what happens to the privacy protections granted under European law once data is sent outside of Europe?

Edward Snowden

The issue of data privacy became a matter of wide discussion after Edward Snowden revealed in 2013 that significant amounts of personal data and personal communications were being scrutinized by US and other national intelligence agencies as part of wide-ranging intelligence-gathering programs.

The *Schrems* Case

In Europe, this concern was brought to the fore by the case of *Maximilian Schrems v. Facebook Ireland Limited,* which came before the European Court of Justice (ECJ).

After Snowden's revelations in 2013, Schrems, an Austrian data protection advocate, filed a complaint with the Irish Data Protection Commissioner claiming that Facebook was violating a number of European Data protection laws by transferring data about its customers to the US.

It was alleged that Facebook was participating in a number of data surveillance programs revealed by Snowden and that this was a violation of European law.

Essentially, the Schrems complaint challenged the Safe Harbor Framework privacy principles that were agreed between 1998 and 2000 between the EU and the US to prevent private firms that store customer data from accidentally disclosing or losing such personal data.

The Irish Commissioner rejected this complaint, and Schrems filed an application for review in the Irish High Court, which referred the issue to the ECJ.

The "Safe Harbor" Struck Down

The European court found that the Safe Harbor did not adequately protect the personal data of private citizens under European law.

On October 15, 2015, the ECJ issued a decision ruling that the EU/US Safe Harbor Framework was not a valid way to comply with EU data protection requirements when transferring personal data from EU countries to the US.[168] The Safe Harbor agreement was found to violate a number of rights available to European citizens under European personal data protection laws and regulations.

The court also held that European NRAs retain the power to review EU/US data transfers.

The EU-US Privacy Shield Framework

As a result, the European Commission and US authorities have sought to develop a new framework for data transfer. A new agreement, called the "EU-US Privacy Shield Framework," was reached between the US Department of Commerce and the European Commission in early 2016. This was believed to be a valid mechanism to comply with EU data protection requirements when transferring personal data from the EU to the US. The US Department of Commerce began accepting certificates of compliance with this mechanism on August 1, 2016.[169]

168. https./2016.export.gov/safe harbour.
169. *Id.*

However, Mr. Schrems and other data privacy activists were not happy with this new agreement. Another complaint was brought that came before the ECJ. The key issue in the new case was whether data that leaves the EU continues to have protection equivalent to that granted under European law.

On July 16, 2020, the ECJ again struck down a personal data transfer agreement between the EU and the US.

That decision could have a wide impact, not only on big tech firms but also on a variety of persons and companies that do international business that requires them to collect cross-border data, such as travel and hotel reservations. The Privacy Shield mechanism had permitted many different companies to transfer personal data internationally.

Because of the court's invalidation of these arrangements, many firms and individuals may have to change the way they do business and how they deal with the data they need and receive.[170]

European Data Protection Supervisor

In September 2015, the EU established that the European Data Protection Supervisor has an independent supervisory authority to make certain that European institutions and bodies respected the rights to privacy and data protection throughout the EU, when those institutions and bodies processed personal data and when they developed policies with respect to the treatment of personal data.[171]

On October 21, 2018, the EU propagated its Regulation on Processing and Transferring Personal Data.[172] The purpose of this regulation was to align the rules for data protection within the EU and to provide a coherent framework for data protection within the EU.

Contract Clauses for International Transfers

Because of the confusion and conflict surrounding the transfer of personal data online between the US and the EU, a set of standard contractual clauses (SCCs) has come into use as the default method of making such transfers.

The original three sets of SCCs were adopted under Data Protection Directive 95/46/EC that came into force in 1995 and was amended by Regulation (EC) No. 1882/2003.

The European Commission implemented Regulation (EU) 2016/679 that repealed Directive 95/46/EC (GDPR) replacing its provisions with new safeguards for data protection when transferring data to a third country.[173]

It provided a new set of SCCs to assure appropriate data protection for international data transfers. Although data controllers or processors are free to use these

170. Adam Santariano, "E.U. Court Strikes Down Trans-Atlantic Data Transfer Pact," *The New York Times*, online, July 16, 2020.
171. EDPS, Europa.EU.
172. Regulation (EU) 2018/1723 of the European Parliament and of the Council of October 23, 2018.
173. Commission Implementing Decision (EU) 2021/914 of June 2021.

clauses, they may also add additional clauses or safeguards that provide additional protection if it does not conflict with the standard EU clauses.[174]

However, these clauses do not illuminate the general responsibilities of the data exporter to provide data subjects with adequate information about the transfer of their data to a third country.[175]

There are eighteen clauses covering the following topics:

(1) Purpose and scope.
(2) Effect and invariability of the clauses.
(3) Third-party beneficiaries.
(4) Interpretation.
(5) Hierarchy.
(6) Description of transfer(s).
(7) Docking clause.
(8) Data protection safeguards.
(9) Use of sub-processors.
(10) Data subject rights.
(11) Redress.
(12) Liability.
(13) Supervision.
(14) Local laws and practices affecting compliance with the clauses.
(15) Obligations of the data importer in case of access by public authorities.
(16) Noncompliance with the clauses and termination.
(17) Governing law.
(18) Choice of forum and jurisdiction.

There are also suggestions of specific language with respect to the following:

- List of Parties.
- Technical and Organizational Measures Including Technical and Organizational Measures to Ensure the Security of the Data.
- List of Sub-Processors.

A new set of SCCs was published by the European Commission in July 2021. These replaced the three sets of SCCs that were introduced by Directive 95/46.[176]

The effective date of the new SCCs was June 27, 2021, but the old clauses could have been used during a transition period that ended on September 27, 2021.

The Implementing Decision containing the clauses and supplementary material will require a fair bit of study in order to be able to effectively and correctly implement the use of these new clauses into commercial contracts that involve the transfer of personal data outside the EU to third countries.

174. Commission Implementing Decision (EU) 2021/914, recitation (3).
175. *Id.*, recitation (4).
176. "Standard Protection Clauses," https://ec.europa.eu/info/law/law-topic/data-protection/international-dimension-data-protection/standard-contractual-clauses-scc_en.

Detailed legal advice from competent legal advisors may be needed.

Some Rulings for Data Violations

Despite the attempts to make concessions for the American nationality of major tech companies such as Amazon, it has recently been brought home to them that they must not forget how important data privacy is under EU law.

Luxembourg

In June 2021, it was reported that the Luxembourg privacy regulator, the National Commission for Data Protection, circulated a draft penalty to twenty-six other EU regulatory authorities proposing to fine Amazon about €350 million ($425 million) for violating provisions of the GDPR.[177] However, their final punishment was much more severe.

In July 2021, the privacy regulator of Luxembourg fined Amazon €746 million (about $887 million) because of violations relating to its advertising activities. This was the largest fine to date under EU data protection regulations. Amazon has its EU headquarters in Luxembourg.[178]

The reason for the fine is apparently data analysis conducted by Amazon that resulted in targeted advertising of which Amazon customers were not made aware. The GDPR requires Internet companies to get users' consent before using their personal data. Failure to do so can attract big fines as the Amazon matter shows.[179]

The fine is certainly huge, but not when compared to Amazon's sales of over $350 billion in 2020. It is within the power of the EU data protection regulator to fine companies as much is 4% of their annual revenue.[180]

Amazon claims that the fine is unjustified and says it will appeal.[181]

France

Another American tech giant, Google, was fined €50 million in 2019 by France's data protection authority. Google's failings were stated to be failures to:

"(1) provide notice in an easily accessible form, using clear and plain language, when users configure their Android mobile devices and create Google accounts," and
"(2) obtain users' valid consent to process their personal data for ad personalization purposes."[182]

177. Callum Jones, "Ämazon Faces Huge Fine for 'Data Breach'," *The Times*, online, June 11, 2021.
178. Sam Schechner, "Amazon Hit with Record EU Privacy Fine," *The Wall Street Journal*, online, July 30, 2021.
179. "Amazon Hit with Record EU Data Privacy Fine," *Reuters*, online, July 30, 2021.
180. Jones, *supra*, June 11, 2021.
181. Sam Schechner, "Amazon Hit with Record EU Privacy Fine," *The Wall Street Journal*, online, July 30, 2021.
182. "France's Highest Administrative Court Upholds 50 Million Euro Fine Against Google for Alleged GDPR Violations," Hunton Andrews Kurth, *Privacy & Information Security Law Blog*, online (huntonprivacyblog.com), June 23, 2020.

This was also for violation of the GDPR. In June 2020, France's top administrative court (*Conseil d' Etat*) upheld the fine.

Germany

In July 2020, Germany's Constitutional Court ruled that current German law allows police to be too intrusive when conducting investigations, even in minor cases. Currently, they are allowed to get names, addresses, birthdates, IP addresses, passwords, and pin numbers.

Privacy advocates challenged the current law on the basis that gathering such data should only be permitted in cases where there is a specific danger or reasonable suspicion of a crime having been committed.

Under existing laws, the police were allowed to get such data not only from telecoms companies but also from hospitals and hotels.

The court ordered the government to revise the Telecommunications Act no later than the end of 2021.

However, it is reported that one concern, which this ruling did not address, is that changes to the law could interfere with the government's efforts to investigate and counter far-right extremism.[183]

It will be necessary to review what changes are made to German law, and whether similar changes are made in other EU Members, or other nations outside the EU.

The Netherlands

In July 2021, the Dutch data protection authority (DPA) hit TikTok with a €750,000 fine because of lack of transparency in protecting the privacy of young children.[184]

Spain

In July 2021, the Spanish data protection authority (AEPD) fined Mercadona, S.A. €2,520,000 for illegal use of a facial recognition system. The supermarket chain was apparently using the system to recognize those with criminal convictions or subject to restraining orders, such as in cases where they had been guilty of assaulting store employees.[185]

However, the AEPD found that the supermarket chain's use of the system did not meet the requirements of Article 9 of the GDPR. In particular, it was found not to comply with the standards of necessity, proportionality, data minimization, transparency, and privacy required. Although the supermarket chain had carried out a data protection impact assessment before employing the system, the AEPD found that to be

183. "Germans Hand Police Too Much Data, Court Rules," *BBC News*, online, July 17, 2020.
184. "Dutch DPA Fines Tik Tok 750,000 EUR for Transparency Violations," Hunton Andrews Kurth, *Privacy & Information Security Law Blog*, online (huntonprivacyblog.com), July 28, 2021.
185. "Spanish DPA Fines Supermarket Chain 2,520,000 EUR for Unlawful Use of Facial Recognition System," Hunton Andrews Kurth, *Privacy & Information Security Law Blog*, online (huntonprivacyblog.com), July 27, 2021.

inadequate. For example, the assessment did not consider the risks to supermarket employees presented by the use of the system.

The fine imposed was originally €3,150,000 but the AEPD reduced it because the supermarket chain voluntarily paid.[186]

Swiss-US Agreement

On January 17, 2017, the Swiss government announced that it had approved a Swiss/US Privacy Shield Framework as a valid mechanism to comply with Swiss data protection requirements when transferring personal data from Switzerland to the US.[187] Switzerland is not a member of the EU.

G OTHER EU INTERNET CASES

Of course, there is a very large number of Internet-related cases that have come before the ECJ and the courts of the twenty-seven EU nations since the Internet era began. However, it is not possible for this book to list or analyze them all. They can be discovered by online searches and by consulting competent advisors in relevant jurisdictions.

186. *Id.*
187. *Id.*

CHAPTER 6

UK Internet Law

The UK was never too far behind the US in setting up its own version of the Internet. By 1983, it had put in place its own network connecting university computers around the country called JANET. It introduced the dot UK domain name in 1985, and the UK was included in the World Wide Web by 1991.

The first UK consumer-priced Internet subscription service, Demon Internet, was introduced in 1992.

The Internet rapidly expanded in the UK. The government soon became concerned that there were dangers of criminal activity, and other misuse of the Internet, and Parliament began to introduce laws to protect against that and to regulate activity on the Internet.

The first of these laws was the Computer Misuse Act of 1990. It was aimed at preventing and punishing criminal activity on the Internet. It identified three types of Internet activity as criminal:

(1) The first was obtaining unauthorized access to computer materials.
(2) The second was unauthorized access with intent to commit or facilitate the commission of offenses.
(3) The third forbid unauthorized changes to computer material.

This act was introduced in response to a 1988 criminal case, *R. v. Gold & Schifreen.*[188] The defendants were two hackers who surreptitiously learned a British Telecom engineer's password to get unauthorized access to the BT Prestel video data system. The Prestel system offered subscribers access to video information on the Internet. One of its other early services was a messaging service known as Prestel Mailbox that allowed subscribers to send and receive messages.

Using the stolen access keys, Gold and Schifreen were able to access the private Mailbox information of subscribers, including the private Mailbox of the Queen's

188. *Regina v. Gold & Schrifreen,* CACD July 17, 1987.

husband, Prince Phillip. However, the defendants were acquitted because their activities did not constitute a specific criminal offense then.

Because of the high-profile nature of the defendants' hacking into private information on the Internet, and the uproar it caused, Parliament quickly passed the Computer Misuse Act in 1990. However, the Act came under quite a lot of criticism at the time for not distinguishing between curious hackers like Schifreen and Gold and committed cybercriminals. Consequently, Parliament subsequently passed several acts to prevent and punish cybercrime and amended several other Acts and regulations to include Internet activity.

This scrutiny and control of the Internet have become increasingly important in the UK, where it is estimated that over 90% of adults are connected to the Internet, and where over £190,000 a day is lost to cybercriminals.[189]

One of the most important Acts that has been applied to Internet activity is the Competition Act 1998.

Competition in the UK is supervised by the Competition and Markets Authority (CMA). In June 2020, Lord Tyrie, the Chairman of the CMA, resigned claiming that he was not able to act forcefully enough to tackle the big tech companies that abuse their market dominance. He claimed that the CMA needed more powers, writing that "The UK has an analog system of competition and consumer law in a digital age."[190]

Lord Tyrie argued that the CMA was unable to act quickly enough to protect consumers because "byzantine" rules allowed tech company lawyers to "game the system" to delay action. He said that the government had not enacted the reforms he suggested.[191]

In August 2020, in a comment, *The Times* argued that one area that UK Internet regulation has struggled with is the protection of Internet users against harmful content.[192] The author said that although ISPs are required to remove terrorist propaganda and child-abuse material, users are still subjected to harmful material, such as "trolling, disinformation, and self-harm guides," and other content that may be technically legal but "can harm our well-being, our mental health and, in extreme cases, our democracy."[193]

The author, Salma Shah, who is a former advisor to the UK Home Secretary,[194] wrote that recent UK governments have a poor record of dealing with harmful Internet content. The government had prepared a report (a "white paper") on harmful online content that proposed the creation of a new independent regulator that would exclusively deal with this issue and set a new higher standard for online safety. However, Shah argued that the UK government lacked the "courage" to follow through with this groundbreaking plan to regulate the Internet as a special case, and that this

189. BBC.com, January 27, 2019. *See*, Chapter 16.
190. Andrew Elison, "Consumer Champion Quits Amid Digital Tax Row," *The Times*, online, June 19, 2020.
191. *Id.*
192. Salma Shah, "Britain Can't Afford to Miss This Chance to Clean up the Web," *The Times*, online, "Thunderer," Comment, Thursday, August 6, 2020, retrieved August 7, 2020.
193. *Id.*
194. Former Home Secretary, Sajid Javid, 2018-2019.

constituted "a missed opportunity" to affectively regulate harmful content.[195] She laments that it was decided to give responsibility for Internet regulation to the "already over-burdened communications regulator," Ofcom.[196]

A DATA PROTECTION AND PRIVACY

In 2019, British Airways was found guilty of a data breach that leaked the names, addresses and bank card details of over four hundred thousand customers and staff. Consequently, the UK Information Commissioner's Office (ICO) required British Airways to pay a fine of £20 million which is the largest fine it had imposed to date. The matter also went to mediation, instead of a public trial, and a settlement was reached with BA. The terms of the settlement are confidential although lawyers for the claimants said that the outcome was "extremely positive." British Airways was required to pay compensation to the victims of the data breach.[197]

Another important question having to do with online privacy is the issue of the protection of anonymity in the Internet age. In 2014, Lord Neuberger, the President of the UK Supreme Court, addressed this issue in his lecture to a group of lawyers and journalists in London, "What's in a name?"—Privacy and anonymous speech on the Internet.[198] In his speech one of the functions of that he highlighted as most important is "holding power, particularly governmental power, to account." He identified freedom of the press and privacy as crucial in accomplishing that task.

He notes that there is an unavoidable tension between the right to privacy in Article 8 of the European Convention on Human Rights (ECHR) and the right to freedom of expression contained in Article 10 of the ECHR. Consequently, it is often left to the courts to effect a balance between these interests when they come into conflict. The UK Supreme Court described both as "vitally important rights" in the case of *Campbell v. MGN.* Lord Neuberger emphasizes that neither has precedence over the other.[199]

The tension between them is particularly acute when a court is asked to grant a privacy injunction.[200] Although this topic has been important for some time, the Internet has raised additional issues to be considered. To begin his analysis of the new privacy issues, Lord Neuberger begins by referring to the Eighteenth-Century problem of "Junius."

Junius was the author of anonymous letters that were printed by a newspaper called *The Public Advertiser.* Junius was a defender of free speech and a harsh critic of the government. It is believed that his attacks on the government may have led to the

195. Shah, *supra.*
196. *Id.*
197. Jonathan Ames, "British Airways Settles over Record Claim for Data Breach," *The Times,* online, July 23, 2021.
198. https://www.supremecourt.uk/docs/speech-140930.pdf.
199. [2004] 2 AC 457 at [12] per Lord Hoffman.
200. This is a topic upon which a committee on super-injunctions (which Lord Neuberger appointed and chaired when he was Master of the Rolls) reported in 2011. The Report can be found at, http://www.judiciary.gov.uk/.

resignation of the then Prime Minister, the Duke of Grafton, in 1770. He was also a harsh critic of the judiciary, stating in one letter quoted by Lord Neuberger that:

> A judge under the influence of government, may be honest enough in the decision of private causes, yet a traitor to the public.

In 1769, Junius crossed a line in a letter addressed to King George, which began:

> Sir, —It is the misfortune of your life, and originally the cause of every reproach and distress which has attended your government, that you should never have been acquainted with the language of truth, until you heard in the complaints of your people.

This publication caused the publisher of the *Public Advertiser* to be tried for seditious libel. Neuberger points out that the debate over this trial, its verdict and mistrial, led to positive changes in libel law.

However, one issue that caused considerable comment at the time, and which, according to Lord Neuberger, has important implications for the regulation of Internet postings was the importance of privacy and anonymity. Two of the most important political and social commentators of that period, Edmund Burke and Samuel Johnson, defended Junius' anonymity, arguing that it gave Junius the ability to make strong, and often justified and badly needed, public criticisms of the powerful while being protected from prosecution or other harassment by offended powers be they individual or institutional.[201]

Neuberger compares the bloggers of today to Junius.[202] He points out that the Internet has given a huge number of people a low or no-cost opportunity to publish anonymously and widely. Bloggers often take extra steps to protect their anonymity by using Virtual Private Networks (VPNs) and "private browsing" modes. However, because of the search and hacking tools available to users of the Internet, it is becoming increasingly more difficult to maintain one's anonymity when using the Internet.

In this day and age, it may be impossible to remain an anonymous "Junius" forever. One example is the political blogger, Guido Fawkes, who was credited with several political "wins" including against a government minister. But he was able to maintain anonymity for only a few months before *The Guardian* newspaper revealed who he was.[203]

To defend their anonymity, some Internet posters have relied on the legal ruling that one does "have a right to be forgotten."[204] This is also known as the "right to erasure" and there is a right granted under the EU's GDPR that gives individuals the right to ask organizations to delete their personal data. This is found in Recitals 65 and 66 and in Article 17 of the GDPR which states:

---

201. Neuberger, *supra*, pp. 2-5. The identity of Junius has never been discovered, although some of his contemporaries believed that Burke was Junius.
202. Neuberger, *supra*, p. 5.
203. *Id.*, p. 6.
204. *Google Spain SL. And Google Inc. v. Agencia Espanola de Proteccion de Datos (AEPD and Mario Costeja Gonzalez* (C-131/12)).

> The data subject shall have the right to obtain from the controller the erasure of personal data concerning him or her without undue delay and the controller shall have the obligation to erase personal data without undue delay.

Under certain conditions, "undue delay" is about a month. The right to erasure is not without limits. It is available under the following conditions as set out in Article 17:

- The personal data is no longer necessary for the purpose and organization originally collected or processed it.
- An organization is relying on an individual's consent as the lawful basis for processing the data and that individual withdraws their consent.
- An organization is relying on legitimate interests as its justification for processing an individual's data.
- The individual objects to this processing, and there is no overriding legitimate interest for the organization to continue with the processing.
- An organization is processing personal data for direct marketing purposes, and the individual objects to this processing.
- An organization processed an individual's personal data unlawfully.
- An organization must erase personal data in order to comply with a legal ruling or obligation.
- An organization has processed a child's personal data in order to offer their information society services (in violation of Article 8.1).

However, there are circumstances in which an organization's right to process someone's data could override that person's right to be forgotten. Such circumstances are the following:

(1) The data is being used to exercise the right of freedom of expression and information.
(2) The data is being used to comply with a legal ruling or obligation.
(3) The data is being used to perform a task that is being carried out in the public interest or when exercising an organization's official authority.
(4) The data being processed is necessary for public health purposes and serves the public interest.
(5) The data being processed is necessary to perform preventative or occupational medicine:
    - This only applies when the data is being processed by a health professional who is subject to a legal obligation of professional secrecy.
(6) The data represents important information that serves the public interest, scientific research, historical research, or statistical purposes and where erasure of the data would likely impair or halt progress toward the achievement that was the goal of the processing.
(7) The data is being used for the establishment of a legal defense or in the exercise of other legal claims.

It should be noted that an organization can request a "reasonable fee" or deny a request if the organization can justify that the request was unfounded or excessive.[205]

However, as Lord Neuberger points out, there is sometimes a public interest to be served by identifying certain people in stories in newspapers on the Internet. Consequently, courts will sometimes override the right to privacy to permit the publishing of the names of persons in the appropriate circumstances. That is considered necessary to protect free speech and freedom of the press. If, in the interest of privacy, publishers were prevented from naming individuals associated with certain situations relating to public safety or other strong public interest:

> Ultimately such an approach could threaten the viability of newspapers and magazines ... because stories about particular individuals are simply much more attractive to readers than stories about unidentified people ... Newspapers and magazines ... can only inform the public if they attract enough readers and make enough money to survive.[206]

Of course, exposing the identity of bloggers may make them reluctant to express themselves candidly on the Internet. This effect cuts both ways.

On the one hand, it can have a "chilling effect" on their postings that can deprive the public of information that may be important or useful to know.

On the other hand, it may make them more careful in their postings so that they do not publish information that is defamatory to individuals or harmful to the public such as when highly confidential government information is exposed.

True, it is sometimes important to reveal information that the government considers "secret," such as the Pentagon Papers or the Watergate Tapes, but there are instances when doing that can create situations that endanger lives.

For example, Lord Neuberger points to a situation in which a blogger known as "NightJack" published various allegations and observations about police activity. In a case relating to that, the court ruled that this activity was not a "private activity" where the blogger could have a reasonable expectation of privacy, but was rather an activity of public interest in public information. In that case, the blogger was revealed to be a police detective constable.[207]

It is important to note here that under English common law, a poster's identity may be protected by well-established principles of confidentiality in addition to any protections provided by the Convention.

For example, legal professional privilege, regarding information received from a client, has been held to override a person's legitimate interest in pursuing remedies

205. https://gdpr.eu/?s = right + of + erasure.
206. Taken from the opinion of Lord Rodger in *In re Guardian News and Media Ltd. and others*, referred to by Lord Neuberger.
207. Decision of Mr. Justice Eady, in *Author of a Blog v. Times Newspapers Ltd.* [2009] EWHC 1358 (QB). However, because a *Times* reporter had resorted to email hacking to discover the blogger's identity, the *Times* later made a public apology to the blogger. Neuberger, *supra*, p. 9.

against the blogger who had revealed confidential information belonging to a person.[208]

It cannot be ignored that, because the Internet currently reaches about 40 % of the world's population, it offers unmatchable opportunities to make one's views known around the world. As the US Supreme Court said in the case of *Reno v. ACLU*[209] in 1997, the Internet represents "the most participatory form of mass speech yet developed":

> Through the use of chat rooms, any person with a phone line can become a town crier with a voice that resonates father then it could from any soapbox.[210]

In that case, the US Supreme Court was considering the justification of a law restricting the publication of sexual material. However, the court held the law to be overbroad, and therefore, unconstitutional. Justice Stevens wrote:

> The interest in encouraging freedom of expression in a democratic society outweighs any theoretical but unproven benefit of censorship.[211]

Lord Neuberger considers how Internet speech interacts with rights under Article 8 of the ECHR. The EU attitude toward Article 8 is that it not only protects privacy per se but also covers personal autonomy and self-development. Lord Neuberger says that "the Internet offers unprecedented opportunities for such self-development."[212]

As Lord Neuberger points out:

> Throughout history, people's willingness to engage in debate on controversial subjects in the public sphere has always been linked to possibilities for doing so anonymously. The Internet allows individuals to access information and engage in public debate without having to reveal their real identities.[213]

Governments Attitudes about Anonymous Blogging

However, the Internet also makes it easier for governments and others to find out information about Internet users. Therefore, the Internet has not only provided opportunities for expression but also made it difficult to be certain that one's posts will remain anonymous. In fact, some government regulators have taken steps to eliminate anonymous blogging.

208. Neuberger, *supra*, p. 9, citing the case of *SRJ v. Person(s) Unknown being the author and commenters of Internet blogs*, [2014] EWHC 2293.
209. 521 U.S. 844.
210. Justice Stevens, delivering the Opinion of the Court at p. 58.
211. *Id.*, p. 91.
212. Neuberger, *supra*, p. 10.
213. *Id.*, p. 11, quoting the Report of UN Special Rapporteur Frank La Rue to the Human Rights Council, A/HRC/17/27.

China

For example, China requires that micro-bloggers on China's "Weibo" platform must register their real names to use the service. South Korea has introduced a similar regulation.

United States

The US has taken a very different approach. The US Supreme Court has ruled that the right to freedom of expression includes a right "to read anonymously."[214] Indeed, tools have been developed to help users protect their anonymity, such as the free "TOR" app.

The US Supreme Court has gone so far as to approve anonymous political pamphleteering as "an honorable tradition of advocacy and dissent [and] a shield from the tyranny of the majority."[215]

Generally, freedom of the press and freedom of expression are protected in the liberal democracies.

However, there is an important difference between the level of protection in the US and the protection given in Article 10 of the Convention governing EU and UK regulation. In the context of a case in which a journalist published an illegally intercepted telephone conversation, the US Supreme Court ruled that the right to privacy was outweighed by the First Amendment right to publish information of substantial public interest.[216]

Article 10 of the ECHR provides no such express protection for the press, but a kind of parallel protection has been found to exist under that Article in European court cases. For example, in the *Goodwin* case cited by Lord Neuberger,[217] although the press has no express right to publish information freely, the public does have the right under Article 10 to receive accurate information, of which the press can be an important source. Lord Neuberger's view is that this protected right to receive accurate information should naturally also extend protection of anonymous Internet bloggers.[218]

Of course, it is difficult or impossible to completely regulate how the Internet is used or what is posted on the Internet, about which Lord Neuberger argues that the law must always be prepared to adapt to new technology in the case of the Internet, despite the difficulties at present because of its international nature and other reasons. Both domestic law and international treaties and conventions can put reasonable limits on the use of the Internet and legislators would be remiss in their duty if they did not make significant efforts to impose such reasonable regulations.[219]

Because of the international nature of the Internet, it is necessary for international organizations and groupings of many countries to develop consistent comprehensive

214. Neuberger, *supra*, p. 11, citing, *United States v. Rumely*, 345 US, 41, 57.
215. *McIntyre v. Ohio Elections Commission*, 514 US 334 (1995). Neuberger, *supra*, pp. 11-12.
216. *Bartinicki v. Vopper*, 532 US 514 (2001). The First Amendment to the US Constitution expressly says that "Congress shall make no law ... abridging the freedom of speech, or of the press."
217. *Goodwin v. UK* (16/1994/463/544) (1996) 1 BHRC 81. Neuberger, *supra*, p. 14.
218. Neuberger, *supra*, p. 14.
219. *Id.*, p. 15.

regulations to control Internet postings of opinions and political information and to prevent dangerous and illegally offensive postings such as racial attacks and insults.

If it is not possible to put together international treaties or conventions that affectively regulate Internet postings in ways that protect freedom of speech and of the press but prevent and punish illegally offensive and false information from being broadcast over the Internet, then it is up to the domestic legislatures of individual countries and jurisdictions to provide those regulations.

The Internet has and is growing so rapidly that it is often the case that legislation will be some way behind the latest activities on the Internet, but this must not discourage legislators from making the effort to protect privacy and free speech without permitting the publication of false or dangerous information.[220]

B ONLINE SAFETY BILL

The UK has proposed to improve its protection from online abuse by introducing an Online Safety Bill. A draft of the bill was proposed in May 2021. However, the main political parties split over who should be members of a "scrutiny committee" to review the bill.

Racial Abuse

The need for such a bill became more urgent since England played in the final of the Euro 2020 football tournament. After England lost in a penalty shootout at the end of the match, several Internet users in the UK directed racial abuse and threats at the England players who had missed their penalty shots.

It is proposed that the bill should place responsibility for the nature of their content on social media platforms. The social media platforms would be required to prevent abusive comments, threats, and harassment from being posted on their platforms.[221]

Although the Online Safety Bill is not yet law, the incident of racial abuse directed at members of the English team has been so widely condemned that the government is making efforts to track down and punish those who posted such abuse. Apparently, the abuse was posted on Instagram, Facebook, and Twitter. The police have said that they will find and punish those who published the abuse and that they are working with the large tech companies mentioned above to get details of the accounts of the abusive posters. Twitter and Facebook have provided details. At least five people were arrested in connection with the abusive posts.[222]

220. *Id.*, pp. 15-16.
221. Tom Knowles, "MPs' Spat Delays Safer Social Media Use," *The Times*, online, July 15, 2021.
222. Tom Knowles, "Bukayo Saka Attacks Social Media Giants over Racist Abuse after Euro 3030 Final," *The Times*, online, July 16, 2021.

The English Prime Minister has condemned the racist Internet attacks and says that those responsible will be banned from attending future football matches.[223]

Racism is not the only abuse that is expressed online. Although the Internet provides access to information and communication that allows users to learn more and express their views more widely than has ever been possible before, it also provides unfortunate opportunities to express hatred, prejudice, and lies to a wider audience than has ever been possible before.

As the public outcry against this kind of behavior grows louder, governments have been taking steps to make certain that the major tech platforms make serious efforts to review and control the kind of information that is disseminated on their systems. The Online Safety Bill is a major step in the direction of forcing tech companies to be more careful about what they allow to be published on their platforms.

Antisemitism

In addition to the outrageous racial slurs that appeared on social media after England's loss in the European football championship, another area of Internet hatred and prejudice that has been widely talked about in the press is the presence of anti-Semitism expressed on social media platforms.

This takes a number of forms. One of the most prevalent is anti-Semitic conspiracy theories making outrageous claims of the existence of harmful conspiracies created by members of the Jewish community, including the absurd claim that Jewish people are somehow responsible for COVID-19.[224]

Other absurd abusive posts include bizarre theories about how certain Jewish individuals or groups are seeking to or already running the world or important parts of the world economy such as the financial system.

There are also expressions of fascist hatred denying or attempting to minimize the horror of the Holocaust.

Many people, both Jewish and non-Jewish, find anti-Semitic posts offensive and in many cases constituting illegal "hate speech."

Many efforts are made to report these to the operators of social media websites, urging the operators of those websites to prevent them from being posted and, if they are discovered to have been posted, to immediately remove them from social media sites.

However, objecting about these posts to the operators of the social media sites is not always effective in getting tech companies to act to prevent or remove these hate speech postings. It has been reported that with respect to 89% of postings alleging Jewish conspiracies, or blaming them for COVID-19, the tech companies have failed to

223. Oliver Wright and Elenia Courea, "PM Pledges Match Bans to Punish Racist Trolls," *The Times*, online, July 15, 2021.
224. "Social Media Giants Fail to Curb 90% of Antisemitism," *The Times*, online, August 2, 2021.

act to remove these posts even where individual employees of the operators have been contacted directly to complain about such posts.[225]

C SOME UK INTERNET CASES

Since it became an important method of communication and commerce, the Internet has been a contentious area of endeavor which has produced numerous disputes and legal cases around the world. That is as true in the UK as much as anywhere because the UK is one of the world's important financial and trading markets.

It would be impossible to give the details of all the Internet cases that have arisen in the UK within this book. Therefore, this volume will discuss only certain UK cases of interest. However, it is certainly possible to search databases of UK legal material by topic to locate additional cases relating to Internet-related disputes. Among the databases that an interested party might wish to consider are the following.

British and Irish Legal Information Institute (BAILII)— an online search of their case database under the word "Internet" reveals thousands of cases and decisions.[226]

The UK Supreme Court. Since 2009, the Supreme Court has replaced the House of Lords as the UK's highest court. Its site includes pdf copies of Decided Cases.[227]

Earlier judgments, in pdf form, from the House of Lords are available online for the years 1996-2009.[228]

UKSC Blog. This is a site, offered by a barristers' group, Matrix Chambers, providing online access to case reports and commentary on the judgments of Supreme Court cases, developments in case law, and "Case Previews" of upcoming Supreme Court cases.[229] The site does provide a search facility. Searching for "internet case" turns up several comments on relevant and often very recent cases.

Current Awareness from the Inner Temple. This is an online source of current information on legal issues, news, case decisions and legislation. It offers helpful resources and tools, including daily alerts.[230]

225. *Id.*
226. https://www.google.com/search?q=BAILII&rlz=1C5CHFA_enFR936FR936&oq=BAILII&aqs=chrome..69i57.4408j0j15&sourceid=chrome&ie=UTF-8. This database is also connected to WorldLII, an online collection of databases of legal information and case reports of courts and tribunals from 123 jurisdictions (both subscription and non-subscription). This includes collections from countries, regions and other groupings, http://www.worldlii.org/. These are made available by the international group of LIIs.
227. https://www.supremecourt.uk/ Note that Supreme Court case decisions are also available on the BAILII website.
228. https://publications.parliament.uk/pa/ld/ldjudgmt.htm.
229. http://ukscblog.com/.
230. https://www.innertemple.org.uk/useful-links/current-awareness-blog/.

Selected UK Internet Cases

Online Privacy

Lloyd v. Google LLC [2021] UKSC 50[231]

In 2014, the High Court ruled that UK Internet users who were suing Google for violating their online privacy could bring the suit in the UK instead of in the US.

The court held that the dispute involves complex issues of English law and therefore England was the appropriate place to bring the case where the issues could be resolved by an English court.

The complainant group of Internet users asserted that Google was secretly tracking their online habits to identify their personal interests in shopping, hobbies, religion, politics, etc., and was selling this information to advertisers without permission. The claimants alleged that this violated their reasonable expectation of privacy under UK and EU privacy law.[232]

In the ultimate decision to the above case, the UK Supreme Court on November 10, 2021, published a judgment in the case of *Lloyd v. Google LLC*,[233] allowing Lloyd to proceed with a collective claim on behalf of about 4 million iPhone users whose Internet activity had been recorded by Google in 2011 and 2012 for commercial purposes without the agreement or knowledge of the users.

However, the court also ruled that damages could not be pursued on a collective basis but would have to be determined separately for each individual claimant.

The court said that in the UK, a "collective action" can be brought under the Data Protection Act 2018. The persons affected by a breach of the DPA have the right to appoint a nonprofit organization to bring a legal action on their behalf.

In the *Lloyd* case, the collection of data by Google led to many claims against Google in both the US and the UK.

In this decision by the UK Supreme Court, there was both good news and bad news for claimants in mass actions against big tech companies in the UK.

The "good news" was that the court recognized that representative actions were a legitimate and useful way to protect the similar data rights of many persons who believe their rights to have been violated.

The "bad news" is that the court ruled that damages, under English law, cannot be assessed on a mass basis but must be determined on an individual basis. This is very good news for big tech companies because it makes it difficult to bring representative actions against them in cases where it is alleged that they have damaged large numbers (millions?) of Internet users.

Ruling that damages can be assessed only on an individual basis means that any damage determination of the members of any group of plaintiffs will be tedious and

231. On appeal from [2019] EWCA CIV 1599.
232. Jane Croft, "Google Loses UK Ruling on Internet Privacy Case," *Financial Times*, online, January 16, 2014.
233. [2021] UKSC 50.

expensive and will probably show that any individual member only suffered very small monetary damage.

That will probably make it difficult for future UK representative actions to be funded by commercial litigation funding because their potential recovery will be too uncertain.

It is unlikely that any individual member of the claimant group will have the funds or the desire to pursue the action without mass financial support, and potential mass financial recovery.

One hopes this case does not hand big tech a license to exploit Internet users at will in the UK without having to worry about the possible financial consequences of collective lawsuit judgment.

The court pointed out that "Parliament has not legislated to establish a class action regime in the field of data protection."

Commentators point out that this recovery gap could be filled by parliamentary legislation, but it remains to be seen whether they will wish to act.[234]

Mass State Data Collection

Judgments in Case C-623/17, Privacy International, and in Joined Cases

In October 2020, the ECJ issued a decision that:

> Confirms that EU law precludes national legislation requiring a provider of electronic communications services to carry out the general and indiscriminate transmission or retention of traffic data and location data for the purpose of combatting crime in general or of safeguarding national security.[235]

Both the UK and various European Member States were found to be collecting the communications data of their citizens. However, according to the ECJ general anti-crime or national security concerns do not provide sufficient excuse to permit the mass collection of communications data by the states.

Genuine serious present or foreseeable threats are required to justify "targeted" data collection as a limited exemption to the general rule stated above.

The challenge to data collection in the UK was brought by an organization called Privacy International. The Legal Director of Privacy International said that this decision would limit the powers of police and security organizations within the UK and EU countries to review the communications data of communications users. The Legal Director said:

> European law applies any time that a national government tries to ask a telecommunications provider to process personal data for the state, including providing access to communications data, or retaining data, even in the context of national security.

234. Gibson Dunn, "UK Supreme Court Overturns Court of Appeal to Disallow Google Data Privacy Class Action," online, November 11, 2021.
235. Court of Justice of the European Union, Press Release 123/20, online, October 6, 2020.

Commentators have said that this decision challenges some significant pieces of UK legislation. For example, the Telecommunications Act 1984 has provisions requiring ISPs to keep and be prepared to provide their customers communications data to UK security agencies.

It also calls into question the Investigatory Powers Act 2016 which contains provisions relating to the collection of communications data in the UK.

Although the UK has now left the EU, this decision may require the UK to modify its surveillance legislation if it wishes to continue to share security data with members of the EU.[236]

Website Blocking Costs

Cartier International AG and others v. British Telecommunications Plc and another

In June 2018, the UK Supreme Court ruled that rights holders such as trademark and patent owners can obtain orders that ISPs should block access to certain websites where counterfeit copies or unauthorized goods of genuine rights holders are being offered for sale. However, the rights holders are required to compensate ISPs for the costs and expenses of blocking certain websites.[237]

The litigation relating to this issue was originally brought by Richemont which owns a number of well-known luxury brands, including Montblanc and Cartier. They obtained an injunction preventing BT and other UK ISPs from hosting websites selling fake copies of luxury goods sold by the rights owners, in this case Richemont. They claimed that they had found thousands or possibly hundreds of thousands of websites where goods and services that infringed the property of rights holders were being offered for sale.

It has been shown that the blocking of such infringing websites is effective protection for rights holders and that blocking is regularly used by owners of valuable trademarks and intellectual property to protect their rights.

The use of website blocking as rights protection requires a significant amount of ongoing maintenance because infringing websites often reappear under new names. Therefore, the rights holders will continually need to request ISPs to update their blocking of infringing websites. Performing these tasks, the court ruled ISPs will need to be compensated by the rights holders for the costs and expenses incurred by ISPs in blocking infringing websites.

Dark Web Drugs

In October 2021, twenty-four people were arrested in the UK as part of an international integration targeting a drugs marketplace on the "dark web."

This was one of the largest operations ever against the criminal use of the dark web.

236. Bill Goodwin, "EU's Top Court Questions Legality of UK Phone and Internet Data Surveillance," *ComputerWeekly.com*, online, October 6, 2020.
237. [2018] UKSC 28. Judgment Date June 13, 2018.

In the UK, the operation, which took over six months, was spearheaded by the National Crime Agency cooperating with police forces in the UK. It resulted in the seizure of a number of drugs, including 50 kilos of cocaine, MDMA, cannabis methamphetamine and ketamine.

The operation began in Germany when authorities there arrested the person who was believed to be the operator of the marketplace, and this gave the German authorities information about how the marketplace was being operated. The German authorities shared their knowledge with enforcement agencies around the world, including those of Australia, Bulgaria, France, Germany, Italy, the Netherlands, Switzerland, the US, and the UK and included cooperation from Europol and Eurojust.[238]

238. National Crime Agency, "International Operation Targets Dark Web Drugs Marketplace," online, October 27, 2021.

CHAPTER 7

French Internet Law

France, because it is a Member State of the EU, is subject to the EU Internet-related law that was discussed previously in Chapter 5. It is also subject to the provisions of the various international conventions and treaties to which it is a party.

However, France also has its own carefully considered laws and regulations that govern the use of the Internet.

Because the Internet has become such an important source of information and entertainment, it is reasonable to ask whether access to the Internet is considered to be a fundamental right in France.

In 2009, France adopted the law on the High Authority for the Dissemination of Works and Protection (HADOPI). This law established that access to the Internet is a protected part of freedom of expression in France. Freedom of expression is considered to include freedom of access to the Internet. Under this law, the publication and protection of information and intellectual property on the Internet are protected.

Of course, there are some restrictions on this right, which permit restriction to Internet access in some circumstances. Where the Internet is being used to commit crimes, to infringe on the rights of others, or to promulgate false or fraudulent information, the persons doing so may be penalized and one of the penalties can include suspension of Internet access.

A ANTI-HATE SPEECH

The Pleven Act

In France, promoting racial hatred had previously been made illegal under the Pleven Act in 1972. This referred to a degree of April 21, 1939, by the then initial Minister of Justice, Paul Machadeau. This decree permitted the prosecutor to bring an action, even in the absence of a third-party complaint, where it found "defamation or insult committed against a group of persons belonging, by reason of their original, to a particular race or religion, if it is intended to incite hatred between citizens or inhabitants."

Freedom of Speech

French law projecting freedom of expression originates from the Declaration of the Rights of Man and of the Citizen that was promulgated in 1881.

But not all expression is free in France. There are laws in France against racism, anti-Semitism, racial hatred and justification of terrorism. These are criminal offenses and punishable by law. Consequently, these kinds of expression on the Internet are unlawful.

Since 2014, incitement to terrorism and public justification of terrorism are punishable by imprisonment for up to seven years.[239]

The Avia Law

In May 2020, France passed a new law that required Internet platforms to delete "hateful content" (such as terrorist or child pornography postings) reported to them by users within twenty-four hours or risk a fine of €1.25 million ($1.45 million).[240] This requires the removal of terrorist and child pornography postings within one hour, and other hateful content within twenty-four hours.[241]

However, in June 2020, a French court, the Constitutional Council of Paris, struck down key revisions of the Avia Law, stating that they were unreasonable restrictions on freedom of expression.[242]

The Constitutional Council ruled that requiring online service providers to make all legal analyses of content, without a judicial ruling, within such a short time, with the threat of such large fine, was a danger to freedom of expression because it may cause service providers to remove any flagged content, regardless of its legal status, rather than risk the statutory punishment.[243]

For the same reasons, the court also struck down hey section of law, requiring platforms to remove content flagged by authorities as child pornography or terrorist

239. France, Government, "Everything You Need to Know about Freedom of Expression in France," online, retrieved August 4, 2020.
240. The original form of this French law was similar to an earlier German law, the NetzDG law, which, although it caused a great deal of controversy, was adopted in January 2018. Online platforms were given responsibility for removing illegal hate speech within twenty-four hours of notification of its existence. Failure to do so could result in a €50 million fine. Within the first year of operation, almost a million postings were reported under the German law as possibly illegal. However, only one fine was imposed. Facebook was fined €2 million for having an inadequate hate speech notification process. The URG Team, "France's watered-down anti-hate speech law enters into force," The Universal Rights Group, online, July 16, 2020.
241. This is known as the "Avia Law," after Laetitia Avia, the member of the French Parliament who drafted and sponsored the bill.
242. Aurelien Breeden, "French Court Strikes Down Most of Online Hate Speech Law," *The New York Times*, online, June 18, 2020, retrieved August 4, 2020.
243. *Id.*

propaganda within one hour because this was a too short time and was being required without any independent review.[244]

However, on a more positive note, the court did state that the law's creation of an official online hate speech watchdog would be allowed to remain in place.[245]

A group representing large tech companies in France and other digital advocacy supporters praised the Council's decision saying that it freed the Internet in France from the law's "abusive censorship."[246]

It should be noted that at the time, the EU also asked France to put off adopting the law because it conflicted with EU law on the "free circulation of services."[247]

The reaction of the government in France was disappointment in the ruling, and statements that the government was determined to introduce new hate speech laws complied with this ruling. A spokesperson said that although France did have laws against hate speech that included criminal penalties, existing laws were introduced at a time before the Internet and were not adequate to deal with the complex new problems that the Internet presented.[248]

The Avia Law did come into effect on July 1, 2020, but in a reduced version. The strict notification procedures were eliminated. The law basically required platforms to streamline their notification processes and included provisions for observing incidents of hate speech on Internet platforms.[249]

In connection with this restriction on illegal content, the French government has indicated its wish that the posting of anti-Semitic content would also be excluded under the policy represented by the Avia Law.

244. *Id.*
245. *Id.*
246. *Id.*
247. The URG Team, "France's Watered-Down Anti-hate Speech Law Enters into Force," *The Universal Rights Group*, online, July 16, 2020.
248. *Id.*
249. *Id.*

CHAPTER 8

Chinese Internet Law

About 54% of Chinese people use the Internet. In a population of about 1.5 billion people, this means that about 800 million people are using the Internet. That is more than Europe and America combined.

However, because almost 80% of the populations of developed Western countries use the Internet, there appears to be a great deal of room for expansion in China. That may mean that in the next decade or so, China will be an enormous power and influence on the Internet.

Given the enthusiastic and growing use of the Internet in China, and the international interaction, personal, commercial, and political, that this entails, the laws and regulations that regulate the Internet in China are an important issue, not only for China but also for the world.

A CHINESE INTERNET POLICY

A fundamental question is "What level of freedom do Internet users have in China?" Freedom House is a private US organization the tracks and ranks countries on issues relating to technology and democracy.[250] In general, they oppose what they say as a "rising tide" of government control over the Internet. To that end, they produce an annual Freedom on the Net report that ranks countries in terms of Internet freedom.

Their 2019 report ranks China the lowest in the world for Internet freedom with a score of only 10 out of 100.[251] Even Russia allows more than three times as much freedom with a score of 31.[252]

This shocking situation begs the question of what exactly China does in terms of restricting Internet freedom.

250. https://freedomhouse.org/.
251. https://freedomhouse.org/report/freedom-net. The next lowest out of the 67 countries ranked is Syria, at 17 out of 100.
252. *Id.*

Freedom House uses three categories to measure Internet freedom:

- The first is "obstacles to access." These judge the legal and ownership barriers to Internet use in a particular country. There is also the question of how independent regulatory bodies are of political control.[253]
- The second issue they analyze concerns "limits on content." They look at such things as: legal regulations on content, technical filters and blocking of websites, self-censorship, the diversity of online News media, and the use of the Internet to mobilize opinion on public issues.[254]
- The third category is examination of whether there are identifiable violations of user rights. This looks at whether there is surveillance online, how privacy is protected, and whether penalties are imposed for online content which might include imprisonment, government harassment, or cyberattacks.[255]

China unfortunately does very poorly with respect to all these tests.

There is very little freedom of information. Censorship is strict. The content of all media, whether on or off the Internet, is closely controlled by the government. Information about significant political or public events, such as protests against government control, is not permitted to be shown on the Internet. There is not really any Internet "neutrality." Sources and content are under the total control of the government.

However, despite the lack of Internet freedom, China does have a keen interest in the Internet. This is shown by the fact that the Chinese government has allowed and encouraged its own gigantic Internet companies to develop including: Alibaba, Huawei, Tencent and China Mobile.

So, all of this begs the question of whether China does publish any formal laws or regulations relating to the Internet which can be a reference point for both Chinese citizens and foreign citizens interested in the Chinese Internet market. The answer is "yes."

B CHINESE INTERNET LAWS

China Cybersecurity Law

In 2017, the Chinese government implemented the China Internet Security Law (also called "the China Cybersecurity Law").[256]

Under the Cybersecurity Law, the government is entitled to undertake a great deal of control over Internet business, and to demand a great deal of cooperation from network operators and other Internet businesses that the Chinese consider "critical" to national security.

253. *Id.*
254. *Id.*
255. *Id.*
256. Jack Wagner, "China's Cybersecurity Law: What You Need to Know," *The Diplomat*, June 1, 2017.

The definitions of those two sectors are very broad:

(1) "Network operators" include network owners, managers and providers of any system consisting of computers and related equipment that gathers, stores, transmits, discovers, exchanges, or processes information. That would seem to include almost all businesses and many individuals that use computers and/or operate on the Internet.
(2) Businesses "critical to national security" include communications businesses; information services; energy, transport, water, financial services; public services; and electronic government services. This puts a large sector of Chinese economic life under scrutiny.[257]

Network operators are required to keep stored within mainland China any data that is gathered or produced within China. This includes any data that is gathered about Chinese citizens within China.[258]

The government is permitted to conduct spot checks and require certifications to ensure that data is being stored within China as required by the law.

Network operators can also be asked to provide source code, encryption data or other important information for review by the government. The law requires network operators to accept supervision from the government into their "social responsibility" and to comply with other standards which are phrased in vague enough terms to permit the network operator very little scope to challenge any government scrutiny and inspection of its computer and data systems.

Internet Administration

In China, the administration of the Internet is overseen by Cyberspace Administration China (CAC). That organization was founded in 2014 and launched its website in December of that year.[259]

Essentially, the function of the CAC is to translate Chinese Communist Party ideology into technical regulations for the Internet.

Controlling Foreign Programs

To encourage the development of Chinese companies, Chinese regulations make serious efforts to reduce the effectiveness of foreign Internet programs.

Tools that they use include restricting search results or asking international companies to eliminate certain kinds of content.

For example, they will sometimes require news aggregating services to remove any content relating to protests against China, such as the Hong Kong protests.

257. *Id.*
258. *Id.*
259. www.cac.gov.cn.

Hong Kong and Macau

It used to be the case that in former European colonies such as Hong Kong or Macau, many Chinese Internet regulations did not apply. This was a product of what was called the one nation two systems approach that was a key feature of the transfer of political control of those territories from Western nations to China.

An important purpose of that system was to permit these affluent former colonies to continue to produce significant amounts of trade and income for China.

However, between 2019 and 2020, this liberality began to disappear. This change was particularly dramatic in Hong Kong when China imposed new laws on the territory, significantly reducing civil liberties there.

The Great Firewall

One of the CAC's most important functions is to operate the Great Firewall of China, previously operated by the State Internet Information Office.

China first connected with the global Internet in 1994. Initially, its priorities were building infrastructure, establishing systems for information security, and aiding industrial development.[260]

Initially, the Internet activity was governed by the Ministry of Information Industry. As the penetration of the Internet grew in China, the government became increasingly concerned about the power of that medium.[261]

China turned its concerns into several regulatory and technical policies which altogether constitute something known as "The Great Firewall of China."

These are several initiatives to regulate the Internet within China. Their goals are to:

- impose Internet censorship;
- block access to several foreign websites that do not conform to Chinese ideology; and
- regulate International Internet traffic to and from China.

Major foreign Internet companies are blocked from operating in China, including Wikipedia, Twitter, Google, and Facebook.

As time has gone on, China has become even more concerned about controlling the Internet. This has the double effect of both:

(1) excluding information and communications which might be contrary to Chinese ideology; and

260. Weishan Miao (Chinese Academy of Social Sciences, China) and Wei Lei (China Radio International, China), "Policy Review, the Cyberspace Administration of China," Book Review, *Sage Journals*, online, December 7, 2016.
261. *Id.*

(2) permitting Chinese competitors to establish themselves within the expanding Chinese Internet market.

Those non-Chinese Internet companies that are permitted to operate within China are required to adapt their systems to Chinese Internet regulations.

The importance of that is not being underestimated by the government.

In 2013, President Xi Jinping said "the Internet directly relates to the national ideology security and the regime security." In recognition of this position, China has taken the following steps.

In 2000, the State Council Information Office created the Bureau of Internet News Regulation. In 2012, China issued a regulation requiring Internet users to give their real names to ISPs.

After the Snowden and Wikileaks developments, China has become even more determined to regulate Internet activity.[262] This ultimately led to the China Internet Security Law of 2017, discussed above.

The Internet Security Law includes several subsidiary regulations that help define its purposes. There is the Core Infrastructure Initiative.

C ANTI-MONOPOLY VIOLATIONS

In 2021, China began cracking down on the power of some of its biggest and most powerful tech companies. One of the tools that it used was Chinese anti-monopoly laws.

In April 2021, China imposed a huge $18 billion fine on Alibaba Group Holdings Limited. This is equal to about two and three-quarter billion US dollars.

In the past, China's enforcement of antitrust laws had been particularly low-key, particularly against big powerful companies that made significant contributions to China's worldwide revenues. In that area Alibaba was certainly a leader.

Alibaba Fine

However, this action by the Chinese government and the size of the fine (almost 5% of Alibaba's Chinese revenues in 2019) indicated a new response to the power of Internet companies, and to any hubris exhibited by their founders.

The Alibaba fine may be as much about the Chinese government's annoyance with Jack Ma, the founder of Alibaba, for publicly criticizing Chinese financial regulation in October 2020, as with any concern about Alibaba's market dominance.[263]

262. *Id.*
263. David Stanway and Scott Murdoch, "China Fines Alibaba Record $2.75 Billion for Anti-monopoly Violations," *Reuters*, online, April 10, 2021, accessed April 12, 2021.

Tencent Punishment

In July 2021, the Chinese government continued its attacks on the market power of Chinese Internet companies by requiring Tencent, the music streaming company, to give up its restrictive music licensing arrangements with international record labels.

China was apparently aiming to end Tencent dominance of online music in China.

Tencent was also fined around $1.5 billion for its practices in the Chinese music streaming market.

Since 2016 Tencent has controlled around 80% of music streaming rights in China. The Chinese state administration of market regulation said it acted because Tencent had broken China's anti-monopoly regulations.

Tencent was required to end any currently existing exclusive streaming rights within thirty days.

Tencent has previously arranged licensing deals with international music giants such as Universal, Sony and Warner.

This government action against Tencent caused its share price to decline on the Hong Kong Stock Exchange.[264]

D MORE CONTROL OF TECH COMPANIES

The Chinese government's punishment of Alibaba and Tencent is apparently just the tip of the iceberg in the government's campaign to exert strict control over tech companies.

The clear policy of the government is that no organization should be more powerful than the Communist Party.

The rapid expansion of the Internet and its dramatic impact on commerce have brought about the rapid expansion of the wealth and influence of companies in the tech sector all over the world.

China, with one of the world's largest economies, has been one of the centers of this growth.

As the Jack Ma of Alibaba example has shown, the growth of some of these companies has been seen as a potential threat to Chinese political leadership.

Immediately after the fine on Alibaba was announced, thirty-four of the most important Chinese tech companies were called in for a talk with government officials that informed them that what happened to Alibaba could happen to them if they were not suitably respectful of Chinese government policies.[265] They were told that they had a month to think about their business and how well they were complying with the government's rules for Internet companies. This made those companies worry that they could be the next target to be made an example of by government regulators.

264. "Tencent Shares Slide after Beijing Crackdown on Music Rights," *BBC News*, online, July 26, 2021.
265. Karishma Vaswami, "Is Alibaba's Fate a Warning to China's Tech Giants?," *BBC News, Business*, online, April 15, 2021.

E CORE STATE DATA REGULATION

Among the details that are being reported of new legislation passed in June 2021 is a regulation that any tech firms that mishandle "core state data" will be forced to cease operations and have their operating license revoked.

Additionally, they can be fined more than $1 million.

Firms will also be punished for leaking "sensitive data" outside of China.

Barring Data to Foreign Law Enforcement

Companies are also forbidden to provide tech data to foreign law enforcement organizations without the Chinese government's permission. Doing so can result in fines of millions of dollars and withdrawal of permission to operate.

Fines for Inappropriate Content

During the same period, China ordered some of its biggest online companies to remove content not considered appropriate for children. The messaging apps providers Kuaishou, QQ (by Tencent), Taobao and Weibo were all fined and told to remove inappropriate content.[266]

Stronger Involvement for Government

The legislation also stipulates that all important decisions relating to data security are to be made by government security officials in the future.[267]

These new laws were effective on September 1, 2021.

Technical standards on the measures that companies will be required to take to comply with these new regulations are expected to be released in the future. It is hoped that these will give detailed guidance to those companies involved in Internet business in China.

F CHINA'S REFOCUS OF TECH POWER

This legislation is another part of China's concerted drive to make the computer data business an important part of Chinese commerce and Chinese security.

The Chinese government has been investing huge amounts of money in electronic infrastructure such as data centers. It is important to the Chinese government to rebalance domination of the tech space away from large private tech companies and in favor of the government.[268]

266. "China: Taobao, Weibo Fined for Illegal Child Content," *BBC News*, online, July 21, 2021.
267. *Bloomberg News*, online, June 10, 2021.
268. *Id.*

This shifting of focus has had a negative impact on the value of publicly traded tech companies. Shortly after this legislation was passed in June 2021, value of some of the largest tech companies listed on the Hong Kong Stock Exchange suffered a decline. Apparently, some shareholders feel that it is not in their interests to be increasingly subject to scrutiny and control by the Communist Party in China.[269]

This also caused a significant fall in the value of Chinese company shares on the NYSE.

This was a serious blow to Chinese companies that wish to raise investment outside of China. More than thirty Chinese companies were listed on the NYSE in the first six months of 2021, raising over $12 billion.[270]

G PUNISHMENT FOR FOREIGN LISTING

As time went on, Chinese policy toward digital business changed significantly. By June 2021, the Chinese government was punishing digital companies that listed their shares for trading on stock exchanges outside of China.

DiDi Ride Hailing App

For example, the Chinese taxi-hailing service DiDi Chuxing was punished for listing American Depository Receipts (ADRs) for the trading of its shares on the New York Stock Exchange. This also caused a significant fall in the value of Chinese company shares on the NYSE.

DiDi had raised over $4 billion from its NYSE public offering.[271]

In July 2021, the CAC ordered online merchants not to offer the ride hailing app of DiDi.

DiDi was accused of unlawfully compiling the personal data of his customers. The government also considered imposing more serious penalties on the DiDi.[272]

H THE LIKELY FUTURE OF CHINESE INTERNET LAW

At the beginning of the Chinese tech boom, the government was happy to let it grow with relatively little regulation. China wanted to encourage economic growth and still does, but only if successful Internet merchants understand that nothing should be more important in the lives of Chinese citizens than the Communist Party.[273]

It appears that this policy will be the most important issue governing Chinese Internet law and regulation for the foreseeable future.

269. *Id.*
270. Yuan Yang and Hudson Lockett, "DiDi Shares Fall 20% as China Tightens Overseas Listing Rules," *Financial Times*, online, July 7, 2021.
271. *Id.*
272. "Tencent Shares Slide ...," *BBC*, online, July 26, 2021.
273. *Id.*

CHAPTER 9
Indian Internet Law

A LAWS AGAINST CYBERCRIME

The principal Indian law regulating electronic commerce and defending against cybercrime is the Information Technology Act 2000 (ITA) that came into force on October 17, 2000, and has been amended since then.

The watching or distributing of child pornography is against the law in India. The penalties can be a fine or imprisonment of up to three years. These offenses are prohibited by the Copyright Act of 1957.[274]

An express definition of "cybercrime" is not found in either the ITA 2000 or the National Cyber Security Policy 2013.

There is no specific regulation prohibiting "cybercrime" as such in India. Cybercrime is brought within the scope of criminal behavior by being recognized as a combination of crime prohibited by criminal legislation in combination with the use of digital technology.

India's laws that can be applied to situations where cybercrime is found are those laws that deal with such things as electronic signatures, intellectual property, or privacy and data protection.

As a practical law enforcement matter in India, cybercrime is recognized as any crime done with the assistance of telecommunication or computer technology or any crime where computers or digital technology is either used in the crime or is the target of the crime. This means that there is really no crime that will not be considered cybercrime if it involves digital or telephonic technology.[275]

274. Indian Copyright Act, 1957, sections 63-65A.
275. Vinit Verma, "Importance of Cyber Law in India," *Legal Service India*, online, retrieved September 9, 2020.

B INTERNET CENSORSHIP IN INDIA

Censorship of the Internet in India covers a variety of online activities and is performed by the national government and the state governments. There are significant efforts by both to regulate and remove content.

There are also court cases brought by content creators seeking court orders to remove content that appears on the Internet in violation of intellectual property laws and regulations.

Blocking Websites

Certain websites have been blocked for political reasons by government orders.

The first such instance occurred in 1999. Following a military conflict between India and Pakistan over control of Kashmir, the website of *Dawn*, Pakistan's daily newspaper, was blocked by the Indian government-owned telecoms company that provided international Internet access to India.[276]

In 2003, all Yahoo groups were banned for about two weeks when the government tried to shut down one Yahoo website that had breached the law by discussing a legal case that was being tried.[277]

Banning Apps

There is also a long list of mobile apps banned in India, including TikTok.[278]

Internet Shutdowns

India also apparently leads the world in Internet shutdowns, with as many as 134 in 2018.[279] Many of these shutdowns are for political and/or public order reasons.

---

276. "India Blocks Pakistani Newspaper Web Site," *Newswatch.in*, July 5, 1999, https://newswatch.write2kill.in/news/1999/07/05/india-blocks-pakistani-newspaper-web-site, online, retrieved September 9, 2020.
277. "India Bans One Yahoo Discussion Group," *Shibu Thomas, InfoWar Monitor*, September 29, 2003, online, retrieved September 9, 2020, https://web.archive.org/web/20110917185442/; http://www.infowar-monitor.net/2003/09/yahoo-groups-blocked-by-indian-government/.
278. "Government Bans 59 Mobile Apps Which Are Prejudicial to Sovereignty and Integrity of India, Defence of India, Security of State and Public Order," *Press Information Bureau*, June 29, 2020, online, retrieved September 9, 2020.
279. "Government Can Switch Off Your Internet in Necessary: The Economic Times," *indiatimes.com*, online, March 8, 2015, retrieved September 9, 2020.

Bhasin v. Union of India

However, in January 2020, the Supreme Court of India declared that it was illegal under Indian law for the government to have indefinite suspensions of Internet services in the case of *Bhasin v. Union of India.*[280]

This case involved Internet restrictions imposed on the provinces of Jammu and Kashmir in August 2019. The government's reason was that these were necessary to protect public order.

The Supreme Court said that to preserve the right of freedom of expression granted under the constitution of India, it was necessary that any government shutdown of Internet service complies with certain key requirements.

Although the court did say that the government had a right to impose Internet shutdowns under certain circumstances in the name of national security, it was necessary that the orders imposing the shutdowns be made public and that they be subject to judicial review.

It was argued that the shutdowns interfered with freedom of expression in that they restricted the travel of journalists and what they would be permitted to publish. The attorney general argued that the restrictions were necessary to prevent terrorists and militants from carrying out terrorist offenses against the public. The court decided that although the government would have the power to impose restrictions under certain circumstances, it was important for a democracy to maintain transparency about the imposition of the restrictions so that the public could know their basis. Also, it was necessary that the reasons for any such restrictions be subject to court review, and it was ultimately up to the court to decide whether such restrictions were permitted under the constitution of India.

2021 Censorship and Surveillance Regulations

In early 2021, India introduced a broad new range of Internet regulations.

Basically, they were aimed at allowing the government to insist that tech companies collect and store billions of messages every day so that they are available for examination by government.

Tech companies must comply with the demands of the government or possibly lose access to the Indian market, which is one of the biggest, if not the biggest in the world.

This is a major problem for companies like Facebook. WhatsApp (owned by Facebook) is believed to have approximately four hundred million users in India. India is its largest market. This is true for other messaging and social media companies as

280. *Anuradha Bhasin v. Union of India,* AIR 2020 SC 1308. Meghana Reddy, "Case Analysis," *legalbites.in,* online, June 17, 2021. Also *see,* "Bhasin v. India," Columbia University, *Global Freedom of Expression,* online, retrieved September 9, 2021.

well.[281] Social media platforms like Twitter, Facebook, and WhatsApp were required to be in compliance with these new rules by the middle of 2021.

In February 2021, Indian government put pressure on Twitter to remove posts that had been put on the platform by political activists about anti-government protests. Twitter initially refused to remove them, saying that this was a freedom of speech issue. However, Twitter caved in and did remove the posts after the government threatened to jail Twitter employees if they did not comply.

Facebook and WhatsApp took a more aggressive approach and went to court to oppose India's new rules. They complained that the new rules required it to keep track of the parties in all chats.

WhatsApp asked the High Court to rule that the new regulation was unconstitutional. They claimed that the new rule would put an end to effective encryption of WhatsApp messages and that this would destroy its users' expectation of privacy.

This change in government attitude toward the Internet is unfortunate because India, which prides itself on being a democratic country, appears to be increasingly authoritarian about controlling the Internet. It remains to be seen what the effect of such attitudes will be on the growth of Internet use in India and the economic impact of diminishing the growth of the online market.[282]

Essentially, these new regulations meant that social media platforms were under direct government supervision.

This situation creates a dilemma for tech companies because India is perhaps the largest market in the world with hundreds of millions of users. It is predicted that there will be nine hundred million users in India by 2025. Therefore, major computer companies do wish to continue to do business there if possible. However, they are concerned that India's regulations essentially give the government a veto power over content.

C PRIVACY AND DATA PROTECTION

It is reported that India makes more requests for user information from tech companies than any other government in the world.

The amount of government intervention in India makes their system comparable to that of China when it comes to strict control of media companies. As in China, much of this regulation appears intended to protect the government from criticism on the Internet. It is a clear restriction on freedom of speech, and a danger to user privacy.[283]

Although India does not have an express Internet data protection law, it does follow international conventions that support rights to privacy.

281. "WhatsApp Facebook-Owned App Goes to Court over India Privacy Rules," *BBC News*, online, May 26, 2021.
282. Billy Perrigo, "India's New Internet Rules Are a Step Toward 'Digital Authoritarianism,' Activists Say. Here's What They Will Mean," *Time*, online, March 12, 2021, accessed April 9, 2021.
283. Sheikh Saaliq and Krutika Pathi, "Ïndia Internet Law Adds to Fears over Online Speech," *AP News*, online, July 15, 2021.

The closest legislation it has to a data protection law are sections 43A and 72A of the ITA that allow persons to seek compensation when there has been improper disclosure of their personal information.

There are also rules which restrict businesses in the disclosure of personal data they have collected.

Also, certain regulated businesses in the financial services and telecommunication sectors are subject to regulations about maintaining the confidentiality of the personal information of customers and using it only for certain limited purposes.[284]

D PLATFORM LIABILITY FOR POSTS

The Alphabet (Google Case)

In the case of *Google India Pvt. Ltd. v. M/S Visakha Industries*, the Supreme Court of India ruled, in December 2019, that Google was not liable for defamatory posts after 2009.

This reaffirmed that Internet service and social media companies are not liable for content posted on their services by third parties. The justices said, any other decision would make it a restriction strangling the free flow of ideas, which is what the Internet is all about.

The case involved a post opposing the manufacture and use of sheets of building material containing asbestos.

Visakha Industries Ltd., a building materials company, claimed that was defamed by an online post, and sued Google for allowing it to be accessed by its search service.

They filed a claim against Google India Private Limited in the form of a Petition under section 482 of The Code of Criminal Procedure, 1973.

However, the Supreme Court of India denied their claim ruling that section 79 of the ITA (Amendment 2008) created an exemption from any other law in respect of third-party posts on computer service and social media platforms.

The court said "Section 79 is a safe harbor provision."[285]

However, Google did not get off completely. The court ruled that the safe harbor of section 79 did not protect Google from prosecution for hosting such posts in time periods prior to section 79's effective date. The trial against Google for offensive posts pre-section 79 would be allowed to proceed.[286]

This 2019 decision was consistent with a decision of the Supreme Court in March 2015 that struck down section 66A of the ITA Prohibiting "Offensive Comments."

Section 66A of the ITA made "offensive" posts a crime punishable by imprisonment.

284. Talwar Thakore & Associates, "Data Protected: India," online, March 2020, retrieved September 11, 2020.
285. *Google India Private Appellant(s) v. M/S. Visakha Industries and Another Respondent(s)*, Supreme Court of India Criminal Appellate Jurisdiction, Criminal Appeal No. 1987 2914. December 19, 2019. Online, retrieved September 10, 2020.
286. *Google v. Visakha*, pp. 147-148.

However, free speech advocates conducted a campaign to have it struck down for being an oppressive restriction on free speech and on the public's right to knowledge.

The Supreme Court ruled, in 2015, that section 66A's prohibitions against "annoying" or "grossly offensive" posts were so vague, subjective, and difficult to enforce that section 66A was unconstitutional.[287]

287. "Sec 66A of IT Act Scrapped: 5 Points Observed by the Supreme Court," *Hindustan Times*, online, March 24, 2015, retrieved September 11, 2020.

CHAPTER 10

Japanese Internet Law

Freedom House, in its chart of Internet scores, rates Japan as having the greatest Internet freedom in Asia with a score of 73 out of 100. That is not far behind the US, which is given a score of 77.[288]

A BACKGROUND

Japan has installed high-quality Internet service to most of the population and virtually all substantial businesses. There are over 117 million Internet users in Japan which represents more than 90% of the population.[289]

Japanese law does go a long way in protecting freedom of speech. This protects most forms of communication, including Internet posts and the press.

Most of the regulation of the Internet in Japan is self-regulation by ISPs. More formal regulation is provided by the Ministry of Internal Affairs and Communications (MIC). However, the MIC avoids an overly intrusive approach.

B NTT DOMINANT ISP

Although there is an open market, the principal ISP in Japan is the formerly state-owned Nippon Telephone and Telegraph Corporation (NTT) that was privatized in 1985. In 1999, a new law separated NTT's Internet services from its mobile and fixed-line telephone services.

Despite the free market, NTT has remained the dominant service provider in Japan. The only other big tech companies to establish themselves in the Japanese

288. The highest among the sixty-five countries surveyed. The top-rated is Iceland with a score of 95. Number two is Estonia with a score of 94, https://freedomhouse.org/countries/freedom-net/scores.
289. International Telecommunication Union, Statistics, Percentage of Individuals Using the Internet, Japan, 91.28%, retrieved online July 27, 2020.

market have been Apple and Samsung which have had success selling mobile phones. But NTT has no serious competitors in the provision of Internet services.

C INTERNET REGULATION

Use of the Internet for both gathering information and posting it largely operates without government restrictions in Japan. In 2001, ISPs were directed to organize a framework of self-regulation by the 2001 Provider Liability Limitation Act.

D PROTECTION OF FREE SPEECH

The Japanese Constitution protects free speech and forbids most kinds of censorship. However, the government has made efforts to block media piracy sites, and there have been arrests and some prosecutions relating to copyright violations using the Internet.

As examples, the government requested ISPs to block certain media piracy sites in 2018. The government also announced that it intends to introduce new laws to increase website blocking powers.

E ANTI-TERRORISM

In June 2017, a conspiracy law was introduced which permits the police to obtain warrants to investigate Internet posts and sites (and other off-line locations) which are likely to have links to terrorism.[290]

F PROTECTION OF TEENAGED USERS

Japan has passed a statute intended to protect teenagers from Internet content that:

- is too sexual;
- provides information about how to commit crimes; or
- contains gruesome descriptions of murder.

The statute applies to telecoms companies providing Internet services, but not to VPNs.[291]

G INTERNET PRIVACY AND DATA PROTECTION

There is no specific statute that recognizes a general right to privacy in Japan. That right has been established by court decisions.

290. www.refworld.org. The UN Refugee Agency retrieved July 29, 2020.
291. Japan, Telecoms, Media and Internet Laws and Regulations, section 6.4, www.iclg.com, retrieved July 29, 2020. Act on the Development of an Environment that Provides Safe and Secure Internet Use for Young People.

In 1964, a decision of the Tokyo District Court ruled that Article 13 of the Japanese Constitution supported a right to privacy.

Article 13 says:

> All of the people shall be respected as individuals. The right to life, liberty and the pursuit of happiness shall, to the extent it does not interfere with the public welfare, be the supreme consideration in legislation and other governmental affairs.

This right was recognized by the Japanese Supreme Court in the 1969 decision. In that case, a police officer took photos of people in a protest march. The court ruled that it was wrong to take photos of people without their consent, unless necessary for public welfare.[292]

A limited kind of Internet privacy is governed by Japan's General Privacy Law. This law applies to businesses that have personal information on five thousand or more people.[293]

There are three principal statutes that protect personal information. They are:

(1) the Act on the Protection of Personal Information (APPI);
(2) the APPI held by Independent Administrative Agencies; and
(3) the APPI held by administrative organs.

These are statutes that apply to all data collection, not only to collection of online information.

The statutes require businesses to protect personal information against loss, or unauthorized disclosure, or destruction.

It is also forbidden to transfer personal information to third parties unless the individual whose data is transferred consents to the transfer.

The government has also instituted a policy that requires all governmental and public administrative bodies to protect the personal data that they collect. The elements of this policy, called the Basic Policy on the Protection of Personal Information, are set out in a set of about forty guidelines that were issued in 2010.[294]

The law also requires businesses that have collections of personal data to make the following information available to all those who are subjects of that data:

(1) The name of the business holding the data.
(2) The purpose for which the data is being used.
(3) How to request corrections, disclosure or file complaints.
(4) Contact information for the entity authorized to accept complaints.

The only cases in which a data collector can disclose personal information without consent are cases where disclosure is:

292. *Id.*
293. Library of Congress, Law, Online Privacy Law, Japan, www.loc.gov, retrieved July 29, 2020.
294. *Id.*

(1) required by law or regulation;
(2) necessary to protect the life, body, or property of someone who is hard to reach to get consent;
(3) necessary for protecting public health; or
(4) necessary for an authorized governmental entity to conduct its legitimate business.[295]

The APPI requires that those business operations handling personal data must have a system for processing complaints about their treatment of personal data and provide for appropriate and expeditious handling of such complaints.

The data holders are also required to have a similarly well-run system to deal with requests to correct or remove data.

Under the APPI, complaints are to be mediated by local government.[296]

However, the remedies available to data subjects who are unhappy with the way that their complaint is being dealt with are limited. They are not permitted to bring private suits or seek civil damages.[297]

In 2009, the Consumer Commission established a Personal Information Protection Special Research Subcommittee. They recommended that there should be unambiguous rules on a data subject's rights to get, correct, and to seek to end use of personal information.

Criminal Sanctions

In addition to laws specifically designed to protect private online data, Japan also has a more general criminal statute that punishes unauthorized computer access.

Such acts can be punished by imprisonment of up to a year or a fine of about $6,000. Someone who steals another's password and access ID and uses it to gain access to a computer will be considered to have violated this statute.[298]

Application to Smartphones

The APPI also applies to the collection of data on smartphones in the same way it applies to data collection on computers.[299]

295. *Id.*
296. *Id.*
297. *Id.*
298. *Id.* The Act on the Prohibition of Unauthorized Computer Access.
299. *Id.*

Data Protection Administration

There is no specific government agency for data protection in Japan. Government ministers who have jurisdiction over business are required to oversee online data protection within their sphere of responsibility.[300]

A 2008 Supreme Court decision ruled that the governmental collection of personal data about persons could violate citizens' rights to liberty in private life if they disclosed the data to third parties or made the data public without a justifiable reason.[301]

Continuing Data Protection Review

There is an ongoing review of the role of protection of personal data in Japan. Several study groups are also examining these issues.[302]

It is fair to say that the state of Japanese law and regulation on online activity, generally, and the important sub-issues of privacy and data protection will continue to evolve as the Internet expands and changes.

300. *Id.*, section III.A.
301. *Id.*, fn. 108.
302. *Id.*, section VI.

CHAPTER 11

South Korean Internet Law

A FIRST INTERNET LAW

South Korea passed perhaps the first Internet regulation law in the world in 1995 with the Telecommunications Business Act (TBA). This law established a regulator for Internet communications entitled "the Information and Communications Ethics Office" (ICEO).[303]

Barring Offensive Posts

The principal functions of the ICEO were to censor posts on the Internet that:

- encroached on public morals;
- might endanger national sovereignty; and
- any other information that could disturb or harm the character, emotions, or sense of values of the youth of South Korea.[304]

The law provided that the Minister of Communication had the power to order service providers to delete or restrict any offensive material.

This was not a power that the Minister ignored. It is reported that in the first months of 1996 more than 220,000 posts were ordered to be deleted from the Internet.[305]

303. Peng Hwa Ang, "How Countries Are Regulating Internet Content," Nanwang Technological University, Singapore, January 1, 1997, https://web.archive.org/web/20160103124414/; https://www.isoc.org/inet97/proceedings/B1/B1_3.HTM.
304. *Id.*
305. *Id.*

Restricting Political Speech and Sympathy with North Korea

In addition, South Korean law contains special restrictions or any political speech, contact with or expression of sympathy for North Korea.

Any such search communications are forbidden, and South Korean prosecutors have indicated that they would punish anyone trying to access North Korean pages on the Internet.[306]

In fact, it has been reported that South Korean government officials stated that if any South Korean encountered a North Korean site on the Internet, he would be required to report this to the police within seven days.[307]

The restrictions on any kind of posting that reflects criticism of the South Korean government in relation to North Korea is forbidden.

For example, it has been reported that with respect to an incident when a North Korean submarine ran aground, and South Koreans had questioned the government's handling of the incident online, those South Koreans were investigated for potential violations of the law.[308]

Court Challenge to TBA

However, the strictness of these restraints was challenged in court by the filing of a complaint in August 1999 claiming that provisions of the TBA and an Enforcement Decree under the Act improperly infringed freedom of expression, violated due process and were an unnecessarily excessive restriction.[309]

In that case, a university student went online to question an incident in which North and South Korea warships briefly exchanged gunfire in 1999. The student posted a note on a message board which accused the then President of South Korea, Kim Dae-Jung, of being sloppy.

The court found that the terms in the statutes in question were too abstract and that different officials could make different judgments about whether the laws were being violated. Consequently, those laws could potentially create a "chilling effect" on communications that should not be regulated.[310]

The Aftermath

In 2002, a revision of the ICEO was passed. However, it did not in any way weaken the government's determination to punish what is improper communication on the

306. *Id.*
307. *Id.*
308. *Id.*
309. Case, 14-1 KCCR 616, 99Hun-Ma480, June 27, 2002, Columbia University, *Global Freedom of Expression*, https://globalfreedomofexpression.columbia.edu/cases/ban-improper-communication-internet-case/.
310. *Id.*

Internet. Political expression is still subject to limits under the National Security Act. Inciting or praising anti-government activities is restricted.[311]

Concern about Strict Korean Law

Some concern has been expressed in the Western media that digital communication is becoming too heavily censored in South Korea.[312]

Freedom House Evaluation

Nevertheless, despite these concerns, Freedom House, that rates 210 countries on their levels of Internet freedom, rated South Korea (at 64 out of 100) as one of the more liberal countries in Asia, ahead of Cambodia (43), China (10), India (55), Indonesia (51), Malaysia (57), Myanmar (36), Sri Lanka (49), Thailand (35) and Vietnam (24).[313]

311. Diane Kraft, "South Korea's National Security Law: A Tool of Oppression in an Insecure World," *Wisconsin International Law Journal*, Volume 24 (2006) 627.
312. David Volodzko, "Is South Korea Sliding Towards Digital Dictatorship?," *Forbes*, online, February 25, 2019.
313. Internet Freedom Scores, Freedom House, https://freedomhouse.org/, retrieved, July 27, 2020.

CHAPTER 12

Singapore Internet Law

A REGULATION BY SBA

In 1996, the Singapore government directed the Singapore Broadcasting Authority (SBA) to monitor activity on and content of the Internet.

The SBA was given the power to regulate ISPs by determining which ISPs should be licensed to operate in Singapore and subjecting them to the Internet Code of Practice.

The Code of Practice described what Internet activity or content is prohibited. Any material that was offensive to public interest, morality, order, security or "National Harmony" was prohibited.

B CENSORSHIP IN SINGAPORE

There are also broader public control laws that can be used against Internet activity or content that is offensive to the government.

For example, Singapore, as a former British colony, kept the British Sedition Act 1861 because it considered the law necessary to act against terrorism/and or ethnic conflicts which might endanger the nation's peace and harmony. This law is sometimes used against Internet users who are considered to have crossed the line into abusive or dangerous use of the Internet.

C REGULATOR CHANGED IN 2000

In 2000, regulation of the Internet was given to a newly created organization, the Media Development Authority.

This regulator frequently censors material that it considers to be politically or racially sensitive, creating concern that this can interfere with freedom of speech.

Satire

Satirical websites are carefully monitored and can be subject to censorship.

D PROTECTION OF INTELLECTUAL PROPERTY

In 2014, Singapore amended its copyright law to provide additional protection to intellectual property. All ISPs were required to block any websites that "flagrantly infringed" intellectual property rights.

Fake News

In 2019, Singapore introduced another law that, although it has some virtues, can also be seen as an additional limitation on free speech. This is a broad fake news law, formally called the Online Falsehoods and Manipulation Law.

Under this law, the spreading of false statements of fact which are considered prejudicial to Singapore's security, public safety, public peace or damaging to Singapore's relations with other countries is prohibited, along with several other types of Internet behavior or content.

The government can decide that certain content needs to be removed or have a correction added to it. The government can also order tech or social media companies to block posts or websites that spread fake news.

The penalties for violating this law can be more than $30,000 for individuals and/or up to five years in jail. If the post is by a fake account or a "bot," the fine can be more than $70,000 and/or ten years in prison.

Companies that violate this law can be fined over $700,000.

Protection under Fake News Law

The government has said that the regulators will be required to explain why a post is considered fake, and the government also promised that appeals under this law will be fast and inexpensive, but many are concerned that it may be used to suppress free speech.

The Prime Minister of Singapore justified this law by saying:

> If we do not protect ourselves, hostile parties will find it a simple matter to turn in different groups against one another and cause disorder in our society.

E PRESS FREEDOM IN SINGAPORE

It is a matter of note that an international journalists' group, Reporters Without Borders, ranked Singapore 158th out of 180 countries on the issue of press freedom in 2020.

F SINGAPORE LAW ON FOREIGN INTERFERENCE

On September 13, 2021, the government of Singapore proposed a parliamentary bill to prevent foreign cyber interference in Singapore politics.

The bill is called the Foreign Interference (Countermeasures) Bill. It is targeted at online content that "can cause immediate and significant harm in Singapore."

Social media providers will be required to comply with the law, and ISPs could be required to block harmful political content.

The bill also would permit the blocking of any computer downloads that aid spreading harmful content.

This law is in addition to the anti-fake news law introduced in Singapore during 2019.[314]

314. Chen Lin, "Singapore Submits Bill to Fight 'Foreign Interference'," *Reuters*, online, September 13, 2021.

CHAPTER 13

Selected Other Countries

It is beyond the scope of this book to list all the Internet laws, online developments, and anti-cybercrime efforts of all of the world's countries. To learn about the Internet activity of a country or legal jurisdiction, one needs to consult qualified legal representatives and other qualified experts in those countries or jurisdictions.

However, several Internet developments in certain countries have been widely reported or might be thought interesting for other reasons. For purposes of information that might inspire readers of this book to seek more information, brief summaries of some reports are set out below.

As with all the other material in this book, the comments below are not legal advice. Legal advice about Internet law can only be obtained from qualified legal professionals in the countries and/or legal jurisdictions in question.

A ABU DHABI

Abu Dhabi has introduced strict legal penalties to deter those who wish to commit crime on the Internet.

Data Theft

In 2012, Federal Decree Law Number Five set out in Article 12 the punishment for digital crimes. Anyone found guilty of violating the anti-Internet crime law:[315]

(1) shall be punished by imprisonment and a fine; or
(2) either of these two penalties for whoever gains access, without legal right to:
  - credit or electronic card numbers; or

315. Yousuf Mohammed Hassan Al Bahar, "How the UAE Is Fighting Cybercrime," *gulfbusiness*, online, November 29, 2020.

- data or bank account numbers; or
- data or any other electronic payment method.

(3) by using the computer networks or an electronic information system or any information technology means;
(4) the punishment shall be imprisonment for a period of at least six months and a fine of not less than DHS 100,000 and not an excess of DHS 300,000; or
(5) either of these two penalties, if it is intended to use the data and numbers to take over the funds of others or benefit from the services which they provide;
(6) if the person takes over the funds of others whether for himself or for others, he shall be punished by:
    - imprisonment for a period of at least one year; and
    - a fine of not less than DHS 200,000; and
(7) "not more than DHS [Emirati Dirhams] 1 million or either of these two penalties."

Cyberattacks on Healthcare

In 2021, Abu Dhabi introduced further measures to protect its healthcare sector from cyberattacks:

- In July of that year, it introduced its "Abu Dhabi Healthcare Information Security Strategy."[316]

  It is stated that Abu Dhabi intends to use both technological innovation and artificial intelligence (AI) to help protect the healthcare sector. The application of these tools will focus on:
  - the governance of cybersecurity;
  - the resilience of cybersecurity;
  - cybersecurity capabilities;
  - partnerships in cybersecurity;
  - the maturity of cybersecurity; and
  - innovation in cybersecurity relating to healthcare facilities.

These new measures will apply to:

- healthcare facilities and professionals;
- insurance companies;
- related health service providers;
- related vendors; and
- all parties that have access to the healthcare data of patients.

316. Rachel McArthur, "Abu Dhabi Working to Fight Cybercrime in Healthcare with New Strategy," *HealthcareITNews*, online, July 16, 2021.

B CHILE

Net Neutrality

In 2010, Chile leapt ahead of other nations by becoming the first country to legislate "net neutrality." This was a result of amending their Telecommunications Act to bar ISPs from discriminating between legitimate contact, posts and business on the Internet.

Privacy and Data Protection

Chilean Internet law focuses on protection of the personal data and privacy of its citizens.

Article 19 of the Constitution of Chile protects citizens' right to privacy and their personal data.

Unsolicited marketing is banned by the Consumer Protection Law.

C CUBA

Internet Protest

In July 2021, protests against the Cuban government were ignited on the Internet by Facebook videos of protests in towns around the country.

People demonstrated against the government, demanded freedom, and demanded the resignation of the President of the country.

The government's response was to arrest hundreds of people and to restrict the Internet.

The problem created for the government by the Internet was that it allowed people throughout the country to see the protests and demonstrations and the government's responses.[317]

Attack on Freedom of Expression

Restricting the communications facilities of the Internet within Cuba raises international human rights issues with respect to freedom of expression.

A US Response

This opens the question of whether a third country has a basis, in international law and policy, to take steps to reopen Internet access in Cuba.

317. Yoani Sanchez, "The New Generation of Cubans Who Won't Be Silenced," *The New York Times*, online, July 19, 2021.

Motivated by both its own political self-interest to undermine the communist government of Cuba and by the human rights question of whether it violates international law for Cuba to restrict the communication options of people by limiting the Internet, the US did consider whether to find a way to provide Internet access to Cubans.[318]

The basic international expression of the human right of free speech is set out in the International Covenant on Civil and Political Rights that was adopted by the UN General Assembly in December 1966. It states "that these rights derive from the inherent dignity of the human person."

The specific section that relates to the use of the Internet is Article 19 of the Covenant, which states the following:

(1) Everyone shall have the right to hold opinions without interference.
(2) "Everyone shall have the right to freedom of expression. This right shall include freedom to seek, impart, and receive information and ideas of all kinds, regardless of frontiers, either orally, in writing or in print, in the form of art, or any other media of his choice."
(3) The exercise of the rights provided for in paragraph 2 of this article carries with it special duties and responsibilities. It may therefore be subject to certain restrictions, but these shall only be such as are provided by law and are necessary:
    (a) For respect of the rights and reputation of others.
    (b) For the protection of national security or public order (*ordre public*), or of public health or morals.[319]

There are 173 countries that are parties to the Covenant that have both signed and ratified the document and accepted that it is part of international law. However, that does not include Cuba. Cuba signed in 2008 but has not yet ratified it.[320]

The US has both signed and ratified the Covenant and regards it as part of international law.

Regarding the question of reopening the Internet in Cuba, the US might rely on the principles of the Covenant.

However, there is little doubt that the real US motivation in seeking to provide Internet service to Cuba from outside the country in some fashion (or perhaps from the

318. Michael Schmitt, "Turning Cuba's Internet Back On: International Legal Options," *Just Security*, online, July 19, 2021.

319. United Nations International Covenant on Civil and Political Rights, Adopted and opened for signature, ratification and accession by General Assembly resolution 2200A (XXI) of December 16, 1966, entry into force March 23, 1976 in accordance with Article 49. Online at, https://www.ohchr.org/en/professionalinterest/pages/ccpr.aspx.

320. Another major country that is in the same position is China. China signed the document in 1998 but has not yet ratified it. There are about twenty countries that have neither signed nor ratified the document. Most of these are in the Middle East or the Far East, although there are some small countries (such as Vatican City) that are not members of the United Nations.

US Naval base at Guantánamo Bay?) is undoubtedly a desire to provide opponents of the communist government with communication facilities.

D EL SALVADOR

Bitcoin as Legal Tender

In June 2021, El Salvador passed a law making bitcoin legal tender in the country.

In response Chainbytes, a manufacturer of bitcoin dispensing machines, moved its manufacturing facilities from China to El Salvador. Eric Grill, the CEO of Chainbytes, plans to export its machines from El Salvador to other countries, including the US.

Risks

Making bitcoins legal tender entails huge risks for El Salvador. The volatility of bitcoin is well known. If bitcoin is legal tender in a country, citizens can pay taxes in bitcoin. The price of bitcoin could crash, causing devastating financial losses to national finances.

US dollars are also legal tender in El Salvador. People could swap bitcoin for dollars increasing the risks to El Salvador's Treasury. Companies and individuals may wish to pay their obligations in bitcoin, receive payments in dollars and keep their dollars.[321]

Gresham's Law needs to be kept in mind: "Bad money drives out good."

Is El Salvador the right country to begin a worldwide adoption of electronic currency? That is a good question, considering that it is reported that only 45 % of its people have access to the Internet.

International Response

There is a significant amount of international unhappiness about El Salvador's decision to adopt bitcoin as a legal currency.

For example, the World Bank rejected El Salvador's request for assistance in making bitcoin legal currency. Their reasons were issues about the transparency of bitcoin creation and the environmental damage caused by the huge amount of electricity used in bitcoin creation.[322]

321. Gian M. Volpicelli, "Ël Salvador Is Racing to the Future of Bitcoin," *Wired*, online, June 30, 2021.
322. "World Bank Rejects El Salvador Request for Bitcoin Help," *BBC News*, online, June 17, 2021.

E IRAN

Censorship and Blocking

Among the most repressive regimes with respect to the Internet is that of Iran. For the past twenty years, the hard-line government of Iran has required the censorship and blocking of thousands of websites that they consider to be offensive.

The blocked sites include YouTube, Twitter and Facebook. Iranians who wish to access such websites need to use VPNs and other "circumvention" software.

Internet users frequently use VPNs to disguise the origin of their computer systems, and this does allow them to use banned social media tools such as WhatsApp. Surveys show that although WhatsApp is banned in Iran, it is still used by over 70% of the population.[323]

Instagram was not blocked initially, and users found it as an effective marketing and business tool. However, the government believes it is better to replace it with a competing Iranian application called Rubica. It is notable that the leaders of the country do themselves use Instagram and Twitter to communicate their political views.

Cyberspace Supreme Council

Iran has a Cyberspace Supreme Council which has the power to make decisions and issue judicially enforced orders blocking access to any social media platforms they consider to be inappropriate.[324]

Registration Laws

The government continues to consider making Internet access even more difficult even though it would damage Iran's already suffering economy and would deny most of its citizens Internet communication with those located in other parts of the world.

In 2021, a new set of laws was proposed that would require any social media networks or messaging apps to register with a newly set up regulatory and supervisory authority. Foreign social media and messaging app companies will be required to appoint an Iranian company as their legal representative and promise to obey the rules set by this new regulator. The foreign companies-designated Iranian representatives could be held legally responsible for the content posted by the foreign companies they represent.

The restrictive legislation proposed is called "Legislation to Protect Cyberspace Users' Rights." However, opponents argue that it does not protect but rather restricts users' rights to the Internet.

---

323. Maryam Sinaiee, "Iran's Parliament Moves Ahead with Internet Censorship Bill," *Iran International*, online, July 28, 2021.
324. Maryam Sinaiee, "Iran Hardliners Introduce New Restrictive Internet Regulations," *Iran International*, online, June 8, 2021.

It is opposed by business leaders as well as members of the public.

A majority of the members of the Parliament of Iran support increasing restrictions on the Internet, but these restrictions are not popular among a population that is already angered by Iran's shortages of water, electricity and medicine such as anti-COVID vaccine.

F KYRGYZSTAN

Threats to Privacy and Press

In August 2021, the Committee to Protect Journalists reported that the Parliament of Kyrgyzstan had approved a bill called the "On Protection from Inaccurate (False) Information" which would go into effect when signed by the country's President.

The bill contains several provisions which are alleged to threaten privacy and freedom of the press.

Under the bill, any person can demand that information about them online that they allege to be false or defamatory. It must be taken down within twenty-four hours and the online publisher must issue a correction.

If these things are not done within twenty-four hours, the complainant can apply to have the website shut down until the content is removed.

No details are given as to how this process is supposed to operate. That is left up to the government officials dealing with a particular complaint.

Website and social media operators are also required to display their names and email addresses. Both ISPs and public Internet providers (like Internet cafés) are required to keep a record of the identities of their users. These proposed regulations are said to threaten both freedom of the press and of privacy.[325]

G PERU

Cybercrime Law and Freedom of Information

Since 2013, Peru has had a controversial cybercrime law called "Ley Beningolea." It identifies a number of criminal offenses, including the following:

(1) Illegally intercepting personal data:
   - Penalty: jail for up to six years.
   - Penalty if the information is "classified": jail for ten years.

(2) Sexual propositions to children over the Internet:
   - Penalty: jail for up to eight years.

(3) Circulating child pornography:
   - Penalty: jail for up to twelve years.

325. "Kyrgyzstan Parliament Approves 'False Information' Bill," *Committee to Protect Journalists*, online, August 10, 2021.

(4) Identity theft:
   - Jail for up to five years.

What made the law "controversial" was that the new law contained provisions that reduced the right to public information and online databases. These provisions were criticized by free-speech advocates on the grounds that they reduced government transparency and made it more difficult to get and use information about government actions. This negatively affected freedom of information.

Guaranteeing Internet Speed

In June 2021, the government of Peru brought in a new law requiring Internet operators to guarantee a minimum Internet speed 30% higher than in the past. A guarantee of a connection speed of 70% of the contracted rate was imposed.

The new requirement (Law 31207) applies whether the customer lives in urban or rural areas.

Customers are also to be supplied with systems that will allow them to accurately measure their Internet speeds.

An important consideration in imposing this requirement was the effect of the COVID-19 pandemic which made Internet use for business education and communication generally much more important to all members of society.

H SWITZERLAND

In the *Swisscom* case of 2019, the Federal Supreme Court held that ISPs are not liable for websites and portals that illegally make movies available for streaming and are not required to block access to search sites.

In this case, Swisscom refused to block access to some streaming sites after being requested by film producers and distributors of movies being illegally streamed.

The court also held that those who stream for their own use are not violating Swiss copyright law.

However, those who provide illegal streams of media are violating Swiss copyright law.

I TURKEY

Turkey has an active Internet environment with over forty-five million users, but it is considered a country that exercises strong censorship of Internet material.

In fact, Turkey has been found guilty of violating the right to free expression in numerous cases before the European Court of Human Rights.

In 2007, Turkey enacted its principal Internet law, Law number 5651, which is called "The Law on the Regulation of Broadcasts via Internet and Prevention of Crimes Committed Through Such Broadcasts" (The Internet Law).

The original purpose of the Internet Law was reported to be to protect citizens from harmful and illegal content. It was intended to prevent abuse of the Internet to promote things like gambling, prostitution, pornography, child abuse, etc.[326]

To accomplish those goals, the Internet Law focuses on four primary areas:

(1) Establishing criminal and civil liability for Internet operators and content providers.
(2) Restricting access for the purpose of preventing crimes, especially in times of emergency.
(3) Defining notice and procedure requirements for blocking access or removing content.
(4) Establishing surveillance and filtering procedures applicable to the Internet.

The Internet Law underwent some major reforms in 2014, including increased focus on social media sites.

Politization of Internet Law

Over time, modifications of the law and its application have increasingly become a political tool, favoring the government of Ahmet Ertegun.

The High Council

In 2018, a law passed giving a media regulator called the High Council for Broadcasting the power to monitor and regulate Internet services.

In 2020, the Internet law was amended once again to further define regulations for social media websites, including requirements that they designate a local representative and that they comply with content takedown requests of the government.

Increasing Internet Restrictions

A website called *VPN Overview* reports that since 2010, freedom of access to the Internet has become increasingly more difficult in Turkey.

They claim that there are some reports that Turkey is responsible for the imprisonment of one-third of all imprisoned journalists throughout the world.

They further report that since 2016, when there was an attempted coup in Turkey, over hundred thousand websites have been blocked, including content

326. This subsection's descriptions of Law 5651 (including an "unofficial" translation) are based on information found at the following website, https://www.mbkaya.com/, accessed September 10, 2021.

published by major Internet sites, including Facebook, Dropbox, YouTube, Twitter, Wikipedia, and others.[327]

With respect to Internet freedom, it appears that this will, at least in the short term, become even more restricted in Turkey.

A report published in August 2021 by the Freedom of Expression Association says that over four hundred thousand websites have been banned in Turkey since 2006 with almost sixty thousand of those bans taking place in 2020.[328]

327. https://vpnoverview.com/unblocking/censorship/internet-censorship-turkey/, online, accessed September 10, 2021.
328. This is reported on the following website, accessed September 10, 2021, https://balkaninsight.com/2021/08/17/turkish-govt-increasing-internet-social-media-censorship-report/.

CHAPTER 14

Intellectual Property

There is no doubt that the Internet has become the most effective and profitable way of delivering intellectual property (IP) to its audience around the globe. Netflix, Spotify and Amazon Kindle are only three of the platforms that have been created to provide it.

Most of the available platforms are operating legally and comply with the many laws protecting the ownership and use of intellectual property.

However, more than $3 billion a year is lost to cybercrime, and much of that represents the theft of intellectual property in various ways whether from ordinary plagiarism or from establishment of platforms that allow Internet users to get access to intellectual property without paying compensatory fees to those that own the legal rights to provide movies, music, books, computer programs, etc.

Therefore, an important question for any intellectual property rights holders or for the legal representatives advising them is what legal protections are there for IP rights holders and what recourse do they have if their Rights are violated? Providing a guide to those resources is the purpose of this chapter.

The protections available for IP fall into three legal categories. First, there are the legal protections that are available for property generally such as contract law, laws against misrepresentation and fraud, and criminal sanctions against theft and other criminal behavior. The second category is the international treaties and conventions that have been put in place to protect intellectual property. Some of the more recent ones deal specifically with intellectual property available over the Internet. The third category is specific national laws and regulations that have been passed to protect the ownership and access to intellectual property within their own jurisdiction, whether by their own citizens or others that are within their legal jurisdiction.

The general legal provisions that are not limited to intellectual property or to the Internet, such as general contract, commercial, and criminal law, will not be covered here. Plenty of information about them is available from other sources.

The subjects of this chapter will be:

- international laws and conventions relating to intellectual property and its use and access on the Internet; and
- national laws of some of the major jurisdictions that relate to the protection of intellectual property and its use and access within their jurisdictions.

The purpose of these discussions will be to give the reader enough of an outline of what issues they should be considering when answering questions about intellectual property and the Internet, and to allow them to seek additional information or advice to satisfy any specific legal questions that they have on those issues:

> The enigma is this: If our property can be infinitely reproduced and instantaneously distributed all over the planet without cost, without our knowledge, without its even leaving our possession, how can we protect it?[329]

A INTERNATIONAL PROTECTION OF IP

History

As far back as there are written records, there is evidence that there were formal protections for intellectual property.

In ancient Mesopotamia, this took the form of limiting those who were allowed to produce certain kinds of IP, particularly writing, to approved scribes.

In ancient Greece, there is evidence dating from about 500 BCE that exclusive rights, essentially ancient "patents," were given to creators of useful inventions and processes.

In the Middle Ages, royal monopolies were granted to specialized "guilds," such as the Stationers Guild in England, whose members were the only people allowed to publish writings.

During the Renaissance, patents were granted to inventors in Florence and Venice.

In England, the monopoly of the Stationers Guild over publishing was ended in 1710 by the world's first general copyright law, the Statute of Anne.

In that statute, authors were given ownership rights to their own publications for a period of fourteen years. The determination of publication rights was transferred, from the Stationers Guild, to the government and to the courts.

As time progressed, national governments around the world established formal procedures that allowed the creators of IP protection for their inventions and media creations by means of patent and copyright laws.

With improvements in transportation, communication and the expansion of international trade, governments became aware that to encourage trade in IP it would be necessary to establish protection that crossed borders and provided IP security outside the home countries of the IP creators.

329. John Perry Barlow, "The Economy of Ideas," *Wired*, online, March 1994.

Consequently, beginning in the nineteenth century, international conventions and treaties were made to provide international IP protection.

The Paris Convention

One of the first of these conventions was signed in 1883 when fourteen countries agreed protections for trademarks, inventions and industrial designs. The full name of this was the Paris Convention for the Protection of Industrial Property.

This allowed inventors to gain some protection for their IP outside of their own countries.

The Berne Convention

The most prominent of these international IP protection efforts was the Berne Convention for the protection of literary and artistic works adopted in Bern, Switzerland, in 1886.

The Berne Convention remains an important guarantee of intellectual property rights, and there are now 177 countries that have adopted the Convention.[330]

The principal terms of the Convention are as follows:

(1) Copyright exists the moment a work is "fixed."
(2) Registration is not required.
(3) The term of copyright is up until fifty years after the author's death:
   - Except for photos and films. For these, the minimum term is twenty-five years.
(4) Convention member nations must treat the copyrighted works of foreign parties at least as well as they treat any work published or performed in their own country.

The Convention provided substantial protection for IP around the world for about a century, but in the 1990s it became obvious that additional protection would be needed.

The coming of the Internet with its rapid expansion of electronic communication and marketing meant that traditional IP protection, which was enough for a time when created media existed in physical form, was insufficient to cope with an expanding world trade in digital versions of IP creations.

Consequently, additional international agreements were created to deal with the digital world.

330. The US finally joined the Convention in March 1989. However the terms of the US adoption limit some remedies (such as certain damages) only to "registered" works.

WTO Agreement and TRIPS

The WTO was set up in 1994 as a culmination of years of negotiations between a number of nations on tariffs and trade. The WTO has 164 members and may be the world's biggest international economic group. Generally, its functions are to determine, agree and revise international rules governing world trade.

In 1994, the members of the WTO entered into the Agreement on the Trade Related Aspects of Intellectual Property Rights (TRIPS).

What made the TRIPS agreement, which came into effect on January 1, 1995, relevant to intellectual property on the Internet was the fact that it emphasized the importance of intellectual property protection in international trade.

Over the next few years, the Internet radically changed world trade. It moved away from being exclusively a physical trade where goods that crossed physical borders were delivered by physical means. It increasingly became an economy without physical borders where digital goods moved instantly from person to person by electronic means through the use of computers connected to the World Wide Web.

Digital data that makes up the transferred goods moves via a universal protocol called the Transmission Control/Internet Protocol (TCP/IP). This protocol can transmit any digital media regardless of its content. It can be written, video, photographic or in any other digital form. The form of the data, where it is coming from and where it is going does not matter. The protocol treats it all the same.

What made the TRIPS a watershed for world trade is that it expanded the discussion of trade beyond only physical goods to include trade in services and the recognition that IP was an important part of world trade. In other words, it began to consider "content" well as things to be important products in commerce. It covered such things as follows:

- Performance rights.
- Sound recordings.
- Broadcasts.
- Trade and service markets.
- Geographical designations.
- Descriptions of origin.
- Designs.
- Patents.
- Organization of integrated circuit boards.
- Trade secrets.
- Confidential data.

TRIPS set out minimum standards for the protection of the IP covered. It provided methods and guides for the enforcement of IP protection. It also provided procedures for settling disputes between signatories.

It is true that TRIPS came into effect before digital trade on the Internet had really taken off, but Article 71 of the agreement gave it the flexibility to review future trade developments.

The WTO and TRIPS dispute settlement procedures have remained important in settling trade-related disputes of all kinds.[331] Recent disputes before the WTO relating to the Internet include:

- measures relating to the exportation of products and technology to Korea;
- tariff treatment on certain goods in the information and communications technology sector; and
- measures concerning the protection of intellectual property rights.

The WTO and TRIPS remain important for the protection of intellectual property rights in all kinds of trade including Internet trade but, of course, they cover nearly every conceivable kind of trade. TRIPS was agreed as part of the negotiations of the Uruguay Round of the General Agreement on Tariffs and Trade (GATT) in 1989/1990.

Because of the expansion of electronic commerce, it was decided that additional agreements would be needed that focused specifically on Internet-based electronic commerce. This has led to several international agreements and national regulations that focus on the Internet.

WIPO

The World Intellectual Property Organization (WIPO) was created in 1967 as a specialized agency of the UN to promote and protect intellectual property. One hundred and eighty countries belong to WIPO.

WIPO is extremely active in the intellectual property sector. It maintains treaties, holds meetings for members to discuss IP issues and since 1994 has established an arbitration and mediation center to provide an alternative to formal court litigation in technology and other IP disputes.

The WIPO Copyright Treaty (WCT) was promulgated in 1996. It provides not only conventional protection for copyrights but also contains provisions to protect information technology. There are 110 parties to this treaty. This along with another treaty the WIPO Performances and Photograms Treaty (1996) are together termed the WIPO "Internet treaties." This reflects their concerns with protecting performances that are available via the Internet.

Under Article 4 of the WCT, computer programs are protected works.

Article 5 protects the arrangement and selection of database material.

Articles 6 through 8 give authors control over the distribution and rental of their works.

Article 11 prohibits circumvention of technological systems to protect works.

Article 12 prohibits unauthorized modification of rights management information contained in media works.

331. The WTO website maintains a chronological list of cases that have come before it along with detailed information about the background and resolution of the disputes, https://www.wto.org.

WIPO Dispute Resolution

WIPO's Alternative Dispute Resolution and Mediation Center provides an impartial forum for resolving IP disagreements between private parties.

It allows them to seek to settle domestic and international IP and technology disputes:

(1) Out of court.
(2) By means of:
  - mediation;
  - arbitration;
  - expedited arbitration; or
  - expert determination.

The WIPO ADR Procedure follows the following steps:

(1) A request for resolution.
(2) A determination of the method for resolution.
(3) Composition of the resolving authorities:
  - Arbitrators (if arbitration).
  - Mediators (if mediation).
  - Experts (if expert determination).
(4) Schedule of fees and costs:
  - A deposit may be required.
(5) Confidential resolution.

European Union

In the EU, there are two major pieces of legislation aimed at modernizing EU Regulation of electronic commerce: the Electronic Commerce Directive 2000 and the EU Copyright Directive of 2019.

Electronic Commerce Directive

This directive was introduced in 2000 for the purposes of reducing obstacles to international online services in the EU market and to provide legal certainty in these areas for both companies and individual users of the Internet within the EU.

The Directive provided common rules on such things as requirements for online service providers, with respect to commercial communications and online contracts and exemptions to liability for ISPs for the posts of their users.

It also urged Member States to create voluntary codes of conduct and sought to enhance cooperation between Member States.

More than twenty years after the passage of this directive, there is discussion within the EU about making revisions to the Directive in a new Digital Services Act.

Digital Services Act and the Digital Markets Act

On December 15, 2020, both the Digital Services Act and the Digital Markets Act were proposed to the European Council.

The purpose of the Digital Services Act is to update the EU's legal framework and in particular to update the E-commerce Directive which was adopted in 2000. One of the issues that is considered particularly urgent is providing clear definitions of harmful conduct in order to counter online harassment faced by social media users.

The purpose of the Digital Markets Act is to improve e-commerce competition within the EU by making it easier for new, small companies to enter the market and by preventing the tech giants from abusing their market power to prevent competitors from entering the market.

It may be the case that neither of these acts is formally enacted into law before sometime in 2023.

EU Copyright Directive 2019

This was proposed in 2018. One of its goals was to implement the WIPO Intellectual Property Treaties. It was finally agreed in February 2019 and came into force on June 7, 2019. Members were given two years to implement the Directive.

Among the stated purposes of the Directive were to:

(1) protect publications;
(2) reduce the gap between the profits of creators of IP and the Internet platforms that market the IP online:
   - Encourage collaboration between them.
(3) provide exemptions from copyright in certain cases.

Article 3 of the Directive provided an exception for text and data mining for purposes of scientific research.

Article 5 provides an exception for use of copyrighted work as part of digital and cross-border teaching activities. Educational institutions can use copyrighted material for noncommercial illustrative purposes.

But Article 5(2) says that the educational exception may not apply where educational institutions can acquire adequate licenses in the market.

Article 14 says that the things in the public domain cannot be subject to copyright unless they represent a reproduction which is an original creative work.

For example, some of Andy Warhol's works that used photographs in the public domain of famous figures such as Queen Elizabeth or Marilyn Monroe would be considered to be original creative works that can be copyrighted.

Article 15 includes a "link tax" which allows newspapers to have control over the reuse of their publications such as by news aggregators on the web. This should allow news publishers to negotiate compensation with aggregators for reuse of their stories.

Articles 18 through 20 were drafted to improve the power of authors and performers. There was included a Rights Reversion Mechanism which allowed authors to cancel copyright transfers if they proved too disadvantageous.

Other provisions in the Directive clarified the legal status of miscellaneous works and activities such as common activities by libraries, etc.

The adoption of the Copyright Directive was controversial because of the different interests of parties in the electronic media sector. For the Directive were newspapers, other print publishers and media creators. Against the Directive were tech companies, Internet users and human rights groups that saw the Directive as too restrictive of access to information.

B NATIONAL LAW PROTECTING INTERNET IP

United States

In 1998, in the US a new copyright statute called the Digital Millennium Copyright Act (DMCA) was passed. The purpose of the Act was to deal with the changes that digital commerce was making to trade, both domestic and international.

One of its purposes was to implement the WIPO 1996 Internet treaties discussed above.

Among its provisions were sections criminalizing:

(1) the production and distribution of any works that violated copyrights;
(2) any actions to circumvents systems that control access to copyrighted material:
   - Such as Digital Rights Management (DRM) systems.
(3) even if the copyright itself is not breached.

There were some exemptions provided to the DMCA, principally for ISPs or other intermediaries. For example, ISPs were protected from direct or indirect liability for any copyright violations by the ISP's users who posted copyright violating material.

China

China, a country that has had a reputation for being a place where enthusiastic unlicensed copying of protected IP was permitted, has been representing that it is making efforts to encourage protection for and respect for IP.

In January 2017, China publicly announced a plan to improve cooperation with other nations on IP protection.

One of its steps was to set up a new Internet court to review cases of alleged improper use of protected IP. To date, that court has accepted about thirty thousand cases. More than 80% of those cases are Internet cases.

In 2021, China announced a supplementary plan to further improve IP protection.[332]

332. Rory O'Neill, "China's New Five-Year Plan Targets 'Hi-Tech' IP," *World Intellectual Property Review, worldipreview.com*, online, April 27, 2021.

One of the important goals of both plans is to improve China's international reputation for IP protection

France

France Enforces EU Neighboring Right

In July 2021, Google was fined €500 million by the French competition regulator because the regulator found that Google had not negotiated "in good faith" with news companies about the use of the content published by those news companies.

In 2020, the French regulation authority had ordered Google to negotiate with news companies in good faith about Google's use of content from those news organizations and from other content providers. The fine was imposed in 2021 because the French competition regulator believed that Google had not negotiated in good faith.

In 2019, France had adopted the new EU Digital Copyright Directive which contained a provision directing compensation for publishers and news organizations for the use of their content. This is the so-called "neighboring rights" provision. This is the law under which the French competition authority sought to compel Google to provide good faith compensation to content providers and which it found Google had failed to comply with.[333]

It remains to be seen whether other tech companies will suffer similar punishment about their use of the content or extracts of the content provided by third parties.

C THE THREAT OF INTERNET PIRACY

"Internet Piracy" constitutes illegal accessing, using copying or sharing of IP via the Internet without permission of the IP owner.

Internet IP piracy is a huge problem:[334]

- There are around 220 billion views of pirated videos annually.
- Pirate streaming sites are responsible for more than 75% of online piracy worldwide.
- Internet video piracy may cost the US economy as much as $60 billion in losses annually.
- A total of 126.7 billion viewings worth of US-produced TV episodes are pirated every year.
- More than 50,000 US jobs are lost a year because of music piracy.
- Around the world, the movie industry loses as much as $75 billion a year from Internet piracy.
- Nearly a quarter of global Internet bandwidth is used to download copyrighted media.

333. "France Fines Google 500 mln Euros over Copyright Row," *Reuters*, online, July 13, 2021.
334. Damjan Jugovic Spajic, "Piracy Is Back: Statistics for 2021," *DataProt*, online, March 19, 2021.

In 2017, in the US alone, there were more than 17 billion visits to Internet piracy sites.

In China, where cheap copies of protected IP products are common, there is even a special name for them, "*Shanzhai.*" There has been significant theft and imitation of popular brands:

> This is a society where, if you open a fake Apple store, people start writing articles about how innovative and creative you are.[335]

An example of how this threat can affect academia is found on a website called the Sci-Hub website, created by a woman in Almaty, Kazakhstan, by the name of Alexandra Elbakyan.

Sci-Hub is a digital database that supposedly has copies of seventy million academic and scientific papers. This is a huge percentage of the number of academic papers that have been produced. It is estimated that this represents around 80% of the existing total. Apparently, this collection has been assembled by hacking into the libraries and databases of universities around the world. Forty-two British universities are alleged to be victims.[336]

The theft of academic research presents the same problem as the theft of other kinds of intellectually produced media such as songs, films and books.

The people who produce such work do so because it is their job from which they expect to earn money. Sometimes it is their sole source of income. Much, if not all, of the papers on Sci-Hub are works for which it is expected that in order to gain access to them one will have to pay a purchase price or subscription fee. Nevertheless, Alexandra Elbakyan from Kazakhstan boasts that she has put together this vast academic library based on her skills as an expert computer data miner without violating the intellectual property rights of the owners or authors. Not surprisingly, law enforcement authorities in several countries have found this hard to believe.

For example, Ms. Elbakyan is currently under investigation by US law enforcement authorities because they suspect her of using her hacking skills on behalf of Russian intelligence to access databases that contain sensitive US military data.[337]

Perhaps the gravest threat to intellectual property is that its production will be curtailed because the hacking and theft of intellectually created material on the Internet will become so extensive that those that produce it will lose interest in doing this kind of work because their ability to earn a profit from this work will be greatly reduced or indeed lost altogether.

Danger from the Internet of Things

The problems that the Internet presents to protecting IP or private data are only growing.

---

335. Kenneth Rapoza, *Forbes Magazine*, online, July 22, 2012.
336. David Brown, "Hacking Fear over Pirated Research Site Sci-Hub," *The Times*, online, March 21, 2021, accessed March 21, 2021.
337. *Id.*

In recent years, we have moved beyond accessing information on the Internet, to allowing the Internet access to a growing list of "connected devices," often without our intervention or even without our knowledge:

> A new study has found that most Internet of things devices routinely deliver an ocean of sensitive data to partners around the world frequently without making these data transfers secure or transparent to the device owner.

A joint collaboration between Northeastern University and Imperial College London looked at eighty-one popular smart TVs, streaming dongles, smart speakers and video doorbells made by Google, Roku, and Amazon, etc.

In 34,000 experiments, they found that 72 of the devices made contact with someone other than the manufacturer.[338]

Protection of IP

What positive steps can be taken to protect IP, and oneself, from illegal Internet intrusion and theft? There are several.

Basic protections include the following:

- Be careful on public networks because others may be able to listen to you and/or get access to your data.
- Make sure that your systems are up-to-date. New threats are constantly coming online.
- Make sure all software and cybersecurity protections are current and are allowed to accept automatic updates.
- Use complex passwords. Make sure all users use complex passwords, all the time, and change them regularly.
- Back up and encrypt key data.

It is also important to get detailed information about the state of legal IP protection in the countries where one does business. There are many online sources of information about this, but the detailed report published online in 2020 by the Office of the US Trade Representative is very useful.[339]

In it there is an extensive description of protection and enforcement of IP rights around the world. It describes the laws, policies, and practices of the world's countries in their treatment of IP.

The report also includes a "Priority Watch List" of the countries that the US considers having the weakest record in IP protection. Those include Algeria, Argentina, Chile, China, India, Indonesia, Kuwait, Russia, Saudi Arabia, Ukraine and Venezuela.

338. Karl Bode, "The Internet of Things Is Still a Privacy Dumpster Fire, Study Finds," *Vice*, online, September 19, 2019.
339. "USTR Releases Annual Special 301 Report on Intellectual Property Protection and Review of Notorious Markets for Counterfeiting and Piracy," *Office of the United States Trade Representative*, online, April 29, 2020.

There is a "Watch List" of countries that cause the US concern about the strength of their IP protection. Those include Bolivia, Brazil, Canada, Columbia, Costa Rica, the Dominican Republic, Ecuador, Egypt, Greece, Guatemala, Jamaica, Lebanon, Mexico, Pakistan, Paraguay, Peru, Romania, Switzerland, Thailand, Turkey, Turkmenistan, UAE, Uzbekistan, and Vietnam.

One may not agree with the conclusions of the Report about the IP protections provided by certain countries, but if one is doing business in those countries, or internationally generally, it does provide things to consider.

It also offers the following strategies for business IP protection:

- Does your business understand the most influential tech changers? Are you investing in any? Are you paying attention to the opportunities they provide you and your competitors?
- Does your company have board-level presence and a business culture that fosters understanding of your IP at every level? Does your head of IP have the ear of the top decision-makers?
- Does your IP strategy match the pace of change in your market by planning for the short, medium and long terms?
- How important is China to your IP marketing? Are you making protective filings in China?

CHAPTER 15
Competition Law

A COMPETITION LAW

The philosophy behind anticompetition laws is that the public benefits from having competition in commerce which allows the public to have more choice and enjoy better prices when purchasing goods and services.

This is a view that has been adopted by the governments of many countries around the world and particularly in those countries where market economies are allowed to operate. In order to enforce this view, those countries have adopted laws and regulations to prevent any commercial operation from being so powerful that it is in the position to exclude competitors from the market in question which would allow that commercial operation to dictate prices and/or terms of service that are beneficial to it but detrimental to the public.

The basic goal of competition law is to prevent any one person or company from becoming so powerful or influential in a market that they can exclude competitors, prevent new competitors from entering the market, and use their market power as the only remaining choice in a market to demand from consumers whatever compensation they wish for their goods and services.

There are different ways that commercial organizations can seek to gain exclusive market power. One way is to conspire with others to exclude new potential competitors from the marketplace. Another way is to purchase other similar companies in the market to reduce the number of competitors or eliminate competitors altogether. Another way is to temporarily make one's prices and/or terms of service so much more favorable than those of competitors, for example, by offering goods and services below cost, that competitors who are less financially strong are forced to leave the market.

Engaging in actions to try and achieve such market power is called anticompetitive behavior, and most developed countries have laws and regulations to protect their markets against this and to encourage the discovery of reasonable prices for goods and services in markets.

Failure to obey these laws and regulations against anticompetitive behavior can result in civil suits, fines, criminal prosecution and possibly being barred from the markets in question.

The competition laws in various countries may differ somewhat, but their essential goals are usually the ones described above. For purposes of this book we will focus on prominent jurisdictions where governments are seeking to enforce tough anticompetition laws such as the US and the EU, although some others will be discussed in the context of particular situations.

US Antitrust Law

The US has a strong history of antitrust enforcement dating from the end of the nineteenth century when Congress took action against the gigantic and powerful oil company called Standard Oil that was owned by John D. Rockefeller.

The legislation that resulted from this effort is known as the Sherman Antitrust Act of 1890.[340]

The Act focuses on preventing two types of anticompetitive behavior. The first is preventing powerful market participants from achieving "monopoly" in their market where they are virtually, or actually, the only company offering particular goods or services to the public. This provision was specifically aimed at Standard Oil which had achieved the position of being so large and powerful in the oil business that no other company could effectively compete with it.

The second is to prevent "combinations and conspiracies in restraint of trade" where business organizations conspire with one or more competitors to fix prices or terms of service to disadvantage other competitors and or to reduce the choices of the public when purchasing goods or services in the markets in question.

From these basic principles, a very large body of antitrust laws, regulations and interpretive court cases has developed. This is not the place to detail all of those. With respect to questions about any particular matter, qualified expert advisors will need to be consulted.

However, because the Internet is a system that operates throughout the world, it is important to remember that many activities will probably involve transactions with US citizens or US residents. That may bring non-US persons and businesses using the Internet within the jurisdiction of US courts.

US courts will often take jurisdiction over matters that directly or indirectly affect the domestic or foreign commerce of the US. A US court may find that a market that is not exclusively a foreign market is part of US commerce.[341]

Also, please note that in US antitrust cases, litigants can request jury trials, and treble damages can be awarded.

340. 26 Stat. 209, 15 U.S.C. sections 1-7.
341. *Transnor (Bermuda) v. BP North America Petroleum*, 738 F. Supp. 1472 (S.D.N.Y. 1990).

EU Antitrust Law

EU antitrust law has essentially the same goals as US antitrust law. The European Commission says:

> Competition encourages companies to offer consumers goods and services on the most favorable terms. It encourages efficiency and innovation and reduces prices. To be effective competition requires companies to act independently of each other, but subject to the pressure exerted by their competitors.[342]

The basic EU antitrust legislation is set out in Articles 101 and 102 of the Treaty on the Functioning of the European Union (TFEU).[343]

TFEU Article 101 prohibits anticompetitive agreements between two or more independent market operators.

TFEU Article 102 prohibits abusive behavior by companies holding a dominant position in any given market.

B CONCERN WITH GIANT TECH

As the size of the major Internet companies Google, Facebook, Amazon, Apple, etc., has grown, there has been growing concern about their power, and, in particular, the power to limit or eliminate serious competitors.

Consequently, there has risen significant concern in the US, the EU and in other countries that large Internet companies are in danger of violating or actually violating legal and regulatory prohibitions against anticompetitive behavior.

This concern is partly due to regulators' perceptions about the difficulty of competing with companies so large and so wealthy, but it is also a result of the fact that big Internet companies have been buying up related companies to increase their reach in their business areas and to eliminate potential competitors.

Another recent and powerful impetus to their growth and wealth has been the recent COVID-19 pandemic.

Because the response of many countries has been to put their populations under lockdown, severely limiting their ability to leave their dwellings or to shop in person, many people have turned to the Internet to order goods and to communicate with friends and relatives.

People have also been working from home to a significant degree, which has increased their need to use the Internet and to have efficient up-to-date computer equipment.

Among the greatest beneficiaries of these unexpected business and personal relationship changes have been the major tech companies, including Apple, Amazon, Facebook, and Google. The pandemic increased usage of their services and products,

342. European Commission, Competition Policy, Antitrust. ec.europa.eu.
343. *See also*, the European Commission, Antitrust Overview, ec.europa.eu.

has made them more essential worldwide, and increased their wealth, making it easier to consolidate and expand their businesses.

These giants have recently made key purchases or commenced business projects that have given competition regulators around the world serious cause for concern.

Facebook's Expansion

Take Facebook, for example. It has been reported in *The New York Times*[344] that Facebook has come under increasing scrutiny by competition regulators for its expansion around the globe.

Facebook reported that it had bought Gojek, an app from Southeast Asia that characterizes itself as a "super app" that allows one to book taxis, do shopping and make payments. Gojek has more than 3.3 million online reviews with an average score of 4.3.

This is one example of Facebook's expansion into the rapidly growing Asian online business market.

Another is Facebook's $5.7 billion investment in Reliance Jo, a major Indian telecommunications company.

It also spent $400 million in May 2020 to purchase Giphy, a company with a catalogue of film clips and animations that can be attached to messages to illustrate ideas that the sender wishes to express. Facebook saw this as an enhancement to Instagram.[345]

Facebook's Fiber Optic Cable

Facebook is also reportedly spending many millions to construct a 37,000-kilometer-long fiber optic cable network around Africa.[346]

Other Internet Giant Moves

The other giant tech companies are engaging in similar expansions.

Amazon

Amazon has hired 175,000 people since March 2020 and it has acquired more airplanes for delivery and has been in talks to acquire a driverless vehicle company.

Microsoft

Microsoft has bought three more cloud computing companies.

---

344. Mike Isaac, "The Economy Is Reeling: The Tech Giants Spy Opportunity," *The New York Times*, online, Monday, June 15, 2020.
345. Kurt Wagner and Sarah Frier, "Facebook Buys Animated Image Library Giphy for $400 Million," *Bloomberg News*, online, May 20, 2020. In late 2021, the British Competition and Markets Authority (CMA) ruled that Facebook must sell Giphy, but Facebook has appealed that decision.
346. Isaac, *supra*, June 15, 2020.

Apple

Apple has bought at least four other companies during 2020. The accidental boost these companies got from the unfortunate pandemic has not only increased their business but also made them more essential to more people.[347]

C REGULATORY RESPONSES

This extraordinary increase in the reach and the power of the Internet Giants has concentrated the minds of competition regulators throughout the developed world.

EU Antitrust Action

Google Fined

In June 2019, Google was fined $1.7 billion by European competition regulators for requiring online advertisers to sign exclusivity agreements that were found to be unfair to competing online advertising companies.[348]

EU v. Amazon

In June 2020, EU began preparing anticompetition charges against Amazon. The basis of their complaint is that Amazon abused its dominant market position in online commerce by attempting to block out less powerful rivals.[349]

It has been reported that the investigation against Amazon is part of a broader EU investigation into the business practices of Amazon, Apple and Facebook.

There is concern about Amazon's dual role of being both a seller of goods on its own account and a provider of a platform for Amazon competitors to sell goods online. It is reported that Amazon requires these subsidiary merchants to collect data that they are required to share with Amazon as a condition for being allowed to sell on the Amazon platform.[350]

EU v. Apple

On June 17, 2020, *The Times* reported that the European Commission was beginning an investigation into whether rules that Apple imposed on app developers restricted competition and improperly benefited Apple.

This investigation comes from complaints from Spotify, a popular music streaming service, and Kobo, an online bookstore, that Apple let iPad and iPhone users download apps only from Apple's own App Store. Apple then claims a substantial percentage (30% in the first year, 15% thereafter) of any payments or subscriptions made through

347. *Id.*
348. Adam Satariano, "Google Fined $1.7 Billion by E.U. for Unfair Advertising Rules," *The New York Times*, online, March 20, 2019.
349. Adam Satariano, "Amazon Set to Face Antitrust Charges in European Union," *The New York Times*, online, June 11, 2020.
350. Satariano, June 11, 2020, *citing* Prof. William Kovacic of George Washington University.

those apps. Apple also forbids those companies from telling their customers (within those apps) that the goods or subscriptions can be bought more cheaply on the companies' own websites.[351]

Apple reportedly makes about $1 billion a month from app fees. Apple's policy of taking 15% to 30% of purchases through apps causes consumers to pay higher prices because to pay those fees, service providers like Spotify must raise their own prices.[352]

In addition, there is also said to be a conflict of interest created by the fact that Apple has now moved into providing its own music and video streaming services which competes with companies, such as Netflix or Spotify, which are using apps from Apple's App Store to sell their products.[353]

Such tactics by Apple might remind one of the activities of John D. Rockefeller, the nineteenth-century founder of Standard Oil, who forced railroad companies that wanted his business to pay him a percentage of the fees they received from carrying the oil of companies competing with Standard Oil. It was Rockefeller's ruthless domination of the oil business that led to the original US anticompetition law, the Sherman Antitrust Act of 1890.

If Apple is found to have violated EU competition law, the European Commission could fine them an amount equal to 10% of Apple's global revenues. In 2019, those revenues were more than $260 billion.[354]

In 2019, Apple was reportedly charged by Spotify with "limiting choices and stifling innovation" by charging high commission fees in the App Store on "in app" purchases and forbidding companies offering their products on the App Store to offer their customers alternatives. After reviewing the charges, in May 2021, the Commission agreed that Apple was breaking EU competition regulations by the way it was operating its App Store. As a result, Apple may be subject to significant fines and requirements that it modifies the way it operates its App Store.[355]

The EU did not stop its investigation with the Spotify complaint. It has continued its investigation into the possible anticompetitive aspects of the way Apple operates its App Store, including whether its standard 30% commission on apps is a fair price. It is reported that many app developers are unhappy with Apple's App Store connected charges, and a number of them have expressed their concurrence with the preliminary findings of the Commission that Apple is engaging in anticompetitive behavior.[356]

Spotify is not the only developer to complain to the EU about Apple. In March 2020, Rakuten reportedly filed a complaint with the EU claiming that Apple was charging an anticompetitive commission on electronic books sold through its App Store while being in the conflicting position of promoting competing books sales through its Apple Books app.[357]

---

351. *The Times*, online, Business, June 17, 2020.
352. *Id.*
353. *Id.*
354. Statista.com, June 17, 2020.
355. Jane Wakefield, "Apple Charged over 'Anti-competitive' App Policies," *BBC News*, online, accessed May 3, 2021.
356. *Id.*
357. *Id.*

France v. Google

A blow against Google's alleged market dominance has been struck in France.

In June 2020, French anticompetition regulators, under EU antitrust regulations, have fined Google €220 million for taking unfair advantage of its search engine dominance to establish a competitive advantage in sales of online ads.[358]

That is certainly a lot of money but is relatively small compared to the $41 billion in revenue earned by Google in 2020.

The French regulator said that its decision would allow competitors of Google that were disadvantaged to seek damages.[359]

The EU is not the only concerned regulatory jurisdiction. Investigations of the large tech companies have reportedly been commenced in London and Washington as well.

UK Antitrust Action

UK Report on Google and Facebook

In December 2019, the UK CMA published a 283-page interim report from a market study which found that Google accounted for 90% of UK search advertising revenues (amounting to about £6 billion a year), and Facebook accounted for over half of display advertising revenues.

The report also said that Google and Facebook's domination of social media and search is so great that it could be driving up the prices of vacations, electronic goods, and financial services. It said their profits as "well above any reasonable estimate of what might be expected."[360]

The CMA has also begun investigating whether Facebook has been misusing its market power to gain unfair advantages in digital advertising.

If they are found by the CMA to be guilty of this, they could be subject to large fines.

The regulator is concerned that Facebook has prevented less powerful rivals from successfully competing with Facebook and has thereby reduced the choice of digital advertisers available to the public.

One Facebook tactic that concerns the CMA is whether Facebook was unfairly using the data its system provided to create new offerings to compete with others in the market, such as eBay.

Facebook Marketplace is reported to be one such new feature.

Facebook is also using its sign-in procedure to allow its users to sign into multiple Facebook-related apps which are thought to automatically give it a competitive advantage over competing online sites such as dating and advertising sites.

---

358. Mark Sweney, "France Fines Google for Abusing Online Advertising Dominance," *The Guardian*, online, June 7, 2020.
359. *Id.*
360. Andrew Ellison, "Consumer Champion Quits Amid Digital Tax Row," *The Times*, online, June 19, 2020.

If Facebook is found by the CMA to be in violation of applicable competition rules, it could be fined as much as 10% of its worldwide revenues, which could add up to over $8 billion.[361]

UK Blocks Giphy Acquisition

However, a little more than a year later, the UK CMA indicated that it would block the takeover of Giphy. In August 2021, the regulator finished an investigation of the takeover and concluded that allowing the acquisition by Facebook would significantly reduce competition in areas of social media and online advertising which would harm individuals and businesses using the Internet. Should the regulator's final report support these conclusions, Facebook could be forced to sell Giphy.

If Facebook refused to sell, the regulator could take them to court.

Facebook is already in some trouble with the Giphy investigation by the Competition Authority. Facebook was accused of deliberately refusing to supply relevant information and was fined £50.5 million.[362]

The principal advertising market said to be affected by Facebook's acquisition of Giphy is called the "display advertising" market of which Facebook had a 50% share in 2020.

Giphy provides a type of animated images, called "giphs," that are useful in advertising on popular social media platforms such as TikTok, Twitter, Tinder, Slack and iMessage.[363] Facebook has responded that the conclusions of the regulator about the competitive harm of the takeover were "manifestly disproportionate." Facebook denied that it had significant market power in the relevant UK market and said that it would be "grossly unreasonable" for the regulator to block the acquisition.[364] As previously noted, Facebook has appealed the decision.

US Antitrust Action

Amazon, Apple, Facebook, and Google are all under US government investigation about the issue of whether they are restricting competition, particularly when they are also acting as a "gate keeper" through which competing companies get access to potential customers.

In June 2019, the US Justice Department opened antitrust investigation of major technology firms. It was reported that they will be looking into whether their online activities have injured competition, interfered with innovation, or harmed consumers and other ways.

---

361. Tom Knowles, "Facebook Investigated by UK Watchdog over Digital Dominance," *The Times*, online, June 5, 2021, accessed June 7, 2021.
362. Mark Sweney, "Facebook Fined £50.5m for Breaching Order in Giphy Takeover Investigation," *The Guardian*, online, October 20, 2021.
363. Callum Jones, "Facebook Fights Completion and Markets Authority over Giphy Deal," *The Times*, online, September 9, 2021.
364. *Id.*

The Justice Department and the Federal Trade Commission (FTC) are examining possible anticompetitive practices by Amazon, Apple, Facebook, and has already begun a suit against Google.

US Department of Justice Sues "Monopolist" Google

On October 20, 2020, the US DOJ published a notice online entitled, "Justice Department Sues Monopolist Google for Violating Antitrust Laws."[365]

The department stated that its goal was to restore competition in the search and search advertising markets.

It was reportedly the largest antitrust action brought by the DOJ in about twenty years. The department was joined in this action by the state attorneys general of Arkansas, Florida, Georgia, Indiana, Kentucky, Louisiana, Mississippi, Missouri, Montana, South Carolina and Texas.

They reportedly also investigated how Google has used its dominance of Internet searches to move into other areas of Internet business, including video, emails, maps, cloud computing, quantum computing and AI.

Harm to Consumers

A principal question raised by such an action will be establishing how consumers have been harmed.

Obviously, it is convenient for many Internet users to search for information using Google, and that basic service is provided by Google without payment. Nevertheless, Google has allegedly used its market power and the vast amounts of money it has earned from its search engine to pay other major Internet companies, such as Apple, to make the Google search app the default search platform on the devices Apple sells such as MacBooks, iPads and iPhones.[366]

Other International Antitrust Actions

Apparently, the large companies of the tech industry have become so powerful that they are attracting the attention of competition regulators in other parts of the world as Australia, Brazil, and India.

Investigations, suits and regulatory fines in the EU, the UK and the US may be only the start of the regulatory hurdles that may be imposed on large and rapidly growing tech companies.[367]

365. Justice.gov.
366. Simon Duke, "If the Tech Giants Can't Be Tamed by New Laws, Then They Should Be Broken Up," *The Times*, online, October 1, 2020, retrieved October 1, 2020, https://www.thetimes.co.uk/article/breaking-up-big-tech-may-be-the-least-worst-choice-dftfn22jd?shareToken=bb1b6d237a194cb9557e94095918e201.
367. Satariano, June 11, 2020, *citing* Prof. William Kovacic of George Washington University.

It is not the enormous success of these companies that attracts the scrutiny of competition regulators, but the fact that Amazon and the other tech giants use that success to harm competitors and the public.[368]

Bill Baer, who is a fellow at the Brookings Institute, wrote in April 2020 that even during a time of an economic emergency such as that caused by the COVID-19 pandemic, regulators should not relax, but rather focus their market scrutiny on possible anticompetitive practices during such difficult times. He pointed out that although marketers of essential goods might claim that they are not raising prices, but merely "stabilizing" prices, it should not be forgotten that agreements by competitors to fix prices are still illegal under antitrust law.[369]

The concern that the US government along with the EU and other nation regulators have is that tech companies like Apple, Microsoft, Amazon, Google and Facebook have become so dominant in their markets that they are in the position of essentially being monopolies in their primary market sectors.

If this proposition is proved by the regulators that are investigating these tech giants, they may consider it appropriate to pass new laws to limit the power of such companies.

Break up Internet Giants?

If those laws do not accomplish what they are intended to do, the US, the EU and other major market regulators may determine that these giants need to be broken up or restricted to operation only in specific market sectors.[370]

Tax Issues

It is not only market power that concerns regulators when considering whether their size creates unfair advantages.

The tax authorities in several countries are concerned that the structure of the Internet Giants as large integrated companies allows them to avoid taxes by balancing the losses of some divisions against gains in the others.

Consequently, there is talk of splitting these companies into separate taxable entities to allow taxation of the most profitable divisions of these companies.

For example, it is suggested that it might be useful to treat Amazon's cloud computing division as a separate company to allow taxation of its $1.6 billion in annual revenue.

There has been considerable concern that these companies are able to avoid their taxation by shifting their profits and losses among the different jurisdictions in which they trade which usually have different and/or contradictory tax regimes. To counter

368. Satariano, June 11, 2020, *citing* Bill Baer, former antitrust enforcement head at the US Department of Justice.
369. Bill Baer, "Why We Need Antitrust Enforcement During the Covid-19 Pandemic," *Brookings Institute*, online, April 22, 2020.
370. *Id.*

this, there is currently a proposal before the G7 countries to require large companies to pay taxes where they sell their products instead of where they declare their profits.[371]

Other Regulators

However, antitrust regulators around the world are certainly not finished antitrust laws with reducing the market dominance of giant Internet companies.[372]

China

China had taken dramatic steps to reduce the financial power of the owner of Alibaba (part of Jack Ma's Ant Group).

In September 2021, there were reports that the Chinese government is considering requiring Jack Ma to separate the lending business of the group, AliPay, and turn over user data to a state-owned group.

It is also reported that part of the Ant Group may come under partial government ownership. This is all part of a recent Chinese government effort to reduce the market power of large Chinese Internet companies that have achieved close to monopoly positions.[373]

Russia

It is not only in the Western countries where there is concern about the market dominance of the Internet Giants.

For example, in late August 2021, Russia's anti-monopoly agency fined the online hotel booking company, Booking.com, a record Russian ruble equivalent of €14.9 million, for dominating the hotel booking market.[374]

The Russians concluded that Booking was abusing its dominant market position, and fined that Netherlands company 1.3 billion Russian rubles.[375]

D PRIVATE SUITS

It is not only government regulatory investigations which are examining are concerned about the anticompetitive behavior of the Internet Giants. There are also likely to be a number of private antitrust suits in the future.

371. Simon Duke, "G7 Plans New Approach to Stop Tech Giants Avoiding Tax," *The Times*, online, June 9, 2021.
372. Adam Satariano, "Google to Pay $270 Million to Settle Antitrust Charges in France," *The New York Times*, online, June 7, 2021.
373. Andrew Ross Sorkin, et al., "Beijing Reportedly Wants to Break up Alipay," *The New York Times*, "Dealbook Newsletter," online, September 13, 2021.
374. "Russia fines Booking.com Record 14.9 Euros for Alleged Market Dominance," *Euronews*, online, August 27, 2021.
375. *Id.*

EPIC Suit v. Apple

The digital games developer, Epic Games, creator of the popular Fortnite game, has reportedly brought a lawsuit in US federal court against Apple alleging that the commissions that Apple collects on in-app sales by developers using the App Store are "extortionate."[376]

Fortnite reportedly provoked a battle with Apple by creating its own in-app payment system, independent of Apple. When Apple learned of this and banished Fortnite from its App Store, Fortnite claimed that Apple's behavior made it unfairly difficult for Fortnite and other developers to sell their products. Allegedly, Apple's rules were intended to give Apple a virtual "monopoly" over the sale of developers' products by severely limiting the options they could choose as a place to market their products.[377] The case went to trial in April 2021.[378]

In September 2021, it was reported that the federal court published a decision in the *Epic* case saying that although the court could not declare Apple to be a monopoly, Apple was behaving in an anticompetitive manner by refusing to permit app creators that sold their products through Apple's App Store to purchase the products through their own purchase systems rather than exclusively through the App Store.[379]

The judge in the *Epic* case said that although Apple did control approximately 55% of the market, that did not, of itself, constitute a monopoly. The judge wrote "Success is not illegal."[380]

Although they achieved one of their major goals—getting the right to sell their app through their own payment system rather than exclusively through Apple's system—Epic was reportedly still unhappy with the decision and shortly after it was issued, Epic filed an appeal with the Ninth Circuit Court of Appeal.[381]

E OTHER FORMS OF MARKET DOMINATION

Education Market Domination

Google

There is another area that is causing concern because of perceived market domination. A commentator has recently argued that Google is becoming too dominant in the education sector in Britain.

Allegedly, this is being achieved through Chromebooks and their Chrome operating system.

376. James Clayton, "Apple Faces Epic Games in Court," *BBC News*, online, May 3, 2021.
377. *Id.*
378. *Id.*
379. Andrew Ross Sorkin, et al., "Why Apple Didn't Lose in the Epic Games Ruling: A Judge's Split Decision in the Lawsuit Mostly Went in Favor of Big Tech," *The New York Times*, "Dealbook Newsletter," online, September 13, 2021.
380. *Id.*
381. *Id.*

During the pandemic, the Chrome system has expanded its reach because so much education has moved online. Google appears to have sprung into action to take advantage of this.

During this time, Google has promoted a number of its free Google education apps, the use of which has given Google an enormous amount of data about students and their schools.

They have introduced forty new models of Chromebook laptops, many upgrades of its education products and AI tools that allow students to have, in effect, conversations with the Internet through their laptops.

While much of this appears to offer significant benefits to educational institutions and their students, and in many respects probably does offer important benefits, it also raises important privacy and ethical issues.

Among the important ones is the fact that the adoption of the hardware and software of a particular supplier, such as Google, makes an educational system worryingly dependent on that company and raises significant concern about how educational institutions and their individual students use the Internet system.[382]

A question that arises is whether any legislative steps should be taken to limit the amount of penetration that any tech company can be allowed to have into a system influencing the thought and behavior of generations of students.

However, the trade-off that must be considered is whether the benefits of the educational tools provided by any particular tech giant outweigh the dangers that their participation raises? Some thought needs to be given to this by educational authorities and other government officials.

Microsoft

However, it is hard to ignore the parallel between this and the penetration of Microsoft systems software and Internet tools into many aspects of the private and business lives of people all over the world. As the importance of computers grew, Microsoft grew with it, providing tools to help us expand our use of computers and the Internet. Consequently, Microsoft has obtained, whether intentionally or by accident, a huge amount of knowledge and data about how the computing and Internet worlds work.

Although Google has a significant amount of power in the world of computing systems and is apparently making efforts to expand that power, there is little doubt that they are dwarfed by Microsoft in the areas of education, business, and communications.

However, there does not appear to be much debate about the harm this may be doing and whether it makes sense to legally limit such influence to a greater degree than existing legislation permits.

Apple

Certainly, there are similar issues with Apple products.

382. Jawad Iqbal, "Tech Giants Have Gained Too Much Power in Schools," *The Times*, online, June 7, 2021.

These days it is possible for a university professor to look out over a classroom of thirty or more students and be facing a sea of silver-colored laptops during the white apple logo.

Although other companies may have been more subtle about their approach to gaining influence in the educational sector, Apple never has. They have always made open and public efforts to attract students and educational institutions to their products by providing discounts, and tools and operating systems that were compatible with what they believed were the interest and aims of the educational community, as well as the artistic community.

Choices

As societies interested in the intellectual, social and moral development of our children, are we OK with turning our young people over to these tech giants? Do our laws make it plain enough as to what the limits on the influence of these tech companies should be?

CHAPTER 16
Privacy and Data Protection

A PRIVACY AND DATA PROTECTION

One of the earliest restrictions on the use of Internet data has been privacy laws which limited the ability of those who found personal data on the Internet to use that data without the permission of the person(s) it referred to.

The development of the Internet and the appearance on the medium of a variety of personal information about individuals required the addition of laws and regulations, and international treaties and conventions about the protection and use of that data.

Initially, these laws and regulations were directed principally at individuals or private parties using this data without the express permission of the people the date are referred to. However, in recent years, there has been serious additional concern about the use and collection of personal information by government agencies.

This government recording and collection of data on its citizens has increasingly become a subject of debate about whether it interferes with the fundamental rights of citizens. Often, this state data-gathering began as a well-meaning attempt to monitor the activities of potential terrorists and prevent terrorist attacks. However, it quickly became apparent that so much data was being recorded and collected that most of it had nothing to do with terrorist suspects but was about the daily lives of ordinary citizens as they went about their work, interacted with their families, and communicated with their friends.

The scope of this concern was brought to light by the well-known case of Edward Snowden.[383]

383. Edward Snowden was a former CIA employee who leaked highly classified data about the global surveillance programs of Western intelligence agencies that accessed the private data of individual citizens. This surveillance upset Snowden, and in June 2013, Snowden went to the press with his concerns. To support his story, Snowden is reported to have downloaded hundreds of thousands, or even millions, of classified documents. The US revoked Snowden's

In June 2020, the *Times* reported that British intelligence agencies have been illegally retaining the sensitive private data of innocent individuals for years.[384]

There is a significant contrast in the way that the protection of privacy and data on the Internet is dealt with in different countries.

United States

Surprisingly, given its early and rapid development of the Internet, the US does not protect consumers with general federal laws of privacy and data protection relating to the Internet. Most laws aimed at consumer protection are issued by the US states.[385]

However, there are some federal laws dealing with privacy and data of specific kinds.

Privacy Act

For example, there is the Privacy Act of 1974 that deals with citizens' rights regarding data maintained by the government. Under the Privacy Act, US citizens have certain rights with respect to that data. Citizens have the right to access and copy data held by government agencies. If there are errors in this data, citizens have the right to have the errors corrected. The amount of data collected about a citizen should only be that data that is relevant and necessary. There are restrictions on sharing information between government agencies.

Health Insurance Act

With respect to health information, collected in connection with the Health Insurance Portability and Accountability Act, there are rules about protection of patient health information found in the Act's "Privacy Rule." This requires health providers and certain others to get the express permission of patients prior to using any of their health information for marketing purposes. Health providers are also required to put in place safeguards to protect against inappropriate access to patient health information.[386]

Child Protection

Then there is the Children's Online Privacy Protection Rule, which has been issued by the FTC pursuant to the Children's Online Privacy Protection Act (COPPA) of 1998.[387] This imposes requirements on the operators of websites that know they are collecting data on children under the age of 13.

Website operators need to give notice to and obtain the permission of parents prior to collecting personal information of children under 13.

US passport and issued a warrant for his arrest. Snowden fled the United States in 2013 and has since been granted asylum in Russia.

384. "MI5 'Illegally Holds Sensitive Private Data on Thousands'," *The Times*, online, Wednesday, June 12, 2020.
385. Andy Green, "Complete Guide to Privacy Laws in the US," https://www.varonis.com/blog/us-privacy-laws/.
386. *Id.*; Privacy Act of 1974, as amended, 5 U.S.C., section 552a.
387. 16 CFR Part 312, and 15 U.S.C. 6501-6505.

Amendments to this rule over the years have continually expanded it to cover a wider variety of types and methods of obtaining personal data relating to underage children such as pictures, emails, videos, and information from social and chat sites.

Financial Data

US legislation relating to the financial sector has also provided some regulations on data developed in connection with those kinds of transactions. The Financial Modernization Act of 1999, often called the Gramm-Leach-Bliley Act after its sponsors, includes a Safeguard Rule which requires financial institutions to maintain an adequate security program to protect the customer information in its possession or under its control.[388]

B US STATE PRIVACY LAWS

Most of the specific laws dealing with data privacy in the US are state laws. The US, as mentioned above, does not have an overall data privacy statute provided by the Federal Government. So, there is no consistent nationwide protection for personal data in the US.

Some US states have passed their own data privacy laws.[389] However, even states which have not yet passed comprehensive data privacy laws have legislated privacy requirements of various types in other legislation dealing with things such as public records or electronic communications. However, there is no consistency among the states with respect to laws for the disposing of data.

Any individual or firm that is collecting and using personal information, such as client or customer information, across state borders will need to consult the local laws regarding data processing, and this may involve needing to consult local attorneys.

There is, of course, another inconsistency here. Each state has its own rules and regulations for attorney licensing, and attorneys admitted in one state to practice may not generally have a right to practice in another state or advise on the laws of another state except under specific circumstances, often requiring an order by a local court permitting a person to practice under limited circumstances before the courts of that state.

So, a person or company dealing with data processing should be aware of the above and be prepared to consult about the laws of the individual states in which you are operating.

It is not within the scope of this book to give detailed information about the data privacy laws in each of the fifty states. But, summarized below are some of the key data privacy laws of a number of states that have enacted such laws.

388. Pub.L. 106-102, 113 Stat. 1338.
389. Information can be obtained from the website of the National Conference of State Legislatures (ncsl.org), "State Laws Related to Digital Privacy," online, April 30, 2021, accessed May 4, 2021.

California, New York, Massachusetts are states that have some of the most comprehensive data protection laws in the US and the most similar protection to that provided within the EU.

Some states have refused to pass similar personal data protection laws.

Curiously, one of the states which have failed to pass such laws is Washington—home to Microsoft, Amazon, and other important tech companies. In Washington, and perhaps in other states lacking such protective laws, there seems to be a fear that the existence of such laws will permit private individuals to bring "a flood of litigation" seeking to enforce such laws. If that is the case, this problem could be solved by including in the legislation a provision which allows only state regulatory authorities to bring enforcement actions and bars private rights of action.

Arizona

In Arizona, libraries and library systems are forbidden from disclosing any record or information, including e-book information, that identifies users of the library service or how the user is using the library service.[390]

Government agencies and subdivisions are required to have policies on data privacy and procedures incorporated into, and readable on, their websites.[391]

Arkansas

Government agencies and subdivisions are required to have policies on data privacy and procedures incorporated into, and readable on, their websites.[392]

California

Consumer Privacy Act

In 2018, California passed the Californian Consumer Privacy Act. In summary, this law provided six rights to Californians with respect to personal data about them:

(1) They have a right to know what personal data is being collected about them.
(2) They have a right to be informed whether any of their personal data is being sold or disclosed to third parties and who those third parties are.
(3) They have a right to prevent their personal data from being disclosed to third parties.
(4) They have a right to access any personal data that is being collected about them.

390. Arizona Laws: Ariz. Rev. Stat. section 41-151.22.
391. Ariz. Rev. Stat. section 41-4151, 41-4152.
392. Ark. Code section 25-1-114.

(5) They have a right to direct any business to delete any of the personal data that said business has collected about them.
(6) It is illegal to discriminate against anyone who exercises the privacy rights above.

This California privacy law applies to any business (defined as any entity that seeks profit):

- doing business in California that collects personal data about consumers; and
- has more than $25 million in gross revenues; or
- collects, personal information about at least 50,000 consumers or households; or
- receives more than half of its yearly revenue from selling such personal information.

To comply with the law, a business must do the following:

- they must have in place systems to get the consent of the parent or guardian of any minors under 13 and the express consent of any minors under 16 to share any of their personal data;
- they must also provide a link on their homepage which allows consumers to refuse to permit the sale or sharing of their personal information; and
- they are forbidden from requesting consumers in California to permit data sharing within twelve months of the time that any consumers have refused to permit the sharing of their personal data.

In the event that any business violates the provisions of the Act, those injured have the right to bring private civil suits, and the business can be subject to fines and penalties imposed by the California Attorney General.

This California law contains detailed definitions of what constitutes covered personal data.

Government agencies and subdivisions are required to have a policy on data privacy and procedures incorporated into, and readable on, their websites.[393]

Additional information about California data privacy protection can be obtained from a detailed review of relevant California laws, regulations, and cases and from consulting qualified California attorneys.

Colorado

Any state or government subdivision that operates an electronic communication system must have a written policy on conditions under which the monitoring of such communications will be permitted.

393. Cal. Govt. Code section 11019.9.

The policy should inform employees that their correspondence may become part of public records and may be open to public inspection.[394]

Connecticut

Any business that collects Social Security numbers must have a protection policy that protects the confidentiality of those Social Security numbers, limits access to them and prohibits unlawful disclosure of such Social Security numbers.[395]

Delaware

Operators of websites or computing services centers that have personal information about Internet users in Delaware must have a privacy policy posted on its website, or otherwise conspicuously available to its users.

If it does not, it can be notified of its noncompliance, and if it fails to correct the situation within thirty days, it will be in violation of the requirements of this regulation.[396]

Operators of digital services are forbidden from disclosing personal information of users of digital technologies or book services, even to government or enforcement entities, or anyone else except under specific circumstances. Such circumstances can include situations where there is an imminent danger of death or injury to someone.

Electronic book services must post annual reports online about disclosures of personal information if they are not exempted.

Violation of these regulations is subject to investigation by the Consumer Protection Unit of the Delaware Department of Justice.[397]

Child Protection

In Delaware, computer companies and websites are not permitted to advertise anything considered an approach inappropriate for children.

For example, the advertising of alcohol or pornography is illegal. It also prohibits using any information about a child for purposes of marketing or advertising such inappropriate services to children.[398]

Policy Publication

Government agencies and subdivisions are required to have policies on data privacy and procedures incorporated into, and readable on, their websites.[399]

394. Colo. Rev. Stat. section 24-72-204.5.
395. Conn. Gen. Stat. section 42.471.
396. Del. Code Tit. 6 section 205C.
397. Delaware Code section 1206C.
398. Delaware Code section 1204C.
399. Del. Code tit. 29 sections 90117C et seq.

Illinois

Government agencies and subdivisions are required to have policies on data privacy and procedures incorporated into, and readable on, their websites.[400]

Iowa

Government agencies and subdivisions are required to have policies on data privacy and procedures incorporated into, and readable on, their websites.[401]

Maine

Government agencies and subdivisions are required to have policies on data privacy and procedures incorporated into, and readable on, their websites.

Massachusetts

The state of Massachusetts has long been associated with scientific developments in many fields, including technical developments in Internet businesses.

It is the home of the MIT, arguably the leading technical university in the world.

It is also the home of Harvard University. It is reported that Bill Gates of Microsoft and Mark Zuckerberg of Facebook began to formulate their ideas about computer communication when they were students at Harvard.

Massachusetts is also the home to many computing and Internet-related companies and has long been at the forefront of the development of the technical tools and standards used in computing on the Internet.

Therefore, it is not surprising that Massachusetts has developed laws and regulations regarding the protection of the personal information of residents of the state.

Massachusetts Regulation 201 CMR 17.00 provides standards for the protection of personal information of residents of the state (although, for historical reasons, formally called the "Commonwealth") of Massachusetts.

This regulation sets out standards required to be met by persons who own or license personal information about a resident of Massachusetts.[402] Essentially, they must:[403]

- ensure the security and confidentiality of that data in a manner fully consistent with industry standards;

400. Ill. Rev. Stat. ch. 5 section 177/15.
401. Iowa Code section 22.11.
402. Commonwealth of Massachusetts Regulation, 201 CMR 17.01(1).
403. *Id.*

- protect against anticipated threats or hazards to the security or integrity of that data; and
- protect against unauthorized access to or use of such information that may result in substantial harm or inconvenience to any consumer.

The regulations were required to be complied with by March 1, 2010.[404]

The scope of the law appears to be very broad. It does not appear to be restricted to businesses operating within Massachusetts but applies to "all persons that own or license personal information about a resident of" Massachusetts.[405]

The Regulation contains a list of applicable definitions including a definition of "personal information" which applies to the following:

(1) a Massachusetts resident's first name and last name; or
(2) first initial and last name in combination with any one or more of the following data elements that relate to such resident:
   - social security number;
   - driver's license number; or
   - state-issued identification card number; or
   - financial account number; or
   - credit or debit card number, with or without any required security code, access code, personal identification number or password, that would permit access to a resident's financial account.
(3) provided, however, that "personal information" shall not include:
   - information that is lawfully obtained from publicly available information; or
   - from federal, state or local government records lawfully made available to the general public.[406]

Duties to protect, and standards for protecting a person's information, apply to the following:

(1) Persons who own or license personal information about residents of Massachusetts are required to develop, implement and maintain written comprehensive information security programs that are readily accessible and that contain administrative, technical and physical safeguards appropriate to:
   - the persons obligated to safeguard the said personal information;
   - the resources available to such persons;
   - the amount of data being stored;
   - the needs for security and confidentiality of both consumer and employee information.

404. Commonwealth of Massachusetts Regulation, 201 CMR 17.05.
405. *Id.*, 201 CMR 17.01(2).
406. *Id.*, 201 CMR 17.02.

The safeguards must not only comply with Massachusetts requirements but also be consistent with the safeguards for protection of personal information and information of a similar character required by any state or federal regulations that are applicable to persons safeguarding information under Massachusetts regulations.[407]

At a minimum, information security programs must:

- designate one or more employees to maintain the program;
- identify the internal and external risks to the data and continually assess whether program safeguards adequately protect against such risks;
- have policies for storage and access of the data and transport of the data outside the business premises;
- impose disciplinary measures for violation of data security rules;
- make sure that terminated employees cannot access records containing personal information;
- have policies in place to monitor and oversee the selection and work of third-party service providers;
- put in place reasonable restrictions on physical access to records containing personal information;
- regularly monitor the security program to make sure that it is adequately protecting personal information and upgrade as necessary;
- review the security measures at least annually and make any changes reasonably necessary to protect the security and integrity of personal information;
- document any measures taken in response to breaches of security and undertake post-incident reviews of such events and the actions taken.[408]

The prescribed computer systems security requirements mandate a written, comprehensive information security program that, at a minimum, to the extent technically feasible, should have the following requirements:[409]

- Secure user authentication protocols.
- Secure access control measures.
- Encryption for all personal information that will travel on public networks or be transmitted wirelessly.
- Reasonable monitoring of systems to detect unauthorized use or access to personal data.
- Encryption of all personal data stored on laptops or other portable devices.
- Firewall protection for systems connected to the Internet.
- Reasonably up-to-date security software.
- Education and training for employees on the proper use of the security system and its importance.

407. *Id.*, 201 CMR 17.03(1).
408. *Id.*, 201 CMR 17.03(2).
409. *Id.*, 201 CMR 17.04.

Minnesota

Government agencies and subdivisions are required to have policies on data privacy and procedures incorporated into, and readable on, their websites.[410]

Missouri

In Missouri, no one who has a library record may disclose any part of that record except to the person identified in the record unless they are subject to a court order.

eBooks and digital material are defined as part of library material that may be part of or related to library records.[411]

Montana

Government agencies and subdivisions are required to have policies on data privacy and procedures incorporated into, and readable on, their websites.[412]

Nebraska

Nebraska Law forbids making false or misleading statements with respect to privacy policies, either published on the Internet or published in another manner, relating to personal information obtained from the public.[413]

Nevada

Under Nevada law, someone who operates an Internet website or commercial online service or who otherwise gathers and keeps information on Nevada residents needs to make available a place where Internet users can make requests there that any information about them not be offered for sale or otherwise collected by the operator.

Violations can result in injunction or fines being imposed by the State Attorney General.[414]

410. Minn. Stat. section 13.15.
411. Mo. Rev. Stat. section 182.815 and 182.817.
412. Mont. Code. Ann. section 2-17-550-2-17-553.
413. Neb. Stat. section 87-302(15).
414. Nevada Law, NRS section 603A.300.

New York

Any person or business in New York that owns or licenses computerized data which includes private information of residents of New York is required to develop, implement, and maintain reasonable safeguards to protect the security, confidentiality and integrity of that private information and the disposal of any such data.[415]

To be compliant with this regulation, the data security program needs to include the following:[416]

(1) reasonable administrative safeguards, such as:
   - one or more employees designated to coordinate the security program;
   - identification of reasonably foreseeable internal and external risks;
   - assessments of the sufficiency of the safeguards in relation to the identified risks;
   - training and management of employees about the security program practices and procedures.

(2) adequate contracts with service providers capable of maintaining the required safeguards; and

(3) periodic adjustments to the security program to take account of business changes or new circumstances.

The safeguards must also be regularly tested and monitored for effectiveness.

Noncompliance with these regulations can subject any person subject to them to an action by the New York State Attorney General to enjoin violations and to obtain civil penalties against the violator.

However, this regulation does not create a private right of action, allowing individuals to sue the violator.[417]

Breaches of any data systems holding private information must be reported by the operator to any New York residents whose private information was, or is reasonably believed to have been, accessed or acquired by a person without valid authorization. The notification must be made as soon as possible without unreasonable delay consistent with the legitimate needs of law enforcement or any measures necessary to determine the scope of the breach or restore the integrity of the system.[418]

Even if a breach is determined that it will not likely result in misuse of private data or harm to the affected persons, if the breach affects over five hundred people in New York, it must be notified to the State Attorney General within ten days after the determination of harmlessness has been made.[419]

Any breaches of a business data system holding private information must be reported to the New York State Attorney General, the Department of State and the State

415. New York General Business Law, Article 39F, section 899-BB.2(a).
416. *Id.*, section 899-BB.2(b).
417. *Id.*, section 899-BB.2(d) and (e).
418. *Id.*, section 899-AA.2(a).
419. *Id.*, section 899-AA.2(a).

Police wherever there has been notification about such breaches sent to New York residents.[420]

Any breach that affects over five thousand New York residents has to be notified to consumer reporting agencies listed by the New York State Attorney General.[421]

Any business that suffers any breaches of its data systems must report that to the data owners.

Government agencies and subdivisions are required to have policies on data privacy and procedures incorporated into, and readable on, their websites.[422]

Additional information about New York data privacy protection can be obtained from a detailed review of relevant New York laws, regulations, and cases and from consulting qualified New York attorneys.

Oregon

In Oregon, it is unlawful to post on a website assertions about how another party will use, disclose, collect, maintain, delete or dispose of information if their assertion is materially inconsistent with the other parties' statements or representations.[423]

Pennsylvania

In Pennsylvania, it is an illegal, false, or deceptive business practice to make false or misleading statements in privacy policies published on websites or otherwise.[424]

South Carolina

Government agencies and subdivisions are required to have policies on data privacy and procedures incorporated into, and readable on, their websites.[425]

Tennessee

In Tennessee, any state or government subdivision that operates an electronic communication system must have a written policy on conditions under which the monitoring of such communications will be permitted.

The policy should inform employees that their correspondence may become part of public records and may be open to public inspection.[426]

420. *Id.*, section 899-AA.8(a).
421. *Id.*, section 899-AA.8(b).
422. N.Y. State Tech. Law sections 201-207.
423. Oregon law: ORS section 646.607.
424. 18 Pa. C.S.A section 4107(a)(10).
425. S.C. Code Ann. section 30-2-40.
426. Tenn. Code section 10-7-512.

Texas

Government agencies and subdivisions are required to have policies on data privacy and procedures incorporated into, and readable on, their websites.[427]

Vermont

In Vermont, those businesses or "data brokers" that intentionally collect and/or license consumer personal information must register each year with the Vermont Secretary of State.

They also are required to provide contact information which allows consumers to request to be excluded from data information collection or sales and to request other information about potential use of their personal data.

Data brokers also are required to maintain a written description of the security program they have established, setting out the physical, technical and other protections that they have in place to protect the identifiable personal information of consumers.[428]

Utah

In Utah, all nonfinancial businesses must tell their customers in writing or by email how they will share or sell any personal information about the customers to third parties for marketing purposes or for pay.[429]

Government agencies and subdivisions are required to have policies on data privacy and procedures incorporated into, and readable on, their websites.[430]

Virginia

Under the Virginia Consumer Data Protection Act, there are regulations for collecting and processing the personal data of Virginia residents.

This law applies to all businesses that control or process the private data of hundred thousand or more consumers or who receive 50% of their revenue from the sale or processing of the personal data of twenty-five thousand or more consumers.

State or local governmental entities are exempted, and there are other exemptions for certain types of information treated under federal law.

Under the law, consumers have the right to obtain, correct, delete, or copy their personal data and to decline to allow their data to be processed for advertising purposes.

---

427. Tex. Govt. Code Ann. section 10-2054.126.
428. Vermont Law, 9 V.S.A sections 2446-2447 (Protection of Personal Information: Data Brokers).
429. Utah Code section 13-37-201-13-37-203.
430. Utah Code Ann. section 63D-2-101, 63D-2-102, 63D-2-103 and 63D-2-104.

There is in Virginia a Commission on Technology and Science which is tasked with providing a group to review the implementation of the Act and to report on it.

The effective date of this law is January 1, 2023.[431]

Government agencies and subdivisions are required to have policies on data privacy and procedures incorporated into, and readable on, their websites.[432]

Washington

Under the proposed State of Washington Privacy Act, people have the right to delete data that is held about them by large tech companies such as Google or Facebook.

They can also refuse to be included in targeted advertising and can refuse to permit the sale of their personal data.

However, this Act is not a formal part of Washington legislation yet. This legislation is included in Washington senate bill 5062.

This bill has passed the Washington State Senate but has not yet obtained enough support in the Washington House of representatives to achieve full passage into law (as of March 2021).

C EUROPEAN UNION

Although the various US state laws described above do provide consumers with protection of their personal information, the lack of a general federal data protection law in the US contrasts sharply with EU legislation.

The GDPR

In 2016, the EU introduced the General Data Protection Regulation (GDPR).[433]

It should be noted that the GDPR is an extremely detailed regulation. The description below is intended as a general summary of the Regulation; however, understanding the full legal implications of the Regulation does require a detailed study of the text of the Regulation itself.

The principal purpose of this regulation is to give individuals ("natural persons") control over the collection and use of their personal data.[434]

The GDPR provides a single regulation for businesses to comply with when engaging in transactions across borders and throughout the EU. The GDPR expressly states that although protections are required, it is not intended to restrict the free movement of personal data within the EU.[435]

---

431. Virginia Consumer Data Protection Act, 2021 H.B. 2307/2021 S.B. 1352, effective date January 1, 2023.
432. Va. Code section 2.2-3800, -3801, -3802, and -3803.
433. EU 2016/679, gdpr-info.eu.
434. GDPR, Article 1, gdpr-info.eu.
435. GDPR, Article 1.3, gdpr-info.eu.

Personal Data

"Personal data" is defined as "any information relating to an identified or identifiable natural person ('data subject')." "Processing" of personal data can include any operation performed on the data, whether the operation is automatic or performed by other means of organizing and/or using such data.[436]

Application of GDPR

The GDPR applies to the collection of data, under EU law, by automated means that is intended to be part of a filing system.

Although there are additional regulations that apply to the collection of data by EU bodies, those regulations are required to comply with the principles of the GDPR.[437]

The Regulation applies to the processing of personal data by an EU entity, regardless of whether the processing takes place within the EU.[438]

This regulation applies to all businesses with respect to the collection and use of personal information no matter what their home country or where they are dealing with the personal information of individuals in the EU.

Requirements for Data Control and Processing

Those that control and process personal data are required to install the technical and organizational measures to protect data.

Their default settings must be put in place with the protection of privacy as their formal start, and the highest level of data protection needs to be the default on their systems.

"Controllers" are defined as those who determine the purposes and means of processing personal data.[439]

The general principle behind the Regulation is that personal data must be processed lawfully, accurately, and transparently. Controllers must be able to demonstrate compliance with this principle.[440]

Under the GDPR, there are six legal justifications for processing personal data:[441]

(1) The first is that the data was obtained with the provable, freely given consent of the data subject:[442]
  - However, the data subject is permitted to revoke consent at any time.[443]

436. GDPR, Article 4(1) and (2), gdpr-info.eu.
437. GDPR, Article 2, gdpr-info.eu.
438. GDPR, Article 3, gdpr-info.eu.
439. GDPR, Article 4(7), gdpr-info.eu.
440. GDPR, Article 5, gdpr-info.eu.
441. GDPR, Article 6.1, gdpr-info.eu.
442. GDPR, Article 6.1(a), gdpr-info.eu.
443. GDPR, Article 7(3), gdpr-info.eu.

(2) The second is that the data was obtained under a contract with the data subject.[444]
(3) The third is that the data is collected in fulfillment of a legal requirement.[445]
(4) The fourth is that the collection of the data is for the purpose of serving a vital interest.[446]
(5) The fifth is that the processing is done in the public interest or by an official authority.[447]
(6) The sixth is that the controller has a legitimate interest in the processing of the data.[448]

The controller has an obligation to keep the data in a concise, transparent, intelligible, and easily accessible form.[449]

The controller is required to supply the data to the data subject upon request without undue delay.[450]

There is also a substantial menu of obligations that controllers are required to comply with.

These include general obligations relating to the responsibilities of the controller, requirements regarding the security of personal data, the requirement of prior consultation and providing a data protection impact assessment, the requirements to appoint a Data Protection Officer (DPO), and codes of conduct and certification requirements.[451]

Data Subject Rights

The GDPR provides data subjects with an extensive list of rights with respect to data collected about them.[452]

They include:

- the right to have access to their data;[453]
- the right to correct and erase certain aspects of their data;[454] and
- a right to object to the processing of their data.[455]

444. GDPR, Article 6.1(b) and Article 7, gdpr-info.eu.
445. GDPR, Article 6.1(c), gdpr-info.eu.
446. GDPR, Article 6.1(d), gdpr-info.eu.
447. GDPR, Article 6.1(e), gdpr-info.eu.
448. GDPR, Article 6.1(f), gdpr-info.eu.
449. GDPR, Article 12(1), gdpr-info.eu.
450. GDPR, Article 12(3), gdpr-info.eu.
451. GDPR, Chapter 4, Articles 24-43, gdpr-info.eu.
452. GDPR, Chapter 3, gdpr-info.eu.
453. GDPR, Article 15, gdpr-info.eu.
454. GDPR, Chapter 3, section 3, gdpr-info.eu.
455. GDPR, Article 21, gdpr-info.eu.

Member States are required to provide independent, public, supervisory bodies to assure that citizens' rights with respect to their data are protected and that the requirements of the GDPR are complied with.[456]

Penalties

To ensure that data protection is treated with care and serious purpose, the GDPR provides a substantial number of remedies and penalties for liabilities arising from failures to comply with its requirements. These include:

- a right to lodge a complaint with a supervisory authority;
- the right to seek a judicial remedy against the supervisory authority;
- the right to seek a judicial remedy against a data controller or processor; and
- a right to compensation and a finding of liability.[457]

The GDPR provides supervisory authorities with the power to impose fines and penalties which are "effective, proportionate and dissuasive."[458]

Limitations on Data Rights

However, the rights of data subjects with respect to the processing of their data are not unlimited.

The GDPR provides for several limitations and exemptions to its general provisions about data processing. These include:

- data processing situations relating to freedom of expression and information;
- situations relating to public access to official documents;
- processing relating to national identification numbers;
- processing relating to employment; and
- situations regarding the protection of the existing data held by churches and religious associations.[459]

D DATA LOSS

Computer data is an important asset, and the loss of it can be costly, not only in terms of money but also in terms of lost client confidence and lost business. Data losses can be of many different sizes. Most are small and inconsequential, but some, as frequently reported in the news, can be massive and devastating to businesses, individuals or national security. The most serious ones are usually the result of Internet activity. It is

456. GDPR, Chapter 6, gdpr-info.eu.
457. GDPR, Chapter 8, Articles 77-82, gdpr-info.eu.
458. GDPR, Articles 83 and 84, gdpr-info.eu.
459. GDPR, Chapter 9, Articles 85-91, gdpr-info.eu.

worth looking at what the principal causes of data loss are, and what is recommended for preventing or minimizing data loss.[460]

There are several kinds of data loss representing different levels of damage. For example, there is loss of the coding that constitutes a computer program. This can be very damaging because it requires highly skilled experts to replace it. This can be costly. Another kind can be the loss of customer or client data. In most cases, copies of that data exist and can be replaced by contact with clients. That may not be costly in terms of immediate out-of-pocket costs but can be very costly in the long run, in terms of lost customer confidence and public embarrassment, leading to lost future business in terms of both repeat business and business that might be available for future expansion.

There are many causes of lost data, some human, some technical. Only a minority are due to cybercrime, although this is the kind that gets the most publicity in the press because it is the most dramatic and perhaps the most frightening. The most common causes are somewhat more mundane.

The most frequent cause of data loss is hardware problems. This represents around 40% reported incidents of data loss.[461] The next largest is human mistakes. This constitutes about 30% of reported data losses. The third is corruption of software. This accounts for just under 15% of data losses.

Another physical cause of data loss is hardware destruction. When computers or computer desks or other media get destroyed by accident or thrown away, data can be lost which is difficult or impossible to duplicate in the future. This is a particular problem because the development and evolution of computer and computer media systems have been so rapid over the last fifty years. Room-size computers recording information on large spinning tapes have given way to personal computers recording data on floppy disks, which gave way to mini discs, which gave way to CDs and DVDs, which have given way to cloud storage to a significant extent.

Another important component of data storage that is still with us is computer hard disks. These hard disks not only store information that is entered on personal or business computers but also, exist at huge data storage facilities that back up data that is "stored on the cloud."

Hard disks have also changed significantly over the decades. The recording of data on these discs used to be largely physical, but now almost all have been replaced by "digital" recording that has allowed much more data to be stored on hard disks and has allowed faster retrieval, which improves the performance of the Internet.

Alongside these developments have been the developments of small, easily portable devices that allow data to be transferred from computers or the web and easily carried from place to place to be used in other systems. These include USB discs, and memory cards, which permit insertion in portable telephones and cameras, and which have been becoming increasingly smaller in size although their capacity keeps

460. David M. Smith, "The Cost of Lost Data," *Graziado Business Review* (Pepperdine University) Volume 6 (2003), online, retrieved August 27, 2021.
461. *Id.*, Figure 1, Causes of Lost Data.

increasing significantly. Unfortunately, this makes it easier to lose them by physically misplacing them.

The consequences of data loss, particularly to a small business, can be devastating. It is reported that about 70% of small firms that suffer a large data loss go out of business within one year.[462]

462. "10 Common Causes of Data Loss," *Consoltech.com*, online, retrieved, August 31, 2021. Smith, *supra*.

CHAPTER 17
Artificial Intelligence

A THE ELON MUSK EXPERIMENTS

However, there is one expected Internet access tool that will require a significant amount of new and stringent regulation in the future. This is the growing probability that it will be possible to access and use the Internet through electronic devices inserted in the human body.

To some, this may seem surprising and shocking. Others may regard it as something that needs to be forbidden by the most stringent legal regulation. But, at this writing, it is much closer than might be thought.

In August 2020, an article appeared in *The Times* that described how Elon Musk had arranged for a small computer chip to be planted in the brain of a pig that was supposed to be able to interact with the nervous system to cure dementia, Parkinson's disease, and paralysis. This procedure was reported to be "a prototype of the first brain-to-machine interface." According to Mr. Musk, this procedure was the start of "a new era of superhuman cognition."[463]

The results of Mr. Musk's experiment have not yet been published as of this writing, but if the procedure is successful, the potential implications are enormous. If such implantations can be successfully done with human beings, it will not only require significant changes to Internet law but also make enormous differences in the ways that society and life generally are conducted.

It has been reported that the Musk experiment is now moving rapidly beyond its initial stages. It was reported in April 2021 that Musk's company Neuralink released a

463. Charlie Mitchell, "Elon Musk Wires up a Pig 'To Cure Dementia'," *The Times*, online, Monday, August 31, 2020, accessed August 31, 2020, https://www.thetimes.co.uk/article/elon-musk-wires-up-a-pig-to-cure-dementia-55vqpgzkx?shareToken=c9c8b45dcf950cc6e0f81f213e829e81.

film showing a monkey playing the primitive computer game "Pong" by communicating with a computer through a chip planted in the monkey's brain. The commands are apparently sent wirelessly through the skin.[464]

It is probably impossible to imagine all the ways that such a development would affect us.

For example, if it were possible to safely implant communication devices in the human brain, we would not need external physical devices to receive much of the information we get from computers and mobile devices. We may be able to receive telephone calls and written, oral or even pictorial messages without an external device. We may be able to access websites without the need for a physical device. We might be able to access reference sources such as dictionaries, encyclopedias, books, or articles just by activating the implanted chip.

Our ability to speak foreign languages without intensive training might be enhanced or even perfected. Speeches would not require paper or electronic notes. There may be medical benefits such as the ones sought by Mr. Musk's project, and others far beyond those. The possibilities are endless.

However, there are many negative possibilities as well—perhaps too many to permit this kind of thing to be done to humans. If this technology becomes effective, it might be impossible to stop criminal or politically hostile groups from using it to their advantage.

Laws and Regulations Will Be Needed

It becomes obvious that the strictest and most thoughtful legal controls must be imposed on the use of such technology.

Medical Issues

First there are the medical issues. How safe is this technology? Medical regulatory and professional ethical authorities will need to carefully control such things as the following:

- What specifications and limitations will need to be applied to the electronic or chemical implantations?
- Who will be permitted to manufacture, sell, install and service such devices?
- Who will be allowed to have such devices implanted?
- Are there circumstances in which such devices can be implanted in a person without their consent?
- What ethical standards will need to be complied with?
- What signals or information can be transmitted to and from such devices?
- What third parties, if any, will be allowed to communicate with the possessor of such a device?

464. Tom Knowles, "For Musk's Next Trick ... Monkeys Playing Mind Games," *The Times*, online, April 10, 2021, accessed April 10, 2021.

These are only some of the questions that will have to be asked and answered.

One is reminded of reports and even criminal cases where it is alleged that individuals or their parents paid large sums to have clever test takers take professional or educational evaluation exams in place of the persons that were registered to take the exams.

If this technology develops to a sufficient level, paying third-party substitutes for exam takers may no longer be necessary. The original registrants could have correct answers fed directly to their brains as they sit there taking the tests. Alternatively, they may be able to access the Internet to get helpful information while they are taking the exam. It is hard to imagine how invigilators could stop this. The nature of the relevant examinations would have to be completely changed.[465]

Third-Party Brain Access

Beyond asking the question of what the possessor of such implants might be able to access with these devices, there is the more worrying question of what access such devices would give third parties to the body and brain of the possessor?

Is what we are facing a world that becomes like the plot of a Christopher Nolan movie whereby third parties will be able to communicate with the electronic chips implanted in peoples' brains and implant ideas, thoughts, desires, and instructions that the possessors of the chips will believe they thought of themselves and that it is necessary and important for these "inceptions" to be put into practice in the physical world?[466]

The sinister implications of having such power are too broad and too inhuman to fully imagine.

Significant legislation needs to be promulgated throughout the world to limit and control such activities. Otherwise, the negative possibilities are too awful to contemplate.

Cybercrime and Cyberwar Enhanced

This may be the ultimate cybercrime and the ultimate weapon of cyberwar. The potential consequences could be far more deadly and long-lasting than a nuclear strike.

For example, following the "Inception" theme, the consequences could be devastating for business and the financial markets.

---

465. Joey Garrison, "NY Attorney Sentenced to 1 Month in Prison for Paying $75K to Have Daughter's ACT Answers Fixed," *USA Today*, online, December 15, 2019, accessed September 2, 2020, https://eu.usatoday.com/story/news/nation/2019/10/03/college-admissions-scam-lawyer-gordon-caplan-faces-prison-paying-cheat-test/3828754002/; Josie Ensor, "Donald Trump Cheated on Exams to Get into University, Claims His Niece in New 'Tell-All' Book," *The Telegraph*, online, July 8, 2020, accessed September 2, 2020.
466. In 2010, the writer and film director, Christopher Nolan released a "science fiction" film called "Inception," in which persons are hired to implant an idea into the mind of a businessman that will be profitable for other businesspeople. The implanters are required to do this in such a way that the person receiving the implanted idea believes the idea to be his own. This implanted idea is an "Inception" as opposed to a "conception," https://www.imdb.com/title/tt1375666/, online, retrieved September 3, 2020.

Financial analysts frequently fail to accurately predict the direction of financial market moves. But they are generally thought to be relying on their own judgment and analysis when they take positions in the markets. Of course, there have been too many instances where investors have taken a position based on inside information that gives them a better view of the future of prices than those who do not have this information.

However, such conduct is illegal and can be punished with large fines, banning from the market, and even imprisonment. But what happens when market participants are guided not by their own judgment and analysis but by ideas implanted in their brains, which the receiving persons believe to be their own, by people intending to profit from the execution of those ideas. Will there ever be a level playing field in the financial markets again? How will regulators be able to prevent or even investigate such behavior?

Chile: "Inception Law"

In response to the problems that the above scenario presents, there are already attempts to put into place laws to protect people from digital manipulation of their brains.

Chile is apparently seeking to become the first country to pass legislation to protect its citizens from having their brains digitally controlled. This is being called the "inception law" in the press.[467]

The purpose of the law is said to be to protect the "neuro-rights" of Chilian citizens by covering them with statutory legal protection.

Going beyond that, Chilean legislators say that the nation's constitution should be revised to protect all things connected to "fundamental human autonomy."

It is reported that the members of the Chilean Parliament unanimously support the passage of this law and are considering making a part of a constitutional revision that may proceed in 2022.

Health Benefits

However, there is another side to this mind manipulation debate. Apparently, there have been significant technological advances in using digital brain manipulation to diminish the effects of Parkinson's disease and epilepsy. These successes are apparently dependent on accessing and manipulating the brain.[468]

There has even been a program in the US, supported by the Obama administration, seeking to learn more about the causes and cures of brain diseases. This program is itself called "Brain," which stands for brain research through advanced innovative neuro-technologies.

As discussed above, Elon Musk is involved in experiments to plant electrodes in the brains of animals. The nature of these experiments is worrying, but one positive aspect of them is that there is an intention that the knowledge gained from such

467. Stephen Gibbs, "'Inception' Law Aims to Stop Mind Control," *The Times*, online, May 7, 2021, accessed May 8, 2021.
468. *Id.*

experiments may be useful for helping people suffering from paralysis to be able to use computers or telephones by controlling them directly with signals from their brains.

It is also suggested that the treatment of a variety of neural problems such as spine injuries or dementia could be aided by discoveries connected to such technologies. However, despite the possible benefits that have been suggested, achieving those kinds of results is still a long way away.[469]

Mind/Computer Interface Developments

Despite legitimate concerns with the impact of an interface between the brain and digital machines, the mind/computer interface is developing rapidly.

One of the positive effects of the research that is being done is that there is help for people with paralysis in some of these developments. The formal name for this type of technology is brain-machine interface technology (BMI). It is a small field of technology currently, but some of the research being done in the field may provide dramatic results.

Important large tech companies are investing a great deal of money in BMI. So far, there has been at least one human recipient of BMI technology that promises to improve his life.

A US man broke his neck in a car accident and was left a quadriplegic. He now takes part in BMI lab experiments that implant his brain with electronic sensors that allow him to control certain devices with his thoughts. He says "I can control a robotic arm and hand or a computer cursor or I've played some games that use a computer emulator."[470]

A recent story in *The New York Times* told of another man who had been paralyzed in a car accident at the age of 20 and had not been able to speak for nearly twenty years. Now, electrodes have been planted in the speech areas of his brain which allow his brain to transmit signals to a computer that shows the words he wants to say on a screen.

Clearly, this is a use of computer science and AI in coordination with human biology of a type that does need to be encouraged and nurtured in the future.

However, an important element in this situation is that the AI allows the patient to express his own decisions and does not direct him to carry out tasks formulated by a third person who may not have the best interests of the subject of the implantation at heart.[471]

Safer Surgery

In one positive development, AI is being harnessed to make a brain surgery easier and safer.

469. *Id.*
470. Antony Funnell, "The Potential of Brain-Machine Interface Technology Has Silicon Valley Excited, and Ethicists Worried," *ABC News*, online, May 11, 2021, accessed May 27, 2021.
471. Pam Belluck, "Tapping into the Brain to Help a Paralyzed Man Speak," *The New York Times*, online, July 15, 2021. *See also*, "Neuroprothesis for Decoding Speech in a Paralyzed Person with Anarthria," *The New England Journal of Medicine* (2021), 217-227, 385.

It is certainly the case the brain surgery entails significant risks to the patient. Tinkering with the control center of a human being is a dangerous business.

But now AI and computers are progressing to the point where the risks of brain surgery can be reduced by providing surgeons with a virtual, AI created, computer representation of a brain on which the surgeons will be working.

In the UK, the system was first employed in 2021. In its favor, it is believed the system will reduce the stress that surgeons feel during these delicate operations, and that it will save lives and reduce the costs of this kind of complicated surgery.

This "virtual brain" is a product of a British business called Oxford Heartbeat.

The system is employed by taking a scan of the patient's brain from which a 3-D computer model is produced. This model can be used to test the effect of certain procedures (such as the insertion of stents into blood vessels) when applied to the brain of the patient. This eliminates the "hit and miss" trials that are often necessary during the insertion of stents into brain vessels to treat brain aneurysms.

It is believed that this system and other computer modeling systems that can be developed for different kinds of surgery using AI will benefit a huge number of patients in the future.[472]

There are those that worry that BMI technology will allow big businesses to enslave consumers by controlling their minds.[473]

This may be a legitimate concern, but it should be possible to harvest the benefits of such technology while controlling potential abuses through carefully thought-out regulations, laws, and treaties. As there has been with the Internet generally, there will no doubt be a need for careful international cooperation and regulation to use the positive results of this technology and prevent cross-border abuse of BMI.

B PROPOSED EU REGULATION OF AI

The EU is now proposing regulations to govern use of AI. The proposed regulations are outlined in an EU White Paper, entitled "On Artificial Intelligence—A European Approach to Excellence and Trust."[474] The Paper says that the EU's goals are to encourage the adoption of AI while dealing with the risks entailed by certain uses of this technology.[475]

The proposal for harmonized rules on AI within the EU was introduced in April 2021. The purpose of the rules is to try and capture the benefits that may be gained from AI while protecting society against the risks and negative consequences that it can pose for both society and individuals.

The proposal describes AI as having potential beneficial uses in the sectors of climate change, environment, health, public sector, finance, mobility, internal affairs

472. "Artificial Intelligence Gives Surgeons a Practice Run on Virtual Brains," *The Times*, online, September 6, 2021, accessed September 7, 2021.
473. Funnell, *supra*.
474. European Commission, February 19, 2020, COM (2020) 65 final, online, accessed April 27, 2021.
475. EU Paper, p. 1.

and agriculture. However, the same powerful AI tools that could benefit society can also negatively impact society.[476]

The EU has previously expressed its interests and concerns regarding AI in several resolutions that have been introduced in 2020 and followed up with further resolutions in 2021.

In October 2020, the EU adopted resolutions relating to AI on ethics, liability, and copyright.

In 2021, those were followed by proposals on the effect of AI in criminal matters in education, culture, and in audiovisual production.[477]

C AI IN THE UK

The UK government published a national AI policy focusing on the development and use of AI in that country in September 2021. The UK's policy focuses on three main points. The first is on planning and investing for the long-term goals for using AI in the UK. The second is in supporting the application of AI to enhance the economy in all business sectors and regions of the UK. The third is making certain that the UK applies both national and international regulations to the development of AI.[478]

Deep Mind

One stunning British example of AI success is the progress made by a company called Deep Mind.

This is a company, bought by Google in 2014, that is probably best known for beating experts at the games of Go and chess.

Although those things garnered a great deal of publicity for the company and its AI programs, it has also been working on other and perhaps much more significant AI applications.

Alpha Fold

One of its new programs called "Alpha Fold" has made significant progress in describing how proteins are formed. Proteins are coded by our DNA and play a significant role in building our bodies.

Flaws in their structure can lead to serious diseases. Alpha Fold is helping scientists to see how disease structures might be avoided and helping to comprehend the basic structures that create human life.

The AI created by Deep Mind is also helping solve problems in creating usable nuclear fusion projects and in providing more accurate weather forecasting.

476. EC, *AI Regulation Proposal*, p. 2.
477. *Id.*, p. 3.
478. Office for Artificial Intelligence, Department for Digital, Culture, Media & Sport, and Department for Business, Energy & Industrial Strategy, "Guidance: National AI Strategy," online, www.gov.uk, September 22, 2021.

Clearly, these are uses of AI that should be encouraged and which may help us live in better harmony with ourselves, with each other, and with our natural environment.

Google's View

In July 2021, Sundar Pichai, the head of Google, said AI would be "the most profound technology that humanity will ever develop and work on."

The implication is that it will be more important than such previous technologies as electricity, the Internet or even fire.[479]

He stated that the companies that were involved in developing AI, such as Google, needed to do so in a way that makes sure that it is being developed for the benefit of humanity.

This is obviously going to present several complicated problems for governments and society.

Regulation will need to be carefully and thoughtfully formulated, and international cooperation on a wide scale will need to be put in place.

An international law of AI will need to be created.

479. Tom Knowles, "AI Will Have a 'Bigger Impact Than Fire'," *The Times*, online, July 13, 2021.

CHAPTER 18
Cybercurrency

A CYBERCURRENCY

Privately issued digital money, popularly known as "cybercurrency" or "cryptocurrency," is a decentralized peer-to-peer payment system that was created to operate separately from national governments and their central banks.

The best known and perhaps the most popular cybercurrency is bitcoin. It is intended to be a discreet international medium of exchange.

Mining and Blockchains

Bitcoin is "mined" or earned by using computer power to solve complex mathematical problems over the Internet. Theoretically, anyone can become a bitcoin miner, but the process is extremely complex and requires sophisticated electronic equipment.[480]

Once earned, the existence and authenticity of a bitcoin is protected by its entry into a decentralized digital ledger called a "blockchain." Blockchain records the existence and ownership history of a digital asset, such as a bitcoin (or other cybercurrency unit). Once entered, the data in a blockchain ledger cannot be changed.

Once created, a unit of cryptocurrency can be transferred into and expressed as a "token." The creation of a token is entered in a separate blockchain ledger. Tokens make transfer and payment of cryptocurrency easier.[481]

480. More details about the process can be found in specialized publications such as *Investopedia*, online at investopedia.com.
481. Jake Frankenfield, "Crypto Tokens," *Investopedia*, online, October 8, 2021.

Impact of Cybercurrency

Bitcoin's popularity has attracted a flood of competitors. As of November 2021, there were over ten thousand cybercurrencies in existence.[482] The ten most important other than bitcoin[483] are reported to be as follows:

(1) Ethereum (ETH).
(2) Litcoin (LTC).
(3) Cardano (ADA).
(4) Polkadot (DOT).
(5) Bitcoin Cash (BCH).
(6) Stellar (XLM).
(7) Dogecoin (DOGE).
(8) Binance Coin (BNB).
(9) Tether (USDT).
(10) Monero (XMR).

Cybercurrencies, once created and owned, can be bought and sold by individuals in private transactions, but crypto "exchanges" have been created for the purchase and sale of cryptocurrencies. An operation called "Binance" claims to be "the world's largest bitcoin exchange."[484]

Over the last few years, cryptocurrencies have become a well-known and immensely popular medium of exchange and investment.

Crypto Problems

The innovation of bitcoin and similar cybercurrencies over the last few years has caused disruption in the world's financial systems.

The very existence of digital currencies challenges the traditional monopoly of national central banks to produce currencies that can be used to transfer value in commercial transactions.

A major problem of their existence has been their anonymous creation and the difficulties in identifying who owns them and where they are being transferred.

This has made them attractive for international criminals to use when perpetrating online crimes such as ransomware and even off-line crimes where the transfer of money in digital form is demanded by the criminals.

Another major problem of digital currencies and one that affects everyone that invests in or uses them is their volatility. Taking bitcoin as an example, its price has fluctuated from about $10 in 2012 to over $20,000 in 2021, with dramatic rises and falls

482. Luke Conway, "10 Important Cryptocurrencies Other Than Bitcoin," *Investopedia*, online, November 19, 2021.
483. *Id.*
484. www.binance.com, accessed November 30, 2021.

during that period. On June 22, 2021, its price was $2,903,131. On June 23, its price was $3,479,033.[485]

B NATIONAL REACTIONS

Despite the objections to its use and existence, governments are beginning to recognize that cybercurrency or "cryptocurrency" is here to stay and in this increasingly Internet-centric world may be useful to national governments.

Consequently, there have been several discussions within and between national central banks about creating their own digital currencies or adopting one of the existing ones, such as bitcoin.

It is reported that China, the UK and the US are among the countries that have been considering creating their own cryptocurrencies, tied to the value of their existing currencies: the yuan, the pound and the dollar.

China

However, it seems that China's policy of strict regulation will also extend to cryptocurrencies.

In mid-June 2021, it was reported that the Chinese police arrested 1,100 people on suspicion of using cryptocurrency trades to launder money.[486]

Chinese Crackdown on Mining

At about the same time, the government of China began a crackdown on bitcoin creation (mining). This caused the market price of bitcoin to drop about 10%. About two weeks previously, some of the China's largest banks were told that they were not allowed to use or hold cryptocurrency. This was a shock to the market because before that China was judged to be the location of the largest production of cryptocurrency. A state newspaper, *The Global Times*, reported that many bitcoin mines had been shut down. About 90% of China's mining capacity had been shut down.[487]

In addition, there is the increasing problem that cryptocurrency mining diverted huge amounts of electric power from other uses:

> China's National Development and Reform Commission said it will work to cut off financial support and electricity supply for mining, which it said, spawns risks and hampers carbon neutrality goals.[488]

485. Charles Bovaird, "Bitcoin Price Volatility Reached a 14-Month High in June," *Forbes*, online, July 1, 2021.
486. Patrick Hosking, "World's Banks Must Cover Risk of Bitcoin, Says Regulator," *The Times*, online, June 11, 2021.
487. Callum Jones, "Bitcoin Falls as China Clamps Down," *The Times*, online, June 22, 2021.
488. Alun John Samuel Shen and Tom Wilson, "China's Top Regulators Ban Crypto Trading and Mining, Sending Bitcoin Tumbling," *Reuters*, online, September 24, 2021.

China's Crypto Ban

However, it was only in September 2021 that the main Chinese financial regulators cooperated together to impose a comprehensive ban on cryptocurrency:

> [The September 2021 ban] ... is the most detailed and expansive yet from the country's main regulators, underscoring Beijing's commitment to suffocating the Chinese crypto market.
>
> "In the history of crypto market regulation in China, this is the most direct, most comprehensive regulatory framework involving the largest number of ministries," said Winston Ma, NYU Law School, adjunct professor.[489]

While other countries have been trying to find some sort of balanced way to deal with the growing popularity of cryptocurrencies that responds to both their usefulness and the risk that they entail, China decided to ban all cryptocurrency transactions[490] in September 2021.

China's regulators imposed a total ban on all cryptocurrency transactions and mining. Of course, this negatively affected the prices of cryptocurrencies such as bitcoin as well as crypto and blockchain-related shares.

China's negative attitude toward cryptocurrency is not new. Chinese regulators have been placing restrictions on the use of cryptocurrencies since at least 2013. They have placed several bans on providing services relating to cryptocurrency business in that year, another in 2017 and the latest in May 2021.

China like other countries shares the worries that digital currencies were displacing nationally issued mediums of exchange, thus reducing government control of financial markets and financial systems and their regulation and tax revenues.

In addition, digital currencies entailed significant financial risk, aided financial crime, and took investment away from traditional investment vehicles such as stocks and bonds.

China is also planning to introduce its own "digital yuan" and did not want privately created digital currencies to compete with that.

China's hard-line regulatory attitude toward cryptocurrencies has provoked negative comments in other countries. In the US, a prominent Republican Senator tweeted:

> Beijing is so hostile to economic freedom they cannot even tolerate their people participating in what is arguably the most exciting innovation in finance in decades.[491]

On the other hand, China's view is that it must prevent speculation in cryptocurrency to safeguard the property of its people and preserve economic, financial, and social stability.[492]

489. *Id.*
490. *Id.*
491. *Id.*
492. *Id.*

El Salvador

One of the more surprising developments in the world of cryptocurrency has been the decision of Nayib Bukele, the President of the tiny Central American country of El Salvador, in June 2021, to adopt bitcoin as a legal tender.

Making bitcoin legal tender entails huge risks for El Salvador.

The volatility of bitcoin is well known. If bitcoin is legal tender in a country, citizens can pay taxes in bitcoin. If thereafter the price of bitcoin falls significantly, those could cause devastating financial losses to national finances.

US dollars are also legal tender in El Salvador. People could swap bitcoin for dollars, increasing the risks to El Salvador's Treasury. Companies and individuals may want to pay their obligations in bitcoin, receive payments in dollars and keep their dollars.[493]

President Bukele is apparently unaware of "Gresham's Law"—"Bad money drives out good."

Bukele tweeted:

> We must break the paradigms of the past. El Salvador has the right to advance towards the first world.[494]

On the first day that El Salvador officially began allowing bitcoin to be used as legal tender (September 7, 2021), the price of bitcoin collapsed by 15%-20%, causing protestors to gather outside El Salvador's Supreme Court burning tires and setting off fireworks. One critic complained that this cost El Salvador $3 million.[495] This was not good news in a country with fewer than 7 million people, a per capita income of less than $8,500 a year, and a GDP below the top hundred in the world.

Ireland

In Ireland, the crypto business has been expanding in new and innovative ways.

Crypto ATMs

In Dublin, Boinnex ATM machines where one can buy or sell cryptocurrency have been appearing around the city.

Boinnex is an Irish company based in Cork. Their intent is to make it easier for members of the public to access crypto.[496]

---

493. Gian M. Volpicelli, "Ël Salvador Is Racing to the Future of Bitcoin," *Wired*, online, June 30, 2021. *See* Chapter 13.
494. Katie Silver, "Bitcoin Crashed on First Day as El Salvador's Legal Tender," *BBC News*, online, September 8, 2021.
495. *Id.*
496. Nick Webb, "Inside Track: John and Daniel Gleason Make Deposits at Boinnex Bitcoin Cash Machines," *The Times*, online, June 20, 2021.

United Kingdom

The financial regulatory watchdog of the UK, the Financial Conduct Authority (FCA), expressed the belief that cryptocurrencies had no inherent value which meant they entailed significant risks.

There had also been a dramatic rise in the number of people advertising get-rich schemes on the Internet that involved cryptocurrency.[497]

The UK FCA estimated that millions of British had bought cryptocurrencies and warned that those that do buy cryptocurrencies as investments must be prepared to risk losing 100% of their money.[498]

FCA Binance Ban

In June 2021, the FCA banned Binance from engaging in regulated activities in the UK after the FCA concluded that Binance did not comply with money laundering standards.

Binance is reported to have a Chinese/Canadian founder and to be one of the largest crypto marketplaces with more than thirteen million customers.

However, the company, although reportedly registered in the Cayman Islands, apparently has no headquarters, and has attracted investigations by several financial regulators.

TSB Blocks Crypto Trading

In June 2021, during a period of frenzied purchases and sales, and wildly fluctuating values, some powerful opposition to the use of cryptocurrency was building. For example, in June 2021, TSB, a large British bank, with more than five million customers said that it was preparing to block its customers from sending money to cryptocurrency trading sites.

They had noticed that customers were losing money to scammers apparently using the Binance trading site, registered in the Cayman Islands. They reported that over eight hundred of their customers had said they lost money to scams connected to Binance accounts.

Barclays Bank Ban

Following that, another large UK bank, Barclays, banned its UK clients from transferring funds to Binance (although customers could still make withdrawals from Binance).[499]

497. David Byers, "TSB Bans Cryptocurrency Amid Fraud Concerns with Binance and Kraken," *The Times*, online, June 19, 2021.
498. Ben Martin, "Barclays Blocks Customers Moving Cash to Binance after FCA Ban," *The Times*, online, July 6, 2021.
499. *Id.*

Starling Bank

Starling Bank also suspended payments to crypto exchanges to protect customers from fraud.

In September 2021, it was announced that the FCA intended to take a closer look at the regulations of cryptocurrencies.

The Chairman of the FCA, Charles Randell, said that it was important to give consumers greater protection from highly speculative assets like cryptocurrencies.

The FCA has apparently been stimulated to action by the promotion of a digital "token" on Instagram by Kim Kardashian, who has 250 million followers on Instagram and is known as something of an "influencer." Mr. Randall is concerned that such publicity might inspire large numbers of relatively unsophisticated investors to buy highly speculative assets putting themselves in danger of large losses.

As a result, UK government is considering additional regulations of digital assets and their promotions.[500]

Britcoin: Digitalization of Central Bank Currency

However, Britain is considering creating its own cybercurrency, tentatively referred to as: "Britcoin."

Britain, along with other countries, has understood that if the use of cybercurrency offers any national advantages, tying them to national currency issued by central banks may help reduce their volatility.

In June 2021, Andrew Bailey, Governor of the Bank of England, said that the bank has been discussing the prospect of creating digital pounds and these have been given the name "Britcoins."

Bailly reportedly said that he supported the exploration of central bank use of what he considered to be a "critical innovation" in finance. He said he considered this innovation to have created a new era in finance which central banks such as the Bank of England should be considering using.[501]

Britcoin would be tied to the value of Pounds Sterling.

United States

US Efforts to Regulate Cryptocurrency

The current situation in the US is that cryptocurrencies are regulated by a variety of state regulations.

But now the Federal Government is moving to change that.

Prior to September 2021, there was no cohesive effort by the US Federal Government to provide nationwide rules for the use of cryptocurrency.

500. "Financial Conduct Authority Seeks More Powers to Curb Cryptocurrency Promotions," *The Times*, online, September 7, 2021.
501. Callum Jones, "A Central Bank Digital Currency Would Be Historic Innovation, Says Andrew Bailey," *The Times*, online, June 12, 2021.

In September 2021, it was reported that US regulators were making efforts to provide a regulatory framework for cryptocurrency.

Federal regulators have become concerned about the large number of business operations that are seeking to adapt their businesses to accommodate payments in digital currencies.[502]

The initial regulatory effort involves a cooperative effort by the US Treasury and other federal agencies to impose a regulatory system on a digital currency product known as "stable coin."

Stable coin has that name because it is supposedly indexed on a one-to-one basis with so-called stable assets like the US dollar, or other "stable" assets.

This concept itself appears to contain a significant fallacy—that assets such as US dollars and gold are stable. Although the value of these things may not fluctuate as often or as dramatically as something like bitcoin does, the market value of gold, US dollars, etc., does change constantly, not only day to day but also during market operations on any day in which markets for those assets are operating.

So, what "stability" stable coins are meant to have is far from clear.

US regulators are aware of this inherent instability and are becoming concerned that the adoption and use of so-called stable coins such as Tether token, USD coin and PAX dollar could lead to disastrous financial losses if their values fluctuated significantly.

As reported in *The New York Times*, the value of these stable coins in circulation increased from $30 billion to approximately $125 billion between January and mid-September 2021. The US Treasury is leading the effort to provide a sensible framework for regulation of digital currencies like stable coins as soon as possible.[503]

It has not indicated that it has any general regulatory interest in banning cryptocurrency.

US Attitude

In contrast to the Chinese crackdown on cryptocurrencies, in early October 2021, Jerome Powell, the Chairman of the US Federal Reserve, said that the US did not intend to ban cryptocurrencies. He is quoted as saying:

> Stable coins are like money market funds, or bank deposits, but they're to some extent outside the regulatory perimeter, and it is appropriate that they be regulated. Same activity, same regulation.[504]

This caused an immediate rise in the market prices of cryptocurrencies, including bitcoin.

---

502. Eric Lipton, Ephrat Livini and Jeanna Smialek, "Regulators Racing Toward First Major Rules on Cryptocurrency," *The New York Times*, online, September 23, 2021.
503. *Id.*, citing a statement by Treasury under Secretary Nellie Liang.
504. Hamza Khalique-Loonat, "Bitcoin Jumps 9% after US Federal Reserve Gives Cryptocurrencies the All-Clear," *The Times*, online, October 2, 2021.

Binance Investigation

However, the world's largest cryptocurrency exchange, Binance, is reported to be under investigation by US Internal Revenue Service, the US DOJ, the US Commodity Futures Trading Commission, and Japanese, British, and Canadian regulators. These regulators are apparently concerned with tax and money laundering issues among other things.

Binance claims it has no established headquarters. It is alleged that this is because Binance is busy moving from country to country to avoid financial regulations. These policies apparently raise questions in the minds of regulators in the US and elsewhere.

Concern with Influencers

There is also a controversial group of so-called cryptocurrency influencers who are reported to publish information about bitcoin price increases. These "reports" are allegedly published in order to create a positive public view of the advantages of investing in bitcoin, but which are allegedly intended to create profits for these "influencers" and their friends.[505]

Puerto Rico Attracts Crypto

In early 2018, it was reported that several successful cryptocurrency and blockchain entrepreneurs were moving to Puerto Rico to avoid US state and federal taxes on their growing fortunes. It is even reported that they had hoped to build a "crypto utopia" by building a new city in Puerto Rico where all money would consist of cryptocurrency to show the rest of the world how a crypto economy could work.[506]

Other Countries

Other countries are considering different approaches to digital currencies as interest in them continues to expand.

Arguments are being made that digital currencies would offer benefits of faster payments and might make financial services easier for people with low incomes to access.[507]

505. Concoda, "We Are about to Witness the Great Cryptocurrency Reset," *medium.com*, online, July 9, 2021.
506. Nellie Bowles, "Making a Crypto Utopia in Puerto Rico," *The New York Times*, online, February 2, 2018.
507. Jones, *supra*, June 12, 2021.

C A REGULATORY GAP?

Compensation Issues

Most cryptocurrencies are not regulated by financial regulators and are not eligible for financial compensation schemes that may be in place to protect investors with more traditional assets and financial products.[508]

One line of thought that is emerging is that banks that deal in cryptocurrencies must be prepared to cover the risks they pose.

Basel BIS View

One of the international regulators that sets banking rules around the world, the Basel Committee on Banking Supervision, a division of Basel's Bank for International Settlements (BIS), has pointed out that because of the risks that digital currencies pose to world banking stability, banks that hold cryptocurrencies should have a hundred times as much capital to protect against possible dramatic decline in the value of cryptocurrency.

A "risk weighting" for cryptocurrencies of 1,250% has been proposed for every dollar of exposure to cryptocurrencies.[509]

However, this large risk weighting will apply only to privately produced digital currencies and not to digital currencies that may be produced by central banks and tied to the value of traditional currencies such as the pound sterling or the dollar.

Those so-called stable coins would continue to operate under the same rules as applied to existing national currencies.[510]

There is little doubt that there will be a range of developments with respect to digital currencies as time goes on.

Risks Misunderstood

However, despite the risks that have been described in respect of their volatility, the cryptocurrencies have shown their popularity as investment vehicles continues to expand.

It was reported in June 2021 that the number of cryptocurrency buyers had expanded by about four hundred thousand. This rise in ownership was occurring despite what was found to be the public's misunderstanding of the nature of cryptocurrency assets. It was also worrying to regulators that a significant portion of investors in crypto were borrowing money to buy them.

---

508. "Cryptocurrencies Boom as Punters Throw Caution to the Wind," *The Times,* online, June 18, 2021.
509. Patrick Hosking, "World's Banks Must Cover Risk of Bitcoin, Says Regulator," *The Times,* online, June 11, 2021.
510. *Id.*

Since its introduction, there have clearly been different and sometimes contradictory reactions to crypto from individuals, private companies, government organizations, of course from hackers and criminals. Some have been enthusiastic about it, and others have been wary or opposed.

D THOUGHTS ON CRYPTO

Since cryptocurrency was first created and used sometime after 2008, there have been several narratives published extolling the potential virtues of digital currency and predicting that it will not only become an accepted medium of exchange but that it might eventually replace state-created paper currencies.

However, these positive predictions appear not to be coming true.[511]

Cryptocurrencies appear to have become mostly a medium for speculation in which some people make a lot of money and others lose a great deal.

As a result, as shown above, financial regulators and other government agencies have moved to restrict or forbid their use.

One of the principal myths that has grown up around cryptocurrency is that it eliminated the decentralization of currency creation.

It was argued that anyone could acquire the electronic means to create bitcoins and other cryptocurrencies. The truth has been quite different; four or five firms have dominated cryptocurrency creation.

For example, it has been reported that nine Chinese companies controlled 79 % of the bitcoin mining network.

However, one thing is quite clear, the frenetic activity generated by interest in cryptocurrencies is changing the world of finance in a way that may be permanent.

For a long time, national governments have been considered the only legitimate creators of acceptable currency.

Prior to that, currencies had been issued by private banks and other private commercial groups. However, as over time some of these went broke and nations turned to central banks as the sole legitimate issuers of acceptable currency.

The centralization of money issuance also allowed central banks to step in in times of financial crisis and loan or inject money where needed to prop up important financial institutions in times where their collapse would have damaged the entire financial system and put the assets of individual citizens at risk of devaluation.

Now the power of central banks is being threatened by a digital method of creating cryptocurrencies.

Initially, confidence in these cryptocurrencies was created by the fact that blockchain technology supposedly restricted their creation and use in highly restricted ways that would defeat attempts to counterfeit, manipulate or steal them.

Many people saw value in having a payment method that allowed them to engage in transactions free from the interference of government-regulated financial systems.

511. Concoda, *supra*.

These developments have changed the world's view of how instruments of value exchange can be created and have led to the creation of several different kinds. One of these is of course cryptocurrencies of which bitcoin is the best-known example. Another is stable coins, a kind of enhanced digital currency. A third kind is types of electronic payment methods provided by tech companies. One has been created by Facebook, called "Diem."

The public does not seem to be bothered by the fact that their "old-fashioned" electronic payments are only guaranteed by their commercial banks and not by a central government bank. But at least these commercial banks that are backing those electronic transactions are regulated by central government financial regulations.

Old-fashioned cash also has advantages. One of the reasons that people like to use cash is that it provides them with a certain level of privacy in their financial transactions.

If all financial transactions go electronic, how secure will the data surrounding them be?[512]

512. Simon Nixon, "State-Backed Digital Currencies Are a Gamble That Might Not Pay Off," *The Times*, online, July 22, 2021.

CHAPTER 19
Cybercrime

A THE SIZE OF THE PROBLEM

In July 2020, *The Times* reported that cybercriminals extorted more than two hundred million in ransom from British companies during the previous year.[513]

It is estimated that in 2021 more than half the manufacturers in the UK have been victims of cybercrime.[514] It is reported that 63 % lost up to £5,000 and around a quarter lost between £5,000 and £25,000.

Automotive industries have apparently suffered the most. In 2021, around 62 % reported being victimized by cybercrime.[515]

Apparently, this is done by gangs of hackers, believed to be principally from Russia, North Korea, China or Eastern Europe, infecting the commercial computer systems of large companies with malware, shutting down their systems, and then charging those companies large amounts to get back access to their networks. The usual technique of hackers is to encrypt the target's files so that they can be reopened only with a key sold by the attacker.[516]

It is believed that companies that have been attacked are willing to pay the hackers, rather than go to the authorities, because they fear damage to their reputations and possible fines from regulators for failing to adequately protect their computer systems and the data stored there. Worldwide, it is believed that cybercriminals are extorting around $19 billion per year.

In Britain, it is reported that the companies there are suffering around five thousand ransomware attacks per year.[517]

513. Tom Knowles and Lucy Fisher, "Firms Pay £200m in Ransoms to Hackers," *The Times*, online, July 31, 2020, retrieved on day of publication, https://www.thetimes.co.uk/#.
514. MakeUK, "Cyber Resilience the Last Line of Defence," *MakeUK Cyber Security Survey 2021*, online, May 4, 2021, accessed May 7, 2021.
515. *Id.*
516. Byers, *supra*, June 19, 2021.
517. *Id.*

Consequently, about 52 % of companies in the UK have now acquired insurance cover against cyberattacks.[518]

In fact, the payment total may be much higher, but many companies refuse to admit that they have paid ransom to hackers.[519]

Individuals Attacked

The pandemic of 2020-2021 made things even worse. Not only large companies, financial institutions or infrastructure are being attacked by perpetrators of cybercrime but also individuals have been swindled out of a large amount of money by online scams.[520]

Generally, this means situations in which cybercriminals tricked individuals into transferring money to them. Twenty percent more people were victimized by this type of scam in 2020 than had been in the previous year.

There have been approximately 150,000 victims in the UK alone.[521] Although much of this fraud involved the bank accounts of the victims, recently banks have been blaming the large tech companies so much of the problem. The banks are claiming that the tech companies have not been diligent enough in rapidly removing suspicious websites from their platforms. These websites are often used by criminals to lure victims into transferring money to the fraudsters. Some in the banking industry claim that the tech giants are not cooperating enough with the banks to put an end to these scams and that these tech companies are not making enough of an effort to take down the sites that offer fake investments.

Consequently, some in the banking industry are demanding that tech companies should be made financially liable for frauds that are committed using their platforms.[522]

Unfortunately, online criminals continue to expand their activities. It has even been reported that they are offering services to fellow criminals to set up fake websites to serve as platforms for their illegal activities.[523]

The public relations problem that the major tech companies suffer is that they of course make money from increased usage of their platforms. In other words, if criminals are increasing their use of online platforms to defraud people, then this increases the revenue to the tech companies. Tech company critics point out that it cannot be right that criminal activity financially benefits the tech companies if the tech companies are less diligent in removing fraudulent websites from their platforms.

A number of banks have signed on to a voluntary code to make refunds to victims of online financial fraud involving their bank accounts. However, they are coming in for some criticism for not in all cases making it easy for victims to recover their losses.

518. MakeUK.
519. Byers, *supra*, June 19, 2021.
520. David Byers, "Internet Giants Are Profiting from Web Scams, Say Banks," *The Times*, online, March 26, 2021, accessed March 30, 2021.
521. *Id.*
522. *Id.*
523. *Id.*

In some cases, banks have tried to say that the losses are due to the negligence of the victims. So, it is not surprising that banks are trying to shift at least part of the blame for financial losses to the tech platforms where the losses are happening. How this debate is ultimately resolved between the financial and the tech companies remains to be seen.

However, some major tech companies respond that they are making serious efforts to prevent fraud on their platforms. Google has said that it has clear policies on the kind of ads it permits to be placed on its platform. They say that they strictly enforce those policies and remove ads that violate them. Google says that it is working around the clock to remove billions of ads that did not meet its standards.

B US AND UK RESPONSES

In 2001 the US Department of Justice set up a section within its Criminal Division to deal with computer crime and intellectual property, the Computer Crime and Intellectual Property Section (CCIPS). According to the Justice Department, the CCIPS is charged with fighting computer and intellectual property crimes worldwide:

> CCIPS is the cornerstone of the Department's anti-cybercrime efforts and has been involved in one capacity or another in practically every significant cybercrime and intellectual property case that has been in the public eye.[524]

Working within the Justice Department, the FBI is a "lead federal agency for investigating cyber attacks and intrusions."[525]

In the UK, the Bank of England governor, Andrew Bailey, has called for amendments to a new government Online Safety Bill to require tech companies to make greater efforts to prevent child abuse, terrorist activities and online financial fraud.

However, the UK government, and undoubtedly other governments, will continue to examine whether tech platforms are doing enough to prevent fraud on their systems and may impose additional regulations if they find that more should be done.[526]

C SCAMS AND FRAUD

Many of these scams involve investment fraud making false offers for investment in things like digital currencies. Nearly ten thousand people have fallen victim to these kinds of frauds in 2020.

524. US Department of Justice, "Criminal Division's Computer Crime and Intellectual Property Section Celebrates 20 Years," online, accessed February 10, 2022.
525. Federal Bureau of Investigation, "The Cyber Threat," online, accessed February 10, 2022.
526. *Id.*

D CRYPTOCURRENCY AND CRIME

As shown in a previous chapter, cryptocurrency itself is a controversial creation. One of its most controversial aspects is that it plays a major role in cybercrime.

Payments to cybercriminals are usually made in the form of a digital currency, such as bitcoin, and cannot be traced to the persons paid. The anonymity of the payments and the reluctance of companies to admit paying combine to give ransomware criminals an almost unfettered opportunity to profit from their crimes free of punishment.

The growth of cybercrime also begs the question of whether cryptocurrency itself is as unassailable as its promoters claim.

It is impossible to know whether cryptocurrency transactions and accounts are ultimately safe from hackers.

Commentators have pointed out that many hacking groups including those in China and Russia love the challenge of a difficult hack. If cryptocurrency transactions can be altered, then the currency can be stolen and will probably be impossible to recover from the digital universe into which it disappeared.[527]

Potential Manipulation

Cryptocurrency also presents an additional problem of market abuse through price manipulation.

In 2021 it was seen that certain influential persons' comments leading cryptocurrencies would be followed by dramatic rises and falls in their prices.

Those comments may have been innocent.

However, if anyone, knowing they have the power to cause dramatic changes in cybercurrency prices, makes price moving comments with the intention that others in the market are likely to follow their recommendations, this could constitute criminal market manipulation.

Crime to Get Crypto

It has been reported that the desire to own cryptocurrency is motivating some people to expand into other types of crime to get cryptocurrency.

For example, it was reported in May 2021 that a group of cryptocurrency "miners" was stealing electricity needed to power their bitcoin mining.[528]

Having received a tip that a building in an industrial site near Dudley, England, was being used as a marijuana farm, the police raided the building because they had flown a drone over the building and discovered that it was giving off an inordinate amount of heat. This is usually associated with places that are being used as indoor marijuana farms.

The police found about hundred computers apparently being used to mine bitcoins.

527. Martin, May 27, 2021.
528. Arthi Nachiappan, "Stolen Electricity Powered Bitcoin Mine," *The Times*, online, May 29, 2021, accessed June 1, 2021.

Operating these computers and associated cooling fans required an enormous amount of electricity. When they made inquiries with the local power company, they discovered that the bitcoin miners had circumvented the usual methods of attaining power and had stolen the enormous amount of electricity they were using, for which they should have paid thousands of pounds.

Banks' Duties

The growing association of cryptocurrency with ransom attacks, fraud and other kinds of crime is of concern.

This has led some banks block transactions in crypto that look "suspicious."

Banks have a duty of care to their customers. So, it appears reasonable that banks may interfere with transactions in which customers appear to be potential victims of fraud or criminality. Banks also have a regulatory duty to detect and prevent money laundering within their systems. This can involve them in restricting or blocking transactions in cryptocurrencies.

E RANSOMWARE ATTACKS

The Range of Attacks

It is not only companies and individuals but also key institutions that are being attacked. In July 2020, it was reported that thirty-three British universities and many charities such as the National Trust suffered from ransomware attacks.[529]

For companies attacked, the impact of their business can be devastating. For example, the digital watch maker, Garmin, was forced to close most of its services for a week and the foreign exchange company Travelex was forced to shut down its computer system and do transactions on paper. It is believed that both companies paid ransom.[530]

Reasons to Pay

Apparently, the dangers of suffering public embarrassment, losing data and being fined by regulators are enough to make companies want to pay such ransoms without reporting the attacks. The actual total amounts of ransoms being paid may be much higher than is being reported. This also means that risk to cybercriminals of being caught and punished is greatly reduced.[531]

Payment in the UK

In the UK, it is not illegal to pay such ransoms, unless it is known that the payment is going to be used to fund terrorism.

529. Martin, May 27, 2021.
530. *Id.*
531. *Id.*

However, some Members of the British Parliament have demanded that laws should be passed to make the payment of such ransom illegal.[532]

Biggest National Targets

These reports about British problems are disturbing but become even more so when one recognizes that Britain is number six in the list of countries experiencing ransomware attacks. The first five are the US, Italy, Germany, Spain and France. In the US alone, it is estimated that about $1.3 billion dollars are paid out each year as a result of ransomware attacks.[533]

Ransom Funds Crime

A frightening aspect of the success that hacker groups have had in extracting money from victims is that these funds make it possible for the hackers to purchase ever more sophisticated systems for their hacking and to expand their criminal activities to target even more and bigger victims for their crimes. It is reported that their success has encouraged criminal gangs to advertise for new recruits on the "dark web."[534]

F THE SIZE OF THE WEB

The Internet is much more extensive than most users realize.

Most people only use and see the websites that are available to the general public using the popular browsers such as Google, Safari and Bing. However, this gives access to only a very small part of the World Wide Web (Web).

There is a part of the Web that comprises an encrypted network that contains websites that cannot be reached with the popular browsers. This is the "Dark Web," and the websites on that can only be reached using special "anonymity browsers" such as the Onion Router, Freenet and f2P. The Dark Web has many uses, but it is a platform favored by cybercriminals to carry out their operations and keep them anonymous.[535]

However, in September 2020, Europol declared that the "golden age of the dark web marketplace is over," after the arrest of 179 sellers and buyers of illegal drugs on the dark web. Also seized in the raids were $6.5 million and over 1,000 pounds of drugs.

---

532. *Id.*
533. *Id.*
534. *Id.*
535. "The Dark Web Explained," "The Dark Web and How to Access It in 3 Easy Steps," *VPN Mentor*, https://www.vpnmentor.com/blog/whats-the-dark-web-how-to-access-it-in-3-easy-steps/?keyword=&geo=9055710&device=&gclid=EAIaIQobChMIhfa6-a_-6gIVjO3tCh3ZZwuREAAYASAAEgJDh_D_BwE, retrieved August 3, 2020.

Most of the arrests, 121, were in the US, and there were 42 in Germany, 8 in the Netherlands, 3 in Austria and 1 in Sweden.[536]

G INTERNATIONAL ANTI-CRIME EFFORTS

An article published by the World Economic Forum (WEF) suggests that the best way to deal with cybercrime is greater international cooperation at the highest levels.[537] This article urges major countries to take responsibility for helping to defeat cybercrime.

The growing success and sophistication of cybercriminals are going to require greater funding and more resources to protect against it. Individuals and companies may not have the funds and resources necessary. The expanding threat will need to be dealt with at the national and international levels. A number of steps are suggested in order to deal with the problem.[538]

Transparency Needed

One important requirement is that those who are victims of attack should be required to report the attacks, cooperate with authorities, and be transparent about the effects of such an attack.

It was reported by the WEF that at least one important international company has followed this path. Norsk Hydro, a large Norwegian metals and energy company, was subject to a ransomware attack. They decided to refuse to pay, to report the attack immediately, cooperate with officials, and be transparent about the effects of the attack.[539]

The WEF article recommends that commercial institutions and governments need a well thought-out anti-cybercrime strategy to deal with these attacks. This requires that the top management of any organization understands the risks that the organization faces.

Training must be provided to working personnel so that they know how to respond immediately in the face of an attack.

The funding and resources to provide the knowledge and equipment necessary to improve security against cyberattacks need to be provided.

Finally, the reporting of cyberattacks, cooperation with officials and transparency about the effects of the attack are essential to frustrate, defeat, identify and punish cybercriminals.

536. Thomas Brewster, "Dark Web Opioid Bust Sees 179 Arrests and $6.5 Million Seized," *Forbes*, online, September 22, 2020, retrieved September 22, 2020.
537. Marie Sophie Muller and Alois Zwinggi, "Global Leaders Must Take Responsibility Cybersecurity: Here's Why—And How," *World Economic Forum*, Davos, January 19, 2020, https://www.weforum.org/agenda/2020/01/global-leaders-must-take-responsibility-for-cybersecurity-here-s-why-and-how.
538. *Id.*
539. *Id.*

H GROWTH OF CYBERCRIME DURING THE PANDEMIC

One thing that seems to be the case is that in times of social stress and or social disruption, Internet crime rises. For example, it has been reported that in Spain cybercrime has risen by 300% during the COVID-19 pandemic.[540]

In the UK, it is reported that since the pandemic began, 74% of banks and financial institutions have been affected by some type of financial crime. Their average loss has been approximately £600,000.

Police forces in the UK have reported more than six thousand cases of cybercrime and other COVID-related frauds. In total, more than £34 million has been stolen by fraud and cybercrime since the pandemic began.

Part of the problem is that due to the pandemic, so many people are working from home and using their personal IT systems. Therefore, IT security is not as strong as it would be if all the work was being done in offices with professionally constructed and protected systems.

The increase may also be due to increased unemployment or to the fact that the pandemic has led to a significant increase in online activity from more people working from home and more people doing shopping on the Internet because of shop closures during lockdown.

This has meant that many more people are putting information about themselves and their financial transactions online. This provides a bigger population of potential targets for cybercriminals and may provide them with a higher rate of success in their criminal activities.

Part of this vulnerability may be the result of people who previously have not had much experience in conducting business and financial transactions online have suddenly been required to adopt the Internet as a principal method of doing transactions that they used to do in person. This makes them more vulnerable to sophisticated cybercriminals.

There is also a larger population of Internet users that can be vulnerable to the installation of a virus placed on their computer systems by criminals to illegally gather information about the computer owners or to encrypt the users' data and demand that they pay a "ransom" to have the data unlocked.

Although governments and security services are getting better at combating cybercrime, criminals are clever at creating inventive new ways of hacking, staying ahead of law enforcement and locating new locations to practice their illegal activities. It is also the case that the existence of the "dark web" and the expansion of the use of cybercurrencies make it even more difficult to locate and punish cybercriminals.[541]

Although the pandemic has made it difficult or sometimes impossible for many people around the globe to conduct their business and personal activities, it has opened

540. Tony Windterburn, "Cybercrime in Spain Has Risen by 300% During the Pandemic," *EuroWeekly*, online, March 21, 2021, accessed March 23, 2021.

541. *Id.*, reporting on information from Juan Jose Nombela, a computer science expert at the International University of La Rioja (UNIR).

up a myriad of new opportunities for cybercriminals who want to take advantage of the Internet.

Cyber-Attacks Are Growing

Ransomware cyberattacks have continued to grow with some of the worst and most serious coming in 2021 at a time when much of the world was also suffering from the COVID-19 pandemic. It is reported that ransomware gangs are "now routinely targeting schools and hospitals."[542]

In 2020/2021, the UK was reported to have suffered more than nine thousand data security incidents where information was stolen by hackers or mistakenly sent to the wrong recipients.

It was reported that five hundred private and public bodies were the victims of ransomware attacks, and several hundred more were victims of other types of hacking attacks.

Attacks on Health, Education and Law Enforcement

Most of these data system breaches were suffered by healthcare and education organizations. The usual tactic of hacking groups is to encrypt the data in the systems of educational or healthcare organizations to deprive those organizations of the use of this data until the ransom is paid.[543]

Other breaches occurred affecting the systems of police forces in the UK; these law enforcement authority systems had an average of approximately eight data incidents a week which resulted in important data being taken.

These statistics are known because whenever a data breach involves information important to the safety, rights or freedoms of people at risk, the organization holding the data is required to report the breach to the UK Information Commissioner's Office (ICO), which keeps a record of such data incidents.

In May 2021, it was reported that the Irish healthcare system had twice been victimized by cyberattacks.[544] The first was a ransomware attack. The second had caused several cancelations of outpatient services. These were described as the most serious hacking attacks that have been suffered by the country of Ireland. Apparently, harmful software had been inserted in the Irish healthcare IT systems in several locations. The Irish Health Ministry said that this attack led to cancelations of several health services over the number of days before the problems caused by the attack could be solved.[545]

---

542. Joe Tidy, "The Ransomware Surge Ruining Lives," *BBC News*, online, April 29, 2021, accessed, May 11, 2021.
543. Fiona Hamilton, "Hackers on Loose as 9,000 Data Leaks a Year Recorded," *The Times*, online, July 5, 2021.
544. "Cyber-Crime: Irish Health System Targeted Twice by Hackers," *BBC News*, online, May 17, 2021.
545. *Id.*

An example of attacks on educational institutions was experienced by the Harris Federation in the UK which operates fifty schools in and around London involving over thirty thousand students. As a result of a cyberattack, the students lost access to email and lesson plans. Also, the CCTV systems of the Federation were disabled as was the lunch payment system.[546]

In March 2021, it was reported that attacks on universities, colleges, and schools prevented students from being able to return to classrooms in about eighty educational institutions.[547]

I THE TECH RESPONSE

This surge in attacks has motivated tech companies and governments to find ways to counter aggressively and effectively these damaging, and potentially deadly, criminal activities.

In 2021, the US FBI, Amazon, Microsoft, and the National Crime Agency of the UK joined the Ransomware Task Force in issuing a report making approximately fifty recommendations for action that governments should take to counter ransomware and other criminal hacking attacks.[548]

However, although hacking gangs found healthcare and educational institutions to be particularly vulnerable to ransomware attacks, they did not forget to attack other sectors as well.

Health organizations suffered from about 1,500 attacks in 2021, and educational institutions more than 1,200 attacks. In the retail sector, there were nearly 1,000 attacks, also nearly 1,000 in financial businesses and charities were victimized more than 500 times.[549]

J DATA PROBLEMS

Not all data incidents are the result of criminal activity; there are also thousands of computer system incidents where data is not sent to the right person. Although many times such a mistake may not be damaging to the owner of the data and may be easily corrected, there are situations where the missending needs to be reported because of risks the misdirection may pose to the data owner.

There is the additional difficulty of the financial problems suffered by companies as a result of declines of business due to the pandemic and the accompanying lockdowns. This has often meant that cost-cutting measures have been necessary which have reduced the amount of money available for IT system maintenance and security. This, among other things, has made it easier for criminals to gain access to commercial IT systems.

546. Fiona Hamilton and Mark Bridge, "Ban Ransom Payments to Hackers, Urges Ex-GCHQ Boss," *The Times*, online, May 14, 2021, accessed May 17, 2021.
547. Hamilton, *supra*.
548. Tidy, *supra*, April 29, 2021.
549. Hamilton, *supra*.

This represents larger law enforcement issues than simply computer attacks. The money that is paid to criminal gangs resulting from ransomware is used by them to fund other crimes such as human trafficking and child abuse.[550]

There are an increasing number of attacks that affect public services at all levels. For example, in the autumn of 2020, the IT systems of the London Borough of Hackney were affected by a cyberattack that interfered with important public services provided online. It was reported:

> The damage done was really significant with things like housing repairs, benefits payments and land registry all impacted. It's going to be months until we are fully recovered, and I can't understand the motivation behind this for criminals.[551]

K US HACKING AND RESPONSE

In May 2021, the Colonial Pipeline, the largest fuel pipeline system in the US, suffered a ransomware cyberattack. The Colonial Pipeline transports two and a half million barrels a day of fuel, including gasoline, jet fuel and diesel fuel on the East Coast of the US. It was completely shut down by a cyber-hacking gang. Fuel availability in eighteen states was affected.[552]

The problem is that modern infrastructure operations are increasingly sophisticated and increasingly digitalized and increasingly connected to central computer systems. Consequently, criminals have a variety of portals through which they can seek access to the electronic systems that control important infrastructure operations.

Although the name "Colonial Pipeline" may make one think of metal, the fact is that the flow of petroleum-based chemicals through the system to the states on the East Coast of America that depend on it is highly evolved technologically so that almost all of its operations are under the control of electronic systems, switches, gauges and valves that are centrally controlled and monitored by operators on computers. This makes much government infrastructure vulnerable to attack by sophisticated computer criminals. As has been said, a devastating attack can begin from opening a single email.[553]

The Colonial Pipeline hack had serious consequences in the US. There were shortages of fuel in various areas served by the pipeline. In some states, petrol stations ran out of fuel. Rises in the price of fuel were expected to last several months. In some areas there was "panic buying" of fuels.[554]

The Colonial Pipeline hack is believed to have been caused by a criminal gang known as Dark Side. They are reported to have begun attacking computer systems and

---

550. Tidy, *supra*, April 29, 2021.
551. *Id.*, quoting Rob Miller, director of information and communications technology for the London Borough of Hackney.
552. Joe Tidy, "Colonial Hack: How Did Cyber-Attackers Shut Off Pipeline," *BBC News*, online, May 10, 2021.
553. *Id.*
554. Joe Tidy, *BBC News*, online, May 12, 2021.

demanding ransom payments sometime in August 2020. Some sources believe that they are connected to Russia, but there is no certain knowledge that this is true.[555]

It is reported that $4.4 million in ransom was paid to the Colonial Pipeline hackers to get them to release the pipeline. However, in early June 2021, US government officials were able to trace and recover $2.3 million of this ransom, which was being transferred in the form of bitcoin by the criminals. Colonial was happy for the "swift work and professionalism of the FBI" in seeking to recover the ransom.

A key element of the FBI's recovery was the acquisition of something called the "private key" to the "bitcoin wallet" of the hackers. No details of how the FBI obtained this information were given, but there has been considerable speculation over whether it was from some equipment seized by the FBI, from an informant inside the criminal gang or from a company that the hackers might have used as part of their hacking project.[556]

The increase of ransomware attacks, and particularly the devastating nature of the attack on the Colonial Pipeline, has highlighted the issue in the US and caused people to think that the government needs to do more to protect vulnerable and important IT systems.[557]

US Increases Cybersecurity

As a result of the Colonial Pipeline hack, the US government has called emergency meetings and began discussions about issuing an executive order to increase the cybersecurity requirements for federal agencies and government contractors.[558]

Drafts of such an order have been provided to government agencies and government contractors that provide a cybersecurity program to better protect the US.

The order outlines government-mandated cybersecurity standards that government agencies and contractors would be required to put in place. The proposed standards include "multi-factor identification" that requires a second code to be obtained by a different trusted method before a critical system user would be allowed to log in. Government agencies would also be required to introduce a "zero trust" policy with respect to software vendors. Vendors would be allowed access to government IT systems only when absolutely necessary and all contractors would be required to comply with certain conditions before any software they supplied would be accepted. Any violators of the required standards could be banned from government business.[559]

However, huge and damaging hacking attacks did not end with Colonial Pipeline. At the beginning of July 2021, there was a massive and devastating ransomware attack

555. *Id.*
556. Joe Tidy, "Colonial Pipeline, US Recovers Most of the Ransom, Justice Department Says," "A Powerful Message to Hacker Gangs," *BBC News*, online, June 8, 2021.
557. David E. Sanger, Nicole Perlroth and Julian E. Barnes, "Biden Plans an Order to Strengthen Cyberdefenses: Will It Be Enough," *The New York Times*, online, May 9, 2021, accessed May 11, 2021.
558. *Id.*
559. *Id.*

that assaulted hundreds of American businesses and many other businesses around the world, affecting companies in about seventeen countries.[560]

L RUSSIAN-BASED HACKING

The suspicion of US law enforcement authorities was that the Colonial Pipeline attack originated in Russia or in the former Soviet states.

However, huge and damaging hacking attacks did not end with Colonial Pipeline. At the beginning of July 2021, there was a massive and devastating ransomware attack that assaulted hundreds of American businesses and many other businesses around the world, affecting companies in about seventeen countries.[561]

The FBI believes that this more recent attack on US companies has been perpetrated by the Russian hacking group known as REvil. Another clue as to the origin of the attack is that the computer code of the attack is structured to exclude Russian language using computer systems.[562] The attack involved inserting malicious code into software used by many companies.

It has been speculated that the hackers were demanding $70 million to restore service to the companies they attacked. President Biden directed the US security services to do a thorough analysis of the attack to determine who was responsible and how it was done. In a meeting in Geneva shortly before this attack, Biden had warned Putin not to permit attacks on US digital sites to originate from Russia. But it is unclear whether this demand will make any difference to the number or intensity of hacking attacks.

However, the countries that are alleged to sponsor or permit hacking attacks from within their borders should not confidently assume that the hacking abilities within their country are superior to those that can be deployed by the US or its allies.

It seems unlikely that the important infrastructure systems of countries like Russia, China or North Korea are invulnerable to hacking attacks. There seems little doubt that significant damage can be done to their systems by other countries through the use of the Internet.

It is also the case that countries alleged to be sponsoring hacking attacks have financial and physical resources that can be vulnerable to seizure as retribution for damaging hacking attacks on other countries. For example, it has been reported that Mr. Putin has made efforts to compile a significant fortune with financial institutions outside of Russia.[563]

It is possible that President Biden's warning to Putin did produce a positive response. One of the most notorious hacking groups, the allegedly Russian REvil (also

560. Marc Bennetts and Alistair Dauber, "Joe Biden Takes Aim at Russia over Crippling Cyberattack," *The Times,* online, January 5, 2021.
561. Marc Bennetts and Alistair Dauber, "Joe Biden Takes Aim at Russia over Crippling Cyberattack," *The Times,* online, January 5, 2021.
562. Ken Dilanian, "Code in Huge Ransomware Attack Written to Avoid Computers That Use Russian, Says a New Report," *NBC News,* online, July 7, 2021.
563. Adam Taylor, "Is Vladimir Putin Hiding a $200 Billion Fortune? And If So, Does It Matter?," *The Washington Post,* online, February 20, 2015.

called, "Sodinokibi"), suddenly disappeared from the Internet after President Biden's warning. REvil's blog and its payment website stopped being available on July 13, 2021.[564]

Of course, there are several possible reasons why this occurred. REvil may have decided that, given all the scrutiny they were subject to, it might be better for them to lie low for a while. It is also possible that the US or other countries with computer expertise may have successfully hacked their servers and taken them off-line. It is also possible that Russian authorities may have been ordered to take action against them. Time will tell whether they will reappear and, if they do, in what form.

M PROPOSED CRIMINALIZING OF RANSOM PAYMENTS

One somewhat radical solution to solving the problem of ransomware attacks is that laws should be passed making the payment of ransom a criminal offense.[565] The former head of the UK's Cyber Security Center, Ciaran Martin, believes that cybercrime would stop being a way for global Internet criminals to make money if payments to them were banned.

One of the problems for providing effective security against cyberattacks is that a cyberattack on a particular organization creates few, if any, legal obligations on the target. Most are not required to report or publicize the attack, and if payment is made in cybercurrency, it may be completely untraceable. This leaves government institutions which are supposed to provide security against cyberattacks with very little information about how to counter them or enforce punishment on the perpetrators.[566]

Martin suggested that regulations similar to those forbidding ransom payments to terrorists should be considered. He says that it makes no more sense to pay Russian cybercriminals than it does to pay Islamic terrorists. Both types of payments are damaging to society. They encourage the continuation of attacks that may raise money to fund other kinds of criminality and terrorism.

As of May 2021, the estimated cost of ransomware attacks worldwide was about $120 billion annually. The focus of the attacks has become ever more sensitive, aiming increasingly at educational institutions, healthcare facilities and vital infrastructure. Some experts express the view that a ban on payments may be the quickest way to reduce or even solve the problem or at least to stunt the growth of ransomware attacks.[567]

There is, of course, a downside in that those that are attacked may lose valuable data because of their failure to pay.

Another problem is that many hackers, rather than threatening to destroy data, threaten to release highly sensitive or deeply embarrassing data about institutions and individuals onto the Internet. The pain, embarrassment, and cost of having such data be made available publicly is a serious problem and key motivation to make payments

564. "REvil Ransomware Websites Disappear from the Internet," *BBC News*, online, July 14, 2021.
565. Hamilton and Bridge, *supra*.
566. *Id.*
567. *Id.*

to hackers.[568] For example, a chain of clinics that provided cosmetic surgery and weight loss therapy to some well-known public figures was recently threatened with public disclosure of a database of client photographs. The disclosure did not happen, but the threat illustrates the delicacy of the problem.[569] Sensitive ways to deal with this type of thing will need to be found.

Martin also urges insurers that provide promises for payment to compensate clients against ran somewhere attacks to require their clients to put better cyber protection in place. This could be incentivized by tying the level of premiums to the effectiveness of the cybersecurity in place. This would make it more attractive for institutions to improve their cybersecurity.[570]

N US INTERNATIONAL CYBERCRIME PREVENTION ACT

The growth of cybercrime during the pandemic in general, and the devastating Colonial Pipeline cyberattack in 2021, caused the US Congress to reconsider the International Cybercrime Prevention Act (ICPA) which had previously failed to pass in 2018.

The bill aimed at giving law enforcement additional powers to seize computing devices of cybercriminals and created additional criminal violations for which attackers could be prosecuted for disrupting critical infrastructure.

After Colonial Pipeline, additional motivation for support of the bill was provided by an attack on the world's largest provider of meat, JBS. These attacks occurred fairly close together, and it is thought to be because of the fact that COVID has caused governments and businesses to increasingly use the Internet to do business. This gives cybercriminals an opportunity to test and find more vulnerabilities in the security systems of important organizations. During 2020/2021, these kinds of attacks increased by almost 70%.

One provision of the ICPA bill would make any violation of the Computer Fraud and Abuse Act (CFAA) an offense within the Racketeer Influenced and Corrupt Organization (RICO) Act.

The US had previously brought some prosecutions of cybercriminals under RICO. For example, the Justice Department prosecuted RICO charges relating to the Eastern European defendants providing hosting services for the distribution of malware.[571]

Section 5 of the Act creates a specific violation for serious damage to infrastructure of computer systems or for intentionally damaging computers controlling important infrastructure such as election systems, hospitals, power plants and dams.

Section 6 of the bill makes it an offense to use or provide access to a computer infiltrated by criminals within a botnet operated for purposes of cybercrime.

568. *Id.*
569. *Id.*
570. *Id.*
571. Department of Justice, "Four Individuals Plead Guilty to RICO Conspiracy Involving 'Bulletproof Hosting' for Cypercriminals," online, May 7, 2021, https://www.justice.gov/opa/pr/four-individuals-plead-guilty-rico-conspiracy-involving-bulletproof-hosting-cybercriminals.

Section 3 of the IPCA allows the law enforcement authorities to confiscate property used to break data privacy laws.

Section 4 allows provision of injunctive relief against botnets used in cybercriminal activities.[572]

O DEEPFAKES

There now has arisen an exceedingly disturbing form of identity theft known as "deepfakes." This is a process of using AI tools to create fake representations of people, sometimes well-known celebrities, or political figures, in the form of videos, voice recordings or correspondence. This involves the theft of more than personal information about someone. It involves theft of their images, their voices, and key aspects of their personalities. Indeed, as was pointed out in a Comment in *The Times*, this constitutes theft of the very things that "make us human."[573]

The author of the Comment argues that "Now tech can replicate anyone's looks and voice, no person or business is safe from violation."

As an example of how extreme these violations can be, one reads that "deepfakers" have gone so far as to create a porn film using the image of the *Wonder Woman* film star, Gail Gadot. It is often argued that some kinds of pornography can be harmful, but this kind of fraud takes abuse and identity theft to a new level.[574]

Since 2017, deep faking has been appearing on Reddit. Suddenly, all kinds of deepfakes were appearing on that website.

Reddit banished them, but this activity has continued to grow, and many deepfake websites can now be accessed through Google searches. They include fake videos using many celebrities and other public figures. Deepfake apps and tutorials are available.[575]

Deep faking can also be used as a tool of political intimidation. For example, an Indian journalist who has been critical of India's ruling party was attacked by a vicious online hatred campaign in 2018 that included a deepfake porn video of her. The video went viral, and she was bombarded with online threats of rape and death. Since this happened, the journalist said "I have not been the same person."[576]

The writer and commentator Jordan Peterson was ridiculed using deepfakes from a website entitled NotJordanPeterson.com. Peterson took legal action against the site and wrote:

---

572. Stevanovic Igor, "Reintroduced International Cybercrime Prevention Act Would Create New Cybercrime Violations, Increase Forfeiture and Injunctive Relief," *IPWatchdog*, online, June 22, 2021.
573. Nina Schick, Comment, "Deepfakes Threaten What Makes Us Human," *The Times*, online, Thursday, August 6, 2020, retrieved August 7, 2020.
574. *Id.*
575. *Id.*
576. *Id.*

> Wake up. The sanctity of your voice, and your image, is at serious risk. It's hard to imagine a more serious challenge to the sense of shared, reliable reality that keeps us live together relative peace.[577]

In another incident, a British company lost £250,000 when criminals used a deepfake voice imitation of the company's CEO to telephone an employee and order transfer of that money to an account that disappeared before the fraud was realized.[578]

From these incidents, and others, specific controls and legal restrictions need to be put in place to limit the use and abuse of these digital tools.

Estonia's Solution

Estonia is one country that has done so to counter deepfakes, which were believed to be from Russian sources, to create political disinformation in Estonia. Estonia mobilized digital resources to counter these attacks and increased public awareness of what was going on.

The steps have given Estonia a level of protection above than most other countries.[579]

The bottom line is that the deepfake problem arose so quickly and has become so serious that specific regulatory attention needs to be focused on it.

Criminal Public Relations

Things have reached a point where the cybercriminals have become extremely bold, regarding themselves as entrepreneurial heroes to be admired. In August 2020 an article appeared in *The Times* that said:

> Cyberhackers are running sophisticated public relations operations with their own news websites, press releases, Twitter accounts and public updates.[580]

It appears that several hacking gangs have formed PR departments. They have set up new sites where they publicize their ransomware attacks.

They have adopted brand names, and their strategy seems to be to make those brands as well known as possible to cause target companies to believe they cannot be stopped and there was no point in trying to defeat them.

Unfortunately, their financial success has been increasing. In the last two years, the average ransom payment they have been able to extract from target companies has increased from about $7,000 to about $180,000.[581]

---

577. *Id.*
578. *Id.*
579. *Id.* Nina Schick in the of a book on the subject: *Deep Fakes and the Infocalypse: What You Urgently Need to Know.*
580. "Hackers Get into the PR Business," *The Times*, online, August 15, 2020, retrieved August 15, 2020.
581. *Id.*

These gangs apparently love the attention. One calls itself "Evil Corp" and is led by a man who drives a Lamborghini with a license plate that says "thief" in Russian. Another, called "Maze Corp." thought to have caused attacks on Xerox, LG, and Canon, issued publicity that said its "clients" (targets) should get in touch within three days if they were attacked by Maze Corp.; otherwise, they would risk significant "reputational damage."[582]

One criminal group "REvil" actually sponsors competition for hackers offering prizes of $15,000 and an opportunity to work for "REvil." It is not reported who won.[583]

P REPORTING AND PROTECTING AGAINST DATA BREACHES

A key factor in preventing and punishing cybercrime is that the regulators and law enforcement bodies must have as much information as possible about cybercrime, how it is being conducted and how victims are being targeted.

As shown by press reports, Internet crime victims that failed to report their attacks or to take appropriate steps to prevent damaging data breaches can also be charged with violations of law and/or regulations that can result in large fines and other possible penalties.

One dramatic example of this is a report that the French Data Protection Authority fined Uber €400,000, US authorities fined them $148 million, the Dutch fined them €600,000, and the British fined them £385,000 because Uber failed to timely report a large data breach. The breach occurred in 2016 and exposed data of about 57 million Uber customers around the world. Apparently, the fines were so high because Uber delayed reporting the breach for over a year hoping to avoid embarrassment, fines, and lawsuits. Uber was also accused of failing to have in place basic security measures that could have prevented the breach.[584]

It is important that companies engaged in business on the Internet remember that, as demonstrated by the Uber fines discussed above, most legal jurisdictions will have in place laws and regulations that require the reporting of data breaches exposing personal data and penalties for failing to report or prevent data breaches.

These penalties will differ from jurisdiction to jurisdiction, but one example is the EU General Data Protection Regulation (GDPR).[585] The GDPR requires that any organization must report certain data breaches that reveal personal information held by that organization. The GDPR requires that the breach must be reported to relevant regulatory authorities without undue delay, usually within seventy-two hours if that is feasible.[586]

582. *Id.*
583. *Id.*
584. "France Hands Uber €400,000 Fine over Huge Data Breach," https://www.thelocal.fr/20181220/france-hands-uber-400000-fine-over-huge-data-breach#: ~ :text = France's%20data%20protection%20agency%20said,million%20clients%20and%20drivers%20worldwide.
585. Regulation (EU) 2016/679.
586. EU GDPR, Article 34.1.

Under the GDPR, the details of the penalties are left to the individual Member States, but they must be "effective, proportionate, and dissuasive."[587]

Uber is by no means the only commercial organization fined for data breaches. For example, the UK has imposed a number of large fines because of data breaches.

In July 2019, British Airways was fined £183,000 because of a data breach that affected five hundred thousand customers. The regulator found that that the security standards of British Airways were not sufficiently robust.

In the same month, Marriott Homes was fined £99,000 because of a breach that affected over three hundred million customer records. The regulator found that Marriott should have done more to secure its records.

In October 2018, the UK fined Facebook £500,000 (the maximum fine that the UK regulator is permitted to impose for breaches), for incorrectly sharing the data of 87 million customers with a political consultant organization. The regulator found that Facebook had failed to adequately protect the data of its customers.

In September 2018, a company called Equifax was fined £500,000 for failing to make certain that its parent company was adequately protecting the data of Equifax's UK customers. It should be noted that the American FTC fined Equifax's parent company $581 million for the breach which involved the personal data of over 140 million people.

In April 2019, the UK regulator fined a club called Bounty £500,000. Bounty provided personal data of over thirty million people to several credit rating agencies, without permission of the people whose data it was.

These are not the only companies that have been punished for failing to protect against data breaches and/or failing to report them as required by law or regulation.

Others include Cathay Pacific, Dixon's Carphone, Yahoo, Capital One, Tesco Bank, Target, Anthem, Google, 1&1 Telecom, University of Texas MD Anderson Cancer Center, Fresenius Medical Care North America, Cottage Health, Touchstone Medical Imaging, University of Rochester Medical Center, Jackson Health Systems, DSG Retail Limited. Many of these have been fined and/or penalized by multiple regulators in several jurisdictions.

The total of fines and penalties imposed so far is estimated to more than $1.5 billion.[588]

The above is just a selection of examples. There have been many other data breach penalties around the world and that is likely to continue for the foreseeable future.

It can be seen from the selection above that any company or organization that has an electronic database of sensitive personal information about people can find itself the target of a serious data hack.

587. EU GDPR, Article 84.1.
588. CSO from IDG, "The Biggest Data Breach Fines, Penalties and Settlements So Far," *csoonline.com*, August 14, 2020, retrieved August 25, 2020.

Data Needs Protection

It does not matter what industry, business, or institution one is talking about. Criminal hackers consider any large collection of personal data valuable, not least because those that own it or collected it need it to run their operations or to live their lives. Consequently, someone who takes it from them and threatens to make it inaccessible can profit from ransom, blackmail, or from commercial, political, or military advantage.

It is vital that business organizations that hold personal data of people put adequate measures in place to protect that data from improper exposure. Failure to do so can be costly and perhaps devastatingly so. If more than $1.5 billion in penalties seems like a lot, there is a little doubt that the total will keep getting larger.

Q POLITICAL PROPAGANDA

Data Analytica

Since Britton's Brexit referendum in 2015, and the US presidential election of 2016, serious concern has risen about the ethics and legality of using Internet tools to gather information from the social media posts of individuals and use that information to construct campaigns to change the behavior of the individuals whose data has been mined for the purpose of achieving certain political results.

Starting in March 2018, Carole Cadwalladr and Emma Graham-Harrison began publishing a series of articles that accused Cambridge Analytica of taking data from the profiles of fifty million Facebook users and using that information to manipulate Brexit referendum voters in the UK and voters in the US presidential election for the benefit of the Leave campaign and Donald Trump's election team.[589] The articles said:

> The Data Analytics firm that worked with Donald Trump's election team and the winning Brexit campaign harvested millions of Facebook profiles of voters, in one of the tech giant's biggest ever data breaches, and used them to build a powerful software program to predict and influence choices at the ballot box.[590]

The 2019 Netflix documentary entitled, "The Great Hack," agreed with *The Guardian* stories that Cambridge Analytica was hired by both the "Leave" campaign during the Brexit referendum and Donald Trump during the 2016 election to gather data from social media sources, and particularly from Facebook, to create profiles of citizens of the UK and the US to enable the Leave and Trump campaigns to change how undecided people would vote.

---

589. Carole Cadwalladr and Emma Graham-Harrison, "Revealed: 50 Million Facebook Profiles Harvested for Cambridge Analytica in Major Data Breach," *The Guardian*, online, March 17, 2018, retrieved September 27, 2020.
590. *Id.*

After these and other revelations about this use of social media data, the situation changed from being embarrassing stories about the activities of Cambridge Analytica to becoming regarded as cyber-criminality.

In January 2019, the parent company of Cambridge Analytica (SCL Elections) pled guilty to violating the Data Protection Act because it had failed to provide an American citizen, named David Carroll (a Professor at the New School of Social Research in New York City), with copies of the data it held on him. They also refused to comply with an enforcement notice issued by a UK Court and were fined £15,000.

Cambridge Analytica has since gone out of business and been liquidated amidst allegations that they liquidated to avoid having to produce more information about their activities.

Brazil

In Brazil, there was apparently an attempt by President Jair Bolsonaro to interfere with the electoral process by issuing regulations in September 2021 preventing social networks from removing posts that they consider to be disinformation about the future presidential election. However, almost immediately following the introduction of those rules, the Senate and Supreme Court of Brazil canceled those rules because Bolsonaro had been using social media to make the claim that he would only lose the election if it were illegally rigged. He appears to have been taking a page from Donald Trump's book on political manipulation.[591]

Mauricio Santoro, Professor of International Relations at the State University of Rio de Janeiro, was quoted as saying:

> It's a very positive sign that the Brazilian political class reacted … The Brazilian leadership is finally understanding how important the Internet is to political life in Brazil.[592]

China

China's cracking down on political speech in Hong Kong that it judges to be in opposition to government policy has been subject to a significant amount of criticism from around the world.

In September 2021, there was an instance where the people that organized the annual Hong Kong commemoration of the 1989 suppression of protest in Tiananmen Square were ordered to take down the content of their commemorative website and the commemorative comments on social media platforms. In making this order, the government was relying on a security law issued last year that allows the government

591. Jack Nicas, "Bolsonaro's Ban on Removing Social Media Posts Is Overturned in Brazil," *The New York Times*, online, September 15, 2021.
592. *Id.*

to ban any Internet content that the government, "on reasonable grounds," considers to be a security threat.[593]

US

In the US, the Republican administrations of both Texas and Florida have attempted to introduce laws like that promoted by President Bolsonaro in Brazil.

Texas

In September 2021, the Governor of Texas signed a bill that forbid social media platforms from removing posts because of the political views expressed in the posts.[594]

Under this bill, social media sites "cannot remove, play down or otherwise moderate content because of a user's political perspective or ban the user entirely. The companies will also need to publish regular reports showing how often they receive complaints about content and how often they took posts down."[595]

Both the State Attorney General and individual citizens will be allowed to sue social media companies that allegedly breach these rules.

The law will apply to any social media providers with more than fifty million users active monthly and to anyone who lives in Texas, conducts business there or receives or distributes social media posts in Texas.

Similar bills have been proposed in many US states that have Republican administrations claiming that they wish to prevent "censorship." They justify their attempts to control social media firms in this way by claiming that social media platforms have become a kind of utility or "common carrier" similar to a telephone company.

Florida

As another example, Florida introduced a law making it unlawful for social media platforms to ban some political candidates from their sites.

However, social media companies brought suit in opposition to this law, and the court blocked enforcement of the law until legal challenges to the law could be decided.[596]

US District Judge Robert Hinkle of the US District Court for the Northern District of Florida said:

> This order preliminarily joins enforcement of the parts of the legislation that are preempted or violate the First Amendment.[597]

593. Kenji Kwase, "Hong Kong Police Invoke Security Law to Censor Online Posts," *Nikkei Asia*, online, September 17, 2021.
594. David McCabe, "Texas Forbids Political 'Censorship' by Social Media Companies," *The New York Times*, online, September 9, 2021.
595. *Id.*
596. David McCabe, December 9, 2021.
597. Kanishka Singh, "Federal Judge Rules Florida Social Media Law Likely Violates Free Speech," *Reuters*, online, July 1, 2021.

R FOREIGN INTERFERENCE IN ELECTIONS

Using the Internet to interfere with foreign elections has become a significant problem in recent years, and this issue has been raised in many countries, including the recent presidential election of the US.

As a result, several countries have introduced laws to prevent and punish such interference. Because these laws may affect the desire of any Internet user who wishes to use the World Wide Web to express their political views and to persuade others (whether in their own country or in other nations) of the correctness of their political views, it is important to examine the legal status of this problem in the steps that have been taken to correct what is regarded in proper use of the Internet to influence or interfere with elections.

United States

One of the most highly publicized incidents of alleged electoral interference has been highlighted by the conclusion of US intelligence that Russia attempted to influence the US presidential election in favor of Donald Trump during the 2016 presidential election.

After the election, the US Director of the National Counterintelligence and Security Center, William Evanina, issued a report on foreign threats to US elections in which he said:

> Foreign intelligence entities likely view US elections as an opportunity to undermine confidence in our democratic institutions and processes, sow division in our society, weaken our alliances and promote their political, economic or ideological agendas. These entities operate in the seams of our democratic system to advance their interest, using the tools of traditional espionage, in combination with cyber operations to influence campaigns.

The US is not the only country that fears this kind of interference and may not be the only country which has suffered from electoral interference. As a result, several countries have taken steps to prevent and punish this kind of interference.

International Response

An accepted international legal basis for the countermeasures is that such interference can constitute a violation of a country's sovereignty. Several countries (but not the UK) have accepted the principle that respecting a nation's sovereignty is a fundamental element of international law.[598]

598. Michael Schmitt, ed., *Tallin Manual 2.0: On the International Law Applicable to Cyber Operations*, published by the United States Naval War College (Newport, Rhode Island, USA, 2017).

The countries and international organizations that accept that the respect for sovereignty is fundamental to international law are: Austria, the Czech Republic, France, Germany, the Netherlands, Switzerland and NATO.[599]

An accepted definition of what constitutes a nation sovereignty was set out in the 1928 Island of Palms arbitration by Max Huber:[600]

> Sovereignty in the relations between States signifies independence. Independence regarding a portion of the globe is the right to exercise therein, to the exclusion of any other State, the functions of a State.

Singapore

On September 13, 2021, the government of Singapore proposed a parliamentary bill to prevent foreign cyber interference in Singapore politics. The bill is called the Foreign Interference (Countermeasures) Bill. It is targeted at online content that "can cause immediate and significant harm in Singapore."

Social media providers will be required to comply with the law, and ISPs could be required to block harmful political content. The bill also would permit the blocking of any computer downloads that aid spreading harmful content.

This bill follows an anti-fake news law introduced in Singapore during 2019.[601]

S ZERO CLICK SPYWARE

One of the most sinister recent developments in online crime, illicit spying and violation of privacy generally has been the development of "Zero Click" spyware that allows hackers access to iPhones and iPads without the owners having to open or click on a file or a link.

This seems to be specific to the iOS operating system. When this became widely reported in September 2021, Apple took urgent steps to correct this flaw in a system.

In mid-September 2021, Apple announced that it had issued security updates to defend against what is described as a malicious pdf file.

This innovative spyware was apparently first recognized at the University of Toronto's citizen lab. They said that this spyware affected all Apple devices, including iPhones, Macs and Apple watches.

Toronto also claimed that this spyware was first used on Arab activists' iPhones and that they suspected that an Israeli firm, the NSO Group, may have created the spyware.

599. Michael Schmitt, "Talk!," *European Journal of International Law, EIJL* (October 16, 2020).
600. *Id.*
601. Chen Lin, "Singapore Submits Bill to Fight 'Foreign Interference'," *Reuters*, online, September 13, 2021.

NSO refused to either confirm or deny its role in creating the spyware. It stated that it would "continue to provide intelligence and law-enforcement agencies … with technologies to fight terror in crime."[602]

Experts pointed out that the use of the spyware seems to be limited to specific high-value targets, so it may not be a worry to the general population of Apple users. Nevertheless, Apple announced that it had issued defensive software patches in iOS 14.8 and iPad OS 14.8 software.[603]

The zero click spyware exploited a gap in Apple's iMessage, which was previously understood to be one of the safest messaging apps. This was embarrassing for Apple not only because Apple likes to be known as having one of the most secure operating systems but also because it came to public attention during the time of the year when Apple likes to announce new and/or improved products (September). However, Apple did appear to respond quickly with solutions when it became aware of this problem and, as stated above, risk to the average Apple user is thought to be low.[604]

T DEATH FROM HACKING

One of the more frightening aspects of hacking and cybercrime is the fact that many devices and systems critical to healthcare are accessible through the Internet.

In one sense that makes them easier to operate and to gather information from them about how they are working, and how they are contributing to patient care. But on the other hand, this makes them vulnerable to interference from hackers and cybercriminals.

Hospital records, hospital networks, MRI machines and drug infusion pumps are all digitally accessible now. This puts them in danger of being hacked.[605]

One of the most sinister possibilities for hackers is the fact that medically implanted devices could be vulnerable to interference. Among the implantable devices that have been found to be vulnerable are insulin pumps and pacemakers.[606]

There has been a fictional story about this in the popular television series, *Homeland*, where Damien Lewis' character gives terrorists information about the American Vice President's pacemaker, which the terrorists use to hack the pacemaker and kill him.[607]

602. Joe Tidy, A BBC News Reporter, notes that NSO has been subject to accusations that its hacking has affected innocent people. Joe Tidy, "Analysis," *BBC News*, online, September 14, 2021.
603. "Apple Rushes to Block 'Zero Click' iPhone Spyware," *BBC News*, online, September 14, 2021.
604. Tidy, *supra*, September 14, 2021.
605. Joe McKinley, "5 Medical Devices You Didn't Know Could Be Hacked," https://www.thehealthy.com/healthcare/hacked-medical-devices/.
606. Jo Best, "Could Implanted Medical Devices Be Hacked?," *British Medical Journal* (January 14, 2020), https://www.bmj.com/content/368/bmj.m102.full.
607. McKinley, *supra*.

This threat had a real-life parallel in 2013, when the former US Vice President, Dick Cheney, had the wireless connectivity of his pacemaker disconnected so it could not be hacked and put Cheney's life at risk.[608]

In 2019, the US Food and Drug Administration found that some kinds of defibrillations had vulnerability that might allow unauthorized persons to manipulate them remotely.[609]

Unfortunately, this threat is becoming ever more real. In September 2020, it was reported that prosecutors in Dusseldorf, Germany, launched a manslaughter investigation after a woman died in a hospital there after her emergency treatment was delayed for more than an hour.

It is thought that her death may have been caused by hackers shutting down the hospital's IT systems. Dusseldorf University Hospital was locked out of its computer systems, and a blackmail message was received, giving digital directions for contacting the hackers.

The police informed the hackers that they had shut down the hospital systems putting patients in danger.

After that, the attack was abandoned, and systems were restored.[610]

U QUANTUM COMPUTING

Another looming challenge to cybersecurity is the dramatic progress that is being made to computer equipment in the form of "quantum computers."

Computers today, or "classical" computers as they are coming to be known, operate digitally in segments of information that are called "bits." A bit can express one of two possible outcomes, 1 or 0. These values represent states that are on or off. All classical computer programs and operations are created from combinations of those two possible positions. Every computing operation we do now is made up of millions of combinations of on or off (1 or 0).

The necessity to operate computers by instructing them with various combinations of those two numbers, some quite long, places limitations on the speed with which computer operations can be completed. Of course, over the past few decades, the computer chips that perform those operations have become increasingly faster, so computer speed is now much greater than it was decades ago.

Qubits

However, computer scientists are now working on developing a computer instruction system that operates not in "bits" but in "qubits."

608. Best, *supra*.
609. *Id.*
610. David Crossland, "Woman Dies after Hackers Hit A&E," *Times*, online, September 19, 2020, retrieved September 19, 2020.

This qubit computing system is based on the field of physics known as quantum mechanics. This field of physics was created to try to understand the natural world better. Nature does not operate by choosing between only two possible known outcomes. Nature is more unpredictable. A "qubit," short for "quantum bit," permits examination of many more possible outcomes than just two. Employing this device in computing could make computing operations exponentially faster.[611]

Until late in 2019, it was thought that quantum computing was still a long way away.

However, in October 2019, everything changed. In the journal *Nature*, Google announced that a quantum computing system, called Sycamore, developed by Google had achieved "quantum supremacy," meaning that it could complete calculations much faster than the fastest "supercomputers" existing up until then. Sycamore completed a calculation that would take hundred thousand classical computers ten thousand years to complete in less than four minutes. The truly amazing thing is that Sycamore represents quantum computing at its most primitive. It is expected that soon quantum computers will be much more powerful.

Sycamore is a 53-qubit system, but it is believed that future quantum computing systems could operate on billion qubit systems.[612]

In 2021, China claimed to have developed a quantum computer one million times more powerful than Google's.

What does this mean for cybercrime? Far too much!

If criminals are currently able to use all the tools and the skills that enable them to crack the security systems that individuals and even major companies have in place to protect their information, how much more powerful would criminal hacking gangs be if they had quantum computing at their disposal?

There is no reason not to believe that it would improve their ability to crack protective codes and security systems to an exponential degree. That is a frightening prospect and causes one to wonder whether it will be possible to create any truly safe passwords and security systems in the future when quantum computing becomes more generally available.

Protection Against Quantum

Fortunately, scientists are already working to solve this potential problem. Two technological solutions are currently being worked on to provide greater security in the face of potential quantum intrusion.

The first is Quantum Key Distribution. This is a method of agreeing to encryption keys between distant parties to protect security keys from being observed or tampered with.

The second anti-quantum attack protection method is Quantum Random Number Generation. This produces numbers of random numbers at such high speeds that

611. Amit Katwala, "Quantum Computing and Quantum Supremacy, Explained," *Wired*, online, March 5, 2020, retrieved September 3, 2020.
612. Scott Aaronson, "Why Google's Quantum Supremacy Milestone Matters," *The New York Times*, online, October 30, 2019, retrieved September 3, 2020.

the numbers can be unpredictable and can form an important part of hacking-resistant security systems.[613]

One can only hope that the development of security technologies can match the pace of the development of quantum computing and the application of this powerful new technology by criminal hacking groups.

Should Quantum Be Regulated?

This discussion begs the question of whether possession or access to such a powerful computing tool should be legally restricted and/or regulated in some way? That is a difficult question.

Of course, societies have traditionally used their legal powers to restrict the ownership, possession and use of technological advances that are deemed to be particularly dangerous. Such concerns have resulted in restrictions on firearms, explosives, nuclear technology, automobiles, and other technological advances that, although their existence is considered to have benefits, they also present different types and degrees of danger to the public.

V ONLINE ABUSE

It is not news that the Internet, and particularly the social media sites, is full of abusive, insulting and sometimes threatening posts.

For Internet service companies and law enforcement agencies, it is not easy to decide what to do about them.

The first issue has to do with the interstate and international aspects of the Internet. Social media sites operate in a World Wide Web. Who has jurisdiction to control and police them? The second issue has to do with when do these posts cross the line from being offensive to becoming criminal activity?

The type of Internet posts that need reaction can be divided into two basic categories.

The first is those Internet posts that constitute illegal hate activity.

The second constitutes posts which threaten death, destruction, or other physical harm.

The first category of activity will depend on what constitutes illegal speech in any particular jurisdiction. This varies from nation to nation. Sometimes it has to do with insulting or demeaning those of a particular racial or ethnic background. Other times it has to do with insulting or demeaning religious beliefs. It might constitute insulting, demeaning or challenging Government activity. There is no universal standard for controlling offensive Internet posts.

A significant problem in many jurisdictions is that there are often constitutional protections for freedom of speech which excuse a wide range of speech, including

613. UK Government, White Paper, "Quantum Security Technologies," March 24, 2020, https://www.ncsc.gov.uk/whitepaper/quantum-security-technologies, online, retrieved September 7, 2020.

Internet posts, which certain individuals or societies might find offensive. There is a consideration in those jurisdictions of whether a post has crossed the line beyond the protections afforded by freedom of speech regulations.

This all makes the area of what constitutes online abuse and how to deal with it very complicated indeed. The best one can do in this section is to give an outline of when the line of acceptability might be crossed and then refer to the jurisdictional sources that may be able to give a more detailed description of how particular posts will be regarded in various jurisdictions.

W THREATS OF VIOLENCE

With threats of violence, it is true that the majority of these do not lead to actual physical harm.

However, that is not always the case. Sometimes people who threaten physical violence act on it. There have been several cases where people who threatened terrorist activity later went on to carry it out by planting bombs or engaging in personal attacks injuring or killing those they considered to be enemies of their ideology.

The standard for judging threatening posts like these seems to be whether a "reasonable person" would consider that a threat was serious enough that it may be expected to lead to criminal acts.[614]

Law enforcement authorities are in a difficult position of having to judge which threats have crossed the line into criminal behavior. This is often a tricky proposition because several countries, such as the US, have freedom of speech protections written into their constitutions. So, it is generally considered that broad threats, such as "let us put Donald Trump back in power," or "let us arrest all Democrats," are considered too general to justify prosecution.[615]

US Prosecution Standard

In the US, it is uncommon for someone to be criminally prosecuted based on things they have said, written or otherwise expressed as a type of speech. However, there have been a couple of prosecutions that are worth discussing.

First, a California man who wrote on a blog about cutting off the heads of employees of the FBI did face criminal prosecution based on those expressions. He claimed that his blog was satire and therefore protected speech. He went to trial but was ultimately not convicted. His defense made the arguments that he never made any preparations to follow through with such action and that he had no plans to do so. Neither he nor anyone acting on his behalf had purchased any weapons or took any

614. Shira Ovide, "When Is Online Nastiness Illegal?," *The New York Times*, online, April 23, 2021, accessed, April 26, 2021.
615. *Id.*

actions which could reasonably be thought to be following through to carry those thoughts.[616]

The government of the US usually sets a high standard before deciding to prosecute someone for things they have said or written that might constitute threats or would otherwise upset people who are the targets of those things.

Generally, only specific threats that would cause reasonable people to believe that the maker intended to follow through with harming the persons targeted will lead to prosecution. It is believed that speech that does not rise to this level should be controlled by social media companies that allow people to express themselves on their systems.[617]

UK Law

In the UK, the law is similar to that of the US.

There is the Offenses Against a Person Act of 1861, which makes it a criminal offense to make threats against a person to kill them, intending to put them in fear that it will be carried out.[618]

EU Law

Although it is the case that there are no universal protection standards against criminal behavior on the Internet. Protecting people and persons against threats and violence is generally considered the province of the laws of the twenty-seven Member States.

However, the EU is making efforts to create regulations to protect Internet users.[619]

In the EU, there is an effort to introduce specific legislation to protect women against violence, and threats of violence. On November 30, the S&D Group of the European Parliament published a call for legislative action at the EU level to protect women from harassment and threats of violence on the Internet.[620]

X GROWING INTERNATIONAL COOPERATION

One positive development is that the international growth of cybercrime is beginning to inspire parallel growth in international cooperation against cybercrime.

At their meeting in England in June 2021, the G7 countries agreed to increase international cooperation against cybercrime. Ursula van de Leyen, the President of the European Commission, said:

---

616. *Id.*
617. *Id.*
618. Offenses Against a Person Act of 1861, section 16.
619. Edward Lucas, "EU Is Becoming Policeman of the Internet," *The Times*, online, April 26, 2021, accessed April 27, 2021.
620. Socialists and Democrats, EU, online, November 30, 2021.

> We need a robust joint response to cybercrimes especially ransomware. We agreed to step up information sharing and to coordinate more closely on police investigations and diplomatic measures.[621]

The Budapest Convention and Other International Standards

The leading international treaty that provides standards for framing national standards for implementing national anti-cybercrime laws and regulations and guidelines for international cooperation is the Budapest Convention on Cybercrime, and the related Protocol on Xenophobia and Racism online.[622]

The Convention is a binding treaty and there are currently sixty-five signatories (including the US, the UK, France, Switzerland, Canada and most EU countries)[623] and eleven countries that consider themselves observers, such as Ireland, New Zealand, Sweden and Russia. It was signed in 2001, and became effective on July 1, 2004.

The Convention's main objective is to bring about a common legal policy aimed at the protection against cybercrime by encouraging the adoption of relevant laws and regulations and promoting international cooperation against cybercrime.

It was the first international treaty to focus on cybercrime, including crimes relating to the Internet and computer networks generally, dealing with such things as infringement of copyright, Internet-related fraud, child pornography and breaches of network security. It provides guidelines for the interception of offending information and the search of computer networks.[624]

The Convention is made of a Preamble and the following Articles:[625]

- Definitions.
- Illegal access.
- Illegal interception.
- Data interference.
- System interference.

621. United News of India, "G7 Agrees to Co-operate on Cybercrime Cases: EU," online, June 13, 2021.
622. Council of Europe, online portal, https://www.coe.int/en/web/cybercrime/the-budapest-convention.
623. As of this writing, parties: Albania, Andorra, Armenia, Argentina, Australia, Austria, Azerbaijan, Belgium, Bosnia and Herzegovina, Bulgaria, Cabo Verde, Canada, Chile, Columbia, Costa Rica, Croatia, Cyprus, the Czech Republic, Denmark, the Dominican Republic, Estonia, Finland, France, Georgia, Germany, Ghana, Greece, Hungary, Iceland, Israel, Italy, Japan, Latvia, Lichtenstein, Luxembourg, Malta, Mauritius, Moldova, Monaco, Montenegro, Morocco, the Netherlands, North Macedonia, Norway, Panama, Paraguay, Peru, the Philippines, Poland, Portugal, Romania, San Marino, Senegal, Serbia, Slovakia, Slovenia, Sweden, Switzerland, Spain, Sri Lanka, Tonga, Turkey, Ukraine, United Kingdom, and United States of America. The Observer countries are: Benin, Brazil, Burkina Faso, Guatemala, Ireland, Mexico, New Zealand, Nigeria, Niger, Russia (as a Member State of the Council of Europe, South Africa and Tunesia).
624. Council of Europe online portal, https://www.coe.int/en/web/conventions/full-list/-/conventions/treaty/185?module = treaty-detail&treatynum = 185.
625. Council of Europe online portal, https://rm.coe.int/1680081561.

- Misuse of devices.
- Computer-related forgery.
- Computer-related fraud.
- Offenses related to child pornography.
- Offenses related to infringements of copyright and related rights.
- Attempt and aiding and abetting.
- Corporate liability.
- Sanctions and measures.
- Scope of procedural provisions.
- Conditions and safeguards.
- Expedited preservation of stored computer data.
- Expedited preservation and partial disclosure of traffic data.
- Production orders.
- Search and seizure of stored computer data.
- Real-time collection of traffic data.
- Interception of content data.
- Jurisdiction.
- General principles relating to international cooperation.
- Extradition.
- General principles related to mutual assistance.
- Spontaneous information.
- Procedures pertaining to mutual assistance requests in the absence of applicable international agreements.
- Confidentiality and limitation on use.
- Expedited preservation of stored data.
- Expedited disclosure of preserved traffic data.
- Mutual assistance regarding accessing stored computer data.
- Transborder access to stored computer data with consent or where publicly available.
- Mutual assistance regarding the real-time collection of traffic data.
- Mutual assistance regarding the interception of content data.
- 24/7 Network.
- Signature and entry into force.
- Accession to the Convention.
- Territorial application.
- Effects of the Convention.
- Declarations.
- Federal clause.
- Reservations.
- Status and withdrawal of reservations.
- Amendments.
- Settlement of disputes.
- Consultations of the parties.
- Denunciation.

- Notification.

There is also an Additional Protocol to the Cybercrime Convention that deals with criminalization of racist and xenophobic acts online.[626] It contains sixteen Articles dealing with racist and xenophobic threats and insults.[627]

GLACY Project

The original GLACY project (Global Action on Cybercrime) was set up to assist countries around the world in implementing the Budapest Convention. It was hoped that GLACY would result in positive changes in the following areas:

- involvement of decision-makers;
- harmonizing legislation;
- training judges;
- improving law enforcement capacity;
- sharing information; and
- reviewing progress.

Its overall aim was to get states to cooperate on cybercrime using the Budapest Convention as a common guide. The project ran from November 1, 2013, until October 31, 2016.

GLACY + Project

In October 2016, the EU and the Council of Europe set up a new joint project to combat cybercrime around the world named the global action on cybercrime extended "(GLACY + Project)."

Its purpose was to continue and use the experience gained under the original GLACY project.

The principal participants in the project are: Bernin, Burkino Faso, Cabo Verde, Chile, Costa Rica, the Dominican Republic, Ghana, Mauritius, Morocco, Nigeria, Paraguay, the Philippines, Senegal, Sri Lanka and Tonga.

It was hoped that these countries would be "hubs" to educate other countries in their regions about the value of their experiences.

The objectives of the GLACY + project are formulated to improve the ability of countries around the world to have effective legislation against cybercrime, improve ways to use electronic evidence and improve international cooperation. These objectives were to be achieved by:

- promoting consistent legislation, policy, and strategy;

626. Additional Protocol 189: Additional Protocol to the Convention on Cybercrime, concerning the criminalization of acts of a racist and xenophobic nature committed through computer systems. This was adopted in 2003 and came into force in 2006, https://rm.coe.int/168008160f.
627. The link to the text of the Additional Protocol is, https://rm.coe.int/168008160f.

- strengthening police ability to investigate cybercrime, and to encourage cooperation between police forces and cybercrime offices around the world;
- smoothing and improving processes to prosecute cybercrime; and
- improving international judicial cooperation.

The activities of the GLACY + project have included the following:

(1) Holding workshops around the world, such as the one in Burkina Faso in September 2021.
(2) Holding courses in international cooperation for judges and prosecutors, such as the one in Costa Rica in August 2021.
(3) Holding training sessions improving cybercrime prosecution and the use of electronic evidence, such as the one held in Paraguay in September 2021 for thirty-four magistrates, judges, and judicial training schools.

The above are just a few examples of the kinds of activities arranged through GLANCY +.

Others have included anti-cybercrime activities in:

- Portuguese-speaking African countries;
- French-speaking African countries; and
- East Timor, Tonga, Belize, etc.;
- Plus various international meetings to promote the objectives of GLANCY +.

Some of these activities are conducted live; others are held online.

In connection with the project, the Council of Europe also maintains and offers several resources to draw upon such as: reports, webinars, information about connections between cybercrime and COVID-19, and information about cyberviolence. Cyberviolence is a phenomenon that has been getting more law enforcement attention. It is defined as:

> The use of computer systems to cause, facilitate, or threaten violence against individuals, that results in (or is likely to result in) physical, sexual, psychological or economic harm or suffering and may include the exploitation of the individual's.

Y CYBERSTALKING AND CYBERBULLYING

Using the Internet to harass and/or intimidate people has become a widespread problem, and, as a result, several legal jurisdictions have adopted laws and regulations criminalizing such behavior.[628]

Cyberbullying is legally defined in the following ways:

628. International Human Rights and Privacy Protection Association, http://ihprpa.org/bullying.php.

- "Actions that use information and communication technologies to support deliberate, repeated and hostile behavior by an individual or group, that is intended to harm another or others.
- "Use of communication technologies for the intention of harming another person.
- "Use of internet service and mobile technologies such as web pages and discussion groups as well as instant messaging of SMS text messaging with the intention of harming another person."[629]

Cyberstalking, on the other hand, is a repeated pattern of such things as:

- false accusations,
- monitoring,
- making threats,
- identity theft,
- damage to data or equipment,
- solicitation for sex, or
- Harassment.

US Legislation Against Cyberbullying and Cyberstalking

US federal law does not yet include any specific legislation expressly forbidding cyberbullying or cyberstalking, but legislation criminalizing cyberbullying or electronic harassment has been proposed as of mid-2021.

All US states, as well as the District of Columbia, have legislation that criminalizes harassment and/ or stalking. Some specifically refer to such behavior on electronic media, but all are intended to protect the public regardless of the vehicle used.

Z THE DUTIES OF INTERNET PROVIDERS AND SOCIAL MEDIA PLATFORMS

As clearly one of the largest and most successful providers of social media platforms, with billions of users, Facebook has been subject to criticism about its failure to properly police the postings of its users.

The dilemma is that it is not clear exactly what the duties of media companies are when it comes to editing and controlling how their platforms are used to post information, communicate, and access the World Wide Web.

There is no universal legal regulation governing:

- what level of "honesty" they are required to comply with or enforce;
- what definition of "morality" they must aspire to;
- how they should decide what their users can do on their platforms; or

629. *Id.*

- under what circumstances they must restrict, penalize, or ban the activities of their users.

In 2021, publications in *The Wall Street Journal* (WSJ) alleged what the WSJ believed to be an unacceptable level of hypocrisy on the part of Facebook by publicly making a statement that Facebook knew to be untrue.[630]

Among the objections of the WSJ to Facebook's behavior are the following:

- Allowing celebrities to post things that other users are not permitted to post.
- Being slow to respond to charges that Facebook is used by drug dealers and people traffickers.
- Allowing Facebook to become a hotbed of anti-vaccination posting when the Facebook founder Mark Zuckerberg was claiming that Facebook would be site for promoting anti-COVID vaccination.

Also, Facebook has, allegedly for several years, had information that its Instagram subsidiary causes anxiety and depression in teenagers which, in some cases, can lead to self-harm or even suicide.[631]

These allegations have led to demands that effective regulation of social media platforms, such as Facebook and others, be brought into force. One proposal is that that the controlling executives of social media companies should be subject to personal liability, possible prosecution, and punishment if a company "breaches fundamental health and safety" rules leading to "severe harm or death."[632]

These laws have not yet been enacted but given the level of dissatisfaction with the governance of social media platforms that has been expressed by commentators and legislators around the world, several jurisdictions may adopt such regulations in the future.

630. As reported in *The Sunday Times* (which has the same parent company as WSJ), in the following online article, "Facebook's Hypocrisy Has Been Exposed in Painful Detail," September 19, 2021.

631. *Id.*

632. *Id.*

CHAPTER 20
Cyberwar

A CYBERWAR IS HERE

In September 2019, PC Magazine published an article entitled, "Cyberwar Is Here: Are You Ready?"[633]

The article pointed out that the US and its allies and adversaries have powerful digital weapons at their disposal.

But the point of the article was not only that nations are able to deploy these weapons against each other to disrupt military (such as nuclear development projects)[634] and infrastructure systems (such as power grids) that are accessible over the Internet, but that they can be used to affect all of us that use the Internet by disrupting the economic and communication systems that much of the world's population use and depend on.

Given the fact that any device that can connect to the Internet can be hacked and remotely controlled, cyberwar can be used to bring domestic and economic disruption, and perhaps paralysis, to each of us as individuals.

Many people use computer payment systems for shopping, digital security cameras to keep our homes safe, robot vacuum cleaners to clean them, and computer games and media streaming to keep our family members entertained. It is not difficult to imagine how disrupted people's lives could be if these and other Internet accessible items were suddenly controlled by a hostile party.

And all these domestic disruptions could be in addition to infrastructure attacks on communications, power systems, water and gas grids, transportation systems and military operations systems.

These issues have made countries increasingly aware that important battles in the future will be fought not in the dirt of the earth but in the tech sphere. There is

633. https://www.pcmag.com/news/370753/cyberwar-is-here-are-you-ready.
634. Such as the US and Israel are alleged to have done to Iran by deploying the Stuxnet Worm, http://large.stanford.edu/courses/2015/ph241/holloway1/.

considerable concern among the Western nations and the NATO allies that countries that may prove enemies of theirs in the future, particularly China and Russia, are developing increasingly more sophisticated ways of attacking the computer-controlled assets of other countries.

Cyperspace

In 2003, the US published a document entitled, *The National Strategy to Secure Cyberspace,* that set out the US objectives to profit from the importance of cyberspace and to develop effective defenses against cyberattacks from hostile nations.[635]

Attacks on NATO

It is reported that NATO is subject to cyberattacks almost every day from hackers trying to get access to confidential information.

The NATO secretary general, Jens Stoltenberg, has said that in addition the individual cellular phones of military personnel in the Baltic states were being hacked apparently to cause disruption of their activities.[636]

In response, NATO has conducted military exercises simulating mass cyberattacks on military assets. A policy has also been adopted that in the case of heightened military threats, personnel will be told to turn off their cell phones and remove the sim cards so that their movements and communications cannot be tracked.

One of the principal purposes of these hostile cyberattacks seems to be to gather information about NATO's military systems so that they can be remotely manipulated in the event of a future conflict.[637]

In March 2021, *The Times* published a report on a UK Ministry of Defense review of these issues which said:

> Britain risks losing battles of the future to tech savvy China and Russia "without a shot being fired" unless it adapts, a senior military chief warned.[638]

The report pointed out that in the next struggle, the power of large armies and conventional weapons will be less important than cyber-sophistication, including knowledge of the construction and effective use of algorithms.

It has been reported that General Sir Patrick Sanders the head of the UK's Strategic Command believes that:

635. Levon Anderson, "Countering State-Sponsored Cyber Attacks: Who Should Lead?," *information as Power*, online, retrieved October 1, 2020.
636. Larisa Brown, "Enemy Hackers Target Nato with Constant Cyberattacks," *The Times*, online, May 28, 2021.
637. *Id.*
638. Larisa Brown, "Military Chief Warns 'Algorithms Will Be Our Armour in High-Tech Wars of the Future'," *The Times*, online, March 13, 2021, accessed March 15, 2021.

> Cyber "warriors" will be as vital to protecting Britain as F35 pilots on aircraft carriers, special forces soldiers and submarine mariners operating the nuclear deterrent ... .[639]

General Sanders said that included in future defense systems, AI, and machines would play an important role in defending humans:

> Even the best human operators cannot defend against multiple machines making thousands of maneuvers per second at hypersonic speed and orchestrated by AI.[640]

The issue of the importance of Internet-based knowledge in potential future conflicts raises several legal questions having to do with access to and the use of such knowledge.

In the present, little thought has been given to the issue of the spread of sophisticated understanding of computer technology and the Internet.

New Laws and Regulations Needed

This information is generally open to everyone in line with laws widespread in developed Western countries granting and protecting Freedom of Information. The general approach seems to be that laws and regulations as applied to the cybersphere are adequate if they can be used to punish misuse of the skills and information necessary to operate at a sophisticated level on the Internet.

However, given the ability of the Internet to reach and direct the increasingly growing "Internet of Things" which includes those instruments and data sources that are reachable over the Internet, are these laws adequate?

Might there be a need to refashion the legal system applying to the Internet to provide more specialized legal barriers to certain categories of Internet accessible data and information?

Historical Precedent

This is not without precedent. Historically, several societies restricted certain important tools of communication to a limited number of specially trained and approved persons.

For example, in ancient Mesopotamia, the important medium of cuneiform writing was restricted to specially trained and approved scribes who are allowed to use their skills only in the context of certain approved activities—largely not only related to the formation of commercial contracts but also related to governmental and or religious uses. Not everyone was provided with the training or permission to operate within the cuneiform writing system.

In medieval Europe, a similar situation existed with respect to published material. The right to produce publish material was limited to printers' guilds such as the

639. Larisa Brown, "Cyber Warriors as Important to Our Safety as Fighter Jets Says General," *The Times*, online, May 27, 2021, accessed May 31, 2021.
640. *Id.*

Stationers Guild in England. If one wanted to publish any writing at all, it would have to be done through the approved Guild.

The Cloud

It is now virtually impossible to run a nation or individual lives in the developed world without using computer systems connected to the Internet.

In fact, less and less of the data that is important to us as individuals is stored or accessed on our individual computer drives. Increasingly data is stored in vast server farms that make up the infrastructure of "the cloud" that keeps so much of the information we need.

It is true that these "cloud networks" are usually operated by digital giants such as Apple or Amazon.

Of course, they try to protect their cloud servers with sophisticated security systems. But cybercriminals and hackers, including those employed by government organizations, are constantly working to improve their abilities to get access to protected computer systems. Consequently, the press periodically reports huge data breaches affecting millions, a serious power outage, "ransomware" attacks and "denial of service" attacks.

These are much more serious than the almost daily irritations that afflict us all from "fishing" emails, fake "security" alerts, false messages from fake law enforcement officials, and emails from fraudsters using hacked email accounts of our friends and acquaintances.

The point is that the penetration of the Internet has become so widespread that it can be used not only to irritate and defraud individuals but also to effectively disrupt or destroy the governing abilities of nations.

The impact of these cybercrimes is huge, but still nowhere near the potential impact cyberattacks could have, given the huge adoption of Internet use currently ongoing and the future potential of the growth of Internet use.

The Internet Weapon

There are currently 3.9 billion users of the Internet worldwide. There are approximately 800 million users in China, around 500 million users in the EU and about 300 million users in the US.

It is estimated that within the next ten years most of the world's population will be connected to the Internet.

The chief operating officer of SoftBank believes that there will be over one trillion devices connected by the Internet by 2025.[641]

641. https://venturebeat.com/2018/10/16/softbank-believes-1-trillion-connected-devices-will-create-11-trillion-in-value-by-2025/.

The frightening vulnerability of that is that any device that connects to the Internet can be "hacked" and probably controlled by the hacker.[642]

A recent wide-ranging study, done jointly by Imperial College in London and Northeastern University in Boston, Massachusetts, USA, examined over eighty devices that connect to the Internet such as speakers, doorbells, smart TVs, and other things from major suppliers including Amazon and Google.

They discovered that most of these devices collected information such as IP addresses, MAC addresses, user habits and location information and sent it to third parties even if the user of the device did not have any relationship to those parties or any knowledge that this information was being shared with third parties.

More than seventy of the devices were found to be contacting parties other than the devices manufacturer.

Smart but Disloyal TVs

"Smart TV" sellers seem to be particularly guilty of ignoring the privacy of their users. It has been reported that Vizio was sued for secretly recording and marketing usage information about more than fifteen million Vizio owners, and Samsung has been criticized for gathering and storing user data.

You can bet that the vulnerability of all these Internet-connected devices to hacking, data-gathering, and eavesdropping would be of significant interest to national intelligence agencies around the globe.[643]

Attacks on Australia

In June 2020, the Australian government reported that it has been the subject of sophisticated state-sponsored cyberattacks on its businesses and institutions.

The Australian Prime Minister refused to identify the suspected source of these attacks, but there is suspicion that they emanated from China, a country with which Australia had been having difficult relations.

It was pointed out that China, Russia, and North Korea were the only countries with whom Australia was not aligned that had the capabilities of undertaking such attacks.[644]

It was reported that such attacks were aimed at "all levels of government," essential services and a number of businesses.

642. https://www.fastcompany.com/90164031/you-can-hack-almost-any-smart-device-with-a-google-search.
643. https://www.vice.com/en_us/article/gyzjym/the-internet-of-things-is-still-a-privacy-dumpster-fire-study-finds.
644. "Australia Targeted by 'State-Based' Cyber Attacks," *BBC News*, online, June 19, 2020.

The attacks were said to have occurred over many months and were increasing. Attacks were being observed on "government, industry, political organizations, education, health, essential service providers and operators of other critical infrastructure." For example, the Australian National University said it had been attacked by a sophisticated operation that accessed staff and student details.[645]

It was noted that although it has been subject to many attacks, Australia was not unique in this regard and similar attacks have been identified in other countries.[646]

WannaCry Attacks

The overseas threat from hackers that appear to be sponsored by foreign governments is continually increasing. For example, during the summer of 2017, two major computer viruses attacked sites in the Western world.

The first was the WannaCry virus that was believed to be a North Korean backed hacker attack that encrypted the data of target companies and individuals and demanded ransom money to release the target's data.

This affected, among others, parts of the German Railway System and the United Kingdom's National Health System computers.

Not Petya Attack

The second was believed to be a Russian attack aimed at businesses in Ukraine. However, this virus, called "Not Petya," hit what were apparently unintended targets, including the shipping company Maersk and a chocolate manufacturer in Australia.[647]

UK Defense

Several countries have taken formal steps to defend against such attacks.

In 2017, the UK launched its National Cyber Security Centre as part of its national effort to protect the nation against cyberattacks.

Ciaran Martin was its first head. From the three years that he headed the organization, he identified three important lessons from his experiences:

(1) Cyberattacks do not operate on their own. They are often part of a coordinated effort of a foreign nation to undermine the security of a target nation. Therefore, it is important for security services to counter the hostile activities

645. *Id.*
646. *Id.*
647. Ciaran Martin, "GCHQ Chief: The Threat of a Rogue Cyber-Attack Keeps Me Awake at Night," *The Times*, online, August 30, 2020, retrieved August 30, 2020, https://www.thetimes.co.uk/article/gchq-chief-the-threat-of-a-rogue-cyber-attack-keeps-me-awake-at-night-9lf8l6hb0?shareToken=fc12cc7cdfdf136fbe47db90f3361e5.

of foreign nationals that are conducted in more traditional ways as well as being sensitive to a computer threat from a hostile foreign country:

(a) it is important to be aware of the different kinds of penetration that foreign cyberattacks are aimed to achieve. For example, Mr. Martin writes that:

    (i) Russian hacker groups tend to focus on national infrastructure targets such as energy systems, medical research, and electoral processes;
    (ii) Chinese hackers, on the other hand, have usually tended to seek economic advantages through the theft of intellectual property. However, Chinese hackers now also seem to be attacking important strategic technology as well;
    (iii) Iranian hackers look for data that can help them track certain people, and they also try to disrupt services in countries that are suffering from unrest;
    (iv) North Koreans try to use hacking to get money to fund their government.

(2) The second lesson is that a decent level of protection cannot be achieved without careful and skillful security management. For example, hacking is far more likely to be effective against organizations without updated software. So, it is important to keep software up-to-date. Having good quality and regular backups is an excellent defense against ransom attacks based on encryption of the target's data.

(3) Third, it is important to keep barriers to data entry high. This is particularly important if one becomes the target of a hacker that cannot effectively control the virus being released. This can have a devastating effect on the target's systems and on the systems of others to whom the target is connected.[648]

Although Mr. Martin ceased being the head of the NCSC in 2020, he was recently quoted in *The Times* on the sensitive issue of how Chinese technology should be treated.[649]

He predicted that in the future Western countries, including Britain, should be much more cautious about the use of Chinese technology in computing and communication systems.

Mr. Martin said that it had taken the West some time to realize that China was determined to become a strategic competitor and to challenge the West in a way it had not been since the end of the Cold War.

However, Martin pointed out that the situation was different and more difficult than the opposition presented by the Soviet Union because the West did not have the extensive economic links with the Soviet Union that it has built with China.

648. *Id.*
649. Mark Bridge, "We Have Been Confused about China, Says Former GCHQ Cybersecurity Chief," *The Times*, online, March 15, 2021, accessed March 16, 2021.

For example, he pointed to the extensive economic and other links that exist between China and several leading Western universities.

This has provided China with a pathway to both information and technical penetration in some leading areas of developing Western technology. This concern appears to be more than speculation.

In early 2021, the think tank Civitas expressed the view that at least a dozen British universities may be unknowingly helping the People's Liberation Army by exchanging information with universities and companies in China.[650]

This is not a problem that is limited to Britain. Chinese universities and Chinese students have been working hard for many years to establish meaningful relationships and or presence with leading universities throughout the world, including the US, Canada and many countries in Europe.

What level of surveillance and caution is being exercised in those countries today now that there is a greater understanding of China's desire to increase its political and strategic power around the world?

Mr. Martin, who is now a professor at Oxford University, has urged the British government to clarify its policies on security, defense, development, and foreign policy to better define its response to the expansion of Chinese power and to provide a better overall understanding of Britain's place in the world.

Defending Against China

United Kingdom

This increasing awareness of China's aggressive technological role has led to some backlash in Western countries.

For example, in 2020, the British government announced that Huawei, the Chinese telecoms company, would be excluded from providing its equipment to British networks by 2027. However, there is an excellent question as to whether the amount of time that Huawei has had its technology as part of the British system did not provide the Chinese with a long period to learn far too much information about the way that the British communication system is constructed and operated.

Will merely replacing Chinese hardware with other substitutes be enough to undo any damage that was done between 2020 and 2027?

After all, the reason that the British are insisting on the removal of Chinese equipment from its infrastructure was because of the fear that such participation would offer the Chinese a dangerous opportunity to gather intelligence or even conduct sabotage operations in the future.

Does the British government have a detailed record of the extent and location of all Huawei products used in the British communication system?

Will it in fact be possible to find and effectively remove all avenues of Chinese penetration into British communications infrastructure?

650. *Id.*

Will the fact that China has had access to this British system for so long mean that British communications infrastructure will be eternally vulnerable to potential malicious Chinese interference?[651]

United States

In October 2021, there was a similar reaction in America. It was reported that the US had banned the top Chinese telecom's company, China Telecom, from operating in the US because of "national security concerns."

It was reported that US officials thought that the Chinese government's involvement in that company gave them an opportunity to interfere with US communications in harmful ways, including conducting espionage.[652]

The Future with China

United Kingdom

But although the UK considers China the "biggest state-based threat" to Britain's economic security, China is still a critically important trading partner to the UK.[653]

UK government advisors have reportedly prepared a hundred-page report entitled *Global Britain in a Competitive Age* which identifies China's increasing international aggressiveness as an important risk to the interests of the UK.[654]

The report is said to assert that one of the biggest challenges for the UK is to maintain and expand protection of its critical infrastructure in electricity, transportation, and water while simultaneously seeking to establish more extensive trade links with China, including increasing Chinese investment in the UK.

According to Sir Alex Younger, who was formerly head of Britain's intelligence agency MI6, it is a mistake to think that as China becomes more economically powerful that it will change its policies to become more like Western countries. According to Younger, it is more likely that China will become more attached to its Communist Party ideology.[655]

But the trickiest part for Britain is that having left Europe, Britain is searching for a new role in the world.

In that context, they are trying to find the best way to deal with China which is not only a powerful military and political competitor but also on its way to becoming the largest economy in the world, which presents potential trade opportunities that Britain may not be able to find elsewhere. In Britain's post-Brexit situation, these issues

651. *Id.*
652. "US Revokes License of Top Chinese Telecoms Company," *BBC News*, online, October 27, 2021.
653. Larisa Brown and Steven Swinford, "UK Plans Tighter Security to Allow Trade with 'Biggest Threat' China," *The Times*, online, March 16, 2021, accessed March 17, 2021.
654. *Id.*
655. *Id.*

present complex diplomatic puzzles that Britain will have to try to solve very carefully.[656]

To counter this growing Chinese rivalry, and threats from other potential international military and economic competitors which may be tempted to engage in cyberattacks and spreading this information that affects the UK, the government of the UK intends to create a secure "situation room" similar to what exists in the US White House, to allow counterterrorism officials from the police intelligence agencies and legal advisors to gather to evaluate and respond to any cyberattacks or other forms of terrorism.[657]

The presence of representatives from the legal and judicial sectors in the proposed team of counterterrorism experts points up the sensitivity to responding to such threats in a way that is compatible with British legal tradition and policy.

Although it is certainly important for the UK or any nation to respond quickly and forcefully to cyber and physical threats of terrorism or destabilization, it is important that the Western democracies do not lose sight of the policies and limitations which support their commitment to democratic processes and the freedom of their citizens.

However, it must be recognized that there will be some conflict between balancing British desire to maintain a good economic relationship with China in conjunction with:

- protecting itself against cyberattacks to its infrastructure; and
- the desire of some British politicians to punish China for such things as its reported treatment of the Uighur minority in China; or
- China's imposition of new laws in Hong Kong that diminish the abilities of the residents of Hong Kong to be able to rely on the protections of democracy.[658]

B CONDUCTING CYBERWAR

Hackers for Hire

One particularly frightening aspect of cyberwar that exists because of the markets created on the Dark Web is the fact that countries do not necessarily have to develop their own high-level hacking capabilities.

Expert hacking skills are for sale on the Dark Web. There are experienced hackers selling their abilities to use well-developed and especially well-tested hacking tools that can be used for the right price.

656. Catherine Philip, "'Global Britain' Must Tread a Fine Line Between China and America," *The Times*, online, March 16, 2021, accessed March 19, 2021.
657. Brown and Swinford, *supra*.
658. *Id*.

There are also hacking specialists that focus on a particular aspect of hacking, such as "system entry specialists" or skilled "data miners" who can be hired by those that wish to put together a team to launch a cyberattack.[659]

Russian Intentions

Russia apparently has no intention of abandoning its cyberwar on the West.

In September 2020, *The Times* reported that the software giant Microsoft had warned that the Russian military hackers who had interfered with the 2016 US presidential election remained active seeking to penetrate the digital data of US political parties, political issue groups and political consultants who were working on the 2020 presidential election.

There is also evidence that Russia continues to target news websites with opinion comments from pro-Russian trolls to try to influence international public opinion in favor of supporting Russia.

Their method is basically to insert pro-Russian comments in the opinion sections of articles appearing in Western media sites.

The evidence for this is a study done by the Cardiff university crime and security research institute. This study examined over thirty well-known media websites in sixteen countries. For example, the fall of Afghanistan to the Taliban allegedly gave the Russians opportunities to introduce comments that this event was a result of the failure of liberal democracy, and the ineffectiveness of NATO.

The comments also alluded to the weakness of Western countries supporting those institutions in their support of Ukraine against Russia.[660] The researchers indicated that this is a long-running campaign by Russia that shows no signs of tapering off.

China and Iran

Microsoft also reported that China and Iran were attempting to access the email accounts of those affiliated with the November 2020 presidential election.[661]

One thing that is clear is that cyberwar is becoming ever more intensive. Several nations have apparently concluded that it is a low-cost and effective method of disrupting the operations of other countries that they consider to be hostile to them.

659. Martin, *supra*, August 30, 2020.
660. Gordon Corera, "Pro-Kremlin Trolls Target News Website Comments, Researchers Say," *The Times*, online, September 2021.
661. Henry Zefferman, "Russian Hackers Targeting US Poll, Warns Microsoft," *The Times*, online, September 11, 2020, retrieved September 11, 2020.

Foreign Attacks on Microsoft

In September 2019, Microsoft Corp. reported that hackers in Russia are behind the largest number of cyberattacks on Microsoft customers. During the last two years, Microsoft has issued thirteen thousand alerts to its customers relating to hacking accounts by nation-states.

It says that about 52% of those incidents originated from Russian hackers. The attacks have been a variety of things, including elections.

Microsoft also reported that Iran is responsible for about 25% of such attacks, and China for about 12%.

Other nation-state attacks came from North Korea and several other countries.[662]

Attacks on UK

According to a report in *The Times*, the UK military is under daily attack from cyberhackers:[663]

> General Sir Patrick Sanders, Commander Strategic Command, outlined how the Ministry of Defense and its assets were under "constant attack" in cyberspace. Up to ten attacks daily are said to stem from hostile state actors.

The report said that the UK has developed cyber-weapons to counter, disrupt and "even destroy" computer systems and infrastructure of such attackers.[664]

The UK maintains a Joint Cyber Unit in the Ministry of Defense facility in Corsham, Wiltshire, to deal with cyber problems. There is a constant flow that needs attention. General Sanders said:

> Each year, the systems here manage millions of networks and cyber events. Most are dealt with automatically, but around 1,800 per month—or 60 a day—require intervention.[665]

However, the UK does not consider its present defense systems to be enough and is intending to set up a "National Cyber Force" modeled on one in the US, which would:

> Fuse expertise in data analytics, machine learning and artificial intelligence, autonomy and robotics, synthetics, quantum, and 5G.[666]

Nations are increasingly understanding the importance of building and maintaining advanced capabilities to both launch and protect against cyberattacks. A phrase

---

662. *Bloomberg*, September 30, 2020, online, retrieved October 1, 2020, https://www.livemint.com/news/world/microsoft-says-russia-behind-most-nation-state-cyber-attacks-11601444175751.html.
663. Lucy Fisher, "Military under Daily Blitz of 'Significant' Cyberattacks," *The Times*, online, September 26, 2020, retrieved October 1, 2020, scratch https://www.thetimes.co.uk/article/military-under-daily-blitz-of-significant-cyberattacks-5tspjc6nw.
664. *Id.*
665. *Id.*
666. *Id.*

that is now commonly used when describing the importance and impact of cyber capabilities is "Information is Power":

> The core element that drives the digital society is digitalized information. Information is the key to how the digital society adds value and redistributes power.[667]

A very serious matter is that cyberwar may become nuclear war. Indeed, nuclear powers are already considering that. It has been reported that the UK is considering the possibility of using nuclear weapons against any stage that inflicted a devastating cyberattack on British systems or infrastructure.[668] The report discussed above, global Britain in a competitive age, said that the UK would reserve the right to review its policy on the use of nuclear weapons:

> The future threat of mass destruction, such as chemical and biological capabilities, or emerging technologies that could have a comparable impact, make it necessary.

C THE SOLARWINDS ATTACK

And that necessity is getting increasingly intense. One of the most clever, sophisticated, and devastating nation-state attacks on critical software of another country started in 2019 with penetration of the software of a company called SolarWinds.

This attack was still being investigated in 2021, and the US has not yet decided what retaliation to take against the suspected attackers who are believed to be related to Russian intelligence.

SolarWinds is an important US technology firm. They are responsible for creating a software system named "Orion" which is used by thousands of customers across the US in the world to manage their IT systems. SolarWinds has over thirty thousand customers that use Orion.

Like any other major software manufacturer, SolarWinds sends periodic updates to its customers. Many of these customers are large US companies and important federal and state government organizations. The Pentagon, the Department of Homeland Security, the Department of Energy, the Nuclear Security Administration, the State Department, and the Treasury are among the many users of Orion. So are Microsoft, Intel, and Cisco, among many other high-profile tech companies.

What the hackers did was extremely clever. They broke into SolarWinds Orion and planted there well-hidden malicious software in the updates that SolarWinds sent to its customers.

This malicious software allowed the hackers to get access to the IT systems of the customers that received these updates and to gather sensitive and critical information from those IT systems.

667. Sora Park, *Information Is Power*, Springer, 2017, online, retrieved October 1, 2020, https://link.springer.com/chapter/10.1057/978-1-137-59332-0_8#: ~ :text = Information%20is%20the%20key%20to,once%20shared%20on%20digital%20networks.
668. Larisa Brown, Catherine Philip and Kaya Burgess, "Britain Could Respond to Future Cyberattack with Nuclear Strike," *The Times*, online, March 17, 2021, accessed March 18, 2021.

Although Russia has denied any involvement in this penetration, major software companies like Microsoft firmly believe that the hackers are connected to Russian intelligence.

The extent of the damage of this wide-ranging attack has not yet been fully assessed. But it does come as a major shock to those responsible for securing the safety of critical IT systems in the US. The US does fund a Cyber Security Command that has responsibility for protecting America's online networks. However, they do not seem to have been prepared to fend off this kind of attack.

What the full nature of the US's response will be remains to be seen but may involve serious sanctions against Russia and or any other nation-state that is found to have participated in or facilitated this attack.

President of the US, Joe Biden, said in July 2021 that he believed that the President of Russia, Vladimir Putin, could shut down the Russian hackers believed to be responsible for several important hacking attacks if Putin wished to do so.

The Hacking gang and REvil are believed to be operating out of Russia.

They are thought to have targeted around 250 businesses with ransomware attacks between 2019 and 2021. From this criminal activity, they are believed to have extorted around $100 million.

One Russian hacking expert has said that "it only needs one person to come after them Putin ... If he goes after them, they are all done very quickly."

It remains to be seen whether Putin can be persuaded to take decisive action to end the hacking attacks that are believed to originate from Russia. President Biden has said that the US will take action to protect its businesses and infrastructure against hacking attacks and that if Russia took no action to curtail the attacks originating from there, the US would take retaliatory action.[669]

Biden has told Vladimir Putin that the US would take "any necessary action" in response to ransomware attacks suffered by companies in the US and elsewhere during mid-2021.[670] Exactly what that retaliatory action would be is not clear. Biden did say that in his communications with Putin that "I made it very clear to him that the United States experts thought the hacking operation is coming from his soil. Even if it's not sponsored by the state, we expect them to act if we give them enough information to act on who that is."[671]

What is clear is that hacking to damage the information systems of third parties either to cripple important infrastructure assets or to extract money will continue for some time.

Major efforts at international cooperation will be needed to put an end to the serious infrastructure and economic damage that is now being inflicted on hacking targets.

---

669. Marc Bennetts, "Putin Could Call Off Hackers If He Wanted," *The Times*, online, July 11, 2021.
670. David Charter and Tom Parfit, "We Will Retaliate If You Hack Us, Joe Biden Tells Vladimir Putin," *The Times*, online, July 10, 2021.
671. *Id.*

D RUSSIAN HACKING ATTACK ON US FOOD PRODUCTION

Despite the warnings of President Biden to Russian President Putin, Russian hacking attacks on important US resources do not seem to have let up.

In September 2021, a group of cybercriminals called Black Matter, which is believed to be based in Russia, attacked the computer systems of Neo Cooperative, an organization of soy and grain farmers that has over eight thousand members and forced their systems to close down which interrupted food supply and feeding schedules for millions of chickens, hogs and cattle being raised in the US.

The hackers threatened to publish Neo Coop's confidential data unless they were paid nearly $6 million in ransom. In response, Neo Coop said that they took their systems off-line to protect them.[672]

E CHINESE ATTACK ON JAPAN

The US and its NATO allies are not the only countries subject to Chinese military cyberattacks. An employee of the Chinese military was accused by Japan of hacking up to two hundred Japanese organizations, including the Japanese space agency.

Another Chinese hacking group is thought to be guilty of other cyberattacks against South Korea and Japan. Among the tactics used by these alleged Chinese cyberattackers is the theft of sensitive emails to use them for purposes of distributing malware into the systems of important companies and organizations.[673]

F THE NORTH KOREAN HEIST

One of the most audacious allegedly state-sponsored hacking attacks by one country on another was an attempt by a hacking group, allegedly under orders from the government of North Korea, to try to steal about $1 billion from the country of Bangladesh.

The attempt occurred in 2016. The circumstances are far too complex to describe in detail here but an outline of what happened follows. For a more detailed description of the theft, the BBC published an informative report in June 2021.[674]

Using a complex series of transfers, and carefully planned timing, North Korea tried to steal about $1 billion from the National Bank of Bangladesh. They were trying to steal the money from the account of Bangladesh at the US Federal Reserve Bank in New York.

Ultimately, the hackers got away with about $80 million, but they were prevented from getting the whole amount because the name of the small bank in Manila the

672. "Russian Hackers Target US Food and Grain Production," *The Times*, online, September 23, 2021.
673. Gavin Blair, "Japan Accuses Chinese Military Hacker over Cyberattacks," *The Times*, April 20, 2021, accessed May 7, 2021.
674. "The Lazarus Heist: How North Korea Almost Pulled Off a Billion-Dollar Hack," *BBC News*, online, June 21, 2021.

hackers had chosen to send the money to raised suspicions at the Federal Reserve. Nevertheless, losing $80 million was painful to a poor country like Bangladesh.

The worst consequences of the hack were prevented, but this is undoubtedly far from the last North Korean hack attack that the world will experience.

Many reports have been published detailing how North Korea spends a significant part of its national wealth to make itself a powerful force on the Internet. North Korea apparently takes children with remarkable mathematical skills at an early age and places them in programs that teach them sophisticated computer skills. Some of the schools that focus on developing the skills are in China; others are found in North Korea. But the clear intent of these programs is to give North Korea the power to damage and steal from countries that they believe oppose them.

The remarkable thing about this practice is that it gives a relatively small country with fewer resources the power to do significant damage to those who are believed to be its enemies without having the financial, manufacturing, or natural resources to compete with other countries.

The secrecy and clandestine manner of these attacks make it possible for North Korea to continuously deny their involvement in the attacks while still reaping the resources and benefits that such international attacks can bring them.

These factors present serious difficulties for countries that are targeted by North Korea in terms of both proving that the attacks are sponsored by the government of North Korea and deciding how to respond to these hacking attacks.

Because of the international nature of these hacking attacks, it will undoubtedly be necessary to form international organizations and to put in place international treaties to detect, counter and punish such behavior.

G RUSSIAN HACKING GERMAN PARLIAMENT

Apparently, the US is not the only target for Russian hackers. Reuters has cited a report in *Der Spiegel* that German government officials have found that the email accounts of members of the German Parliament have been hacked apparently by a hacking group called "Ghostwriter" which is believed to be a creature of the Russian military intelligence group, the GRU.

This is apparently not the first time that Germany has suffered Russian digital interference.

It is also reported that in 2015, emails from Angela Merkel's office were hacked as was other German Parliament information.[675]

H FORMER US INTELLIGENCE AGENTS HACK FOR UAE

One of the more slippery things about the Internet is that it permits users to operate from anywhere in the world.

675. Reuters Staff, "Russian Hackers Target German Parliament Again: Der Spiegel," *Reuters*, online, March 26, 2021, accessed, September 8, 2021.

In the peaceful commercial sector, the value of this was shown during the COVID-19 pandemic when billions of employees around the world worked from home to avoid unnecessary contact that might have contributed to spreading the virus.

However, this flexible ability to work at a distance also enables the intelligence agencies of any country in the world to employ experts from any other country that suit their purposes—whether peaceful or more sinister.

An unfortunate example of the advantages of this flexibility occurred in 2021 when three former US intelligence personnel pleaded guilty to breaking US laws engaging in hacking projects for the United Arab Emirates.[676]

The men pled guilty to computer fraud, gaining fraudulent access to relevant devices, and violations of export controls for which they were fined a total of $1.7 million.

It is reported that they worked for the UAE allegedly hacking into servers, computers, and phones around the globe.[677]

I REMOTE OPERATION OF CONVENTIONAL WEAPONS

Israel Versus Iran

There is a great deal written above about the power of digital weapons and how they are disrupting the defense, infrastructure, and political systems of targeted countries.

However, one of the most sinister developments in digital warfare is the creation of tools that can control conventional weapons over the Internet from a remote location.

One of the most shocking incidents of this type of cyber warfare took place in 2021 when Israel allegedly assassinated Iran's principal nuclear scientist, Mohsen Fakhrizadeh. It is reported that Israel had wanted to kill him for more than a decade, but in 2021 it finally happened using a remotely controlled machine gun mounted on a truck by the side of the road which unleashed a stream of bullets at Fakhrizadeh's car as he drove it past with his wife as a passenger.

Israeli operatives reportedly smuggled the pieces of this robot machine gun into the country and assembled it to fit in the back of a type of pickup truck commonly seen in Iran. They also packed the truck with bombs so that it could be destroyed after the assassination, thereby eliminating much of the evidence relating to the plan.

The robot was controlled via computer 1,000 miles away, communicating by means of a satellite.

As Fakhrizadeh's car drove by, a remote operator used the machine gun, with the help of computerized cameras also attached to the truck, to target and unleash a stream of bullets that killed Fakhrizadeh almost instantly but left his wife untouched. The truck was then blown up.

676. "Three Ex-US Intelligence Officers Admit Packing for UAE," *BBC News*, online, September 17, 2021.
677. *Id.*

Using this type of setup was unexpected and confusing. Iranian news sources first reported that Fakhrizadeh had been killed by a group of assassins in a furious gun battle with the scientists' bodyguards that left several people dead. It took a while for it to be understood what had really happened.[678]

It is reported that over the years Israel has arranged for the assassination of several Iranian nuclear scientists and military personnel. However, this is the first known instance where the operation was conducted remotely but with extraordinary precision that killed only the target. This is of course very different than the results that occur when remotely controlled drones are used which often cause the deaths of innocent bystanders as well as the target for assassination.

There seems a little doubt that Israel may continue to order assassinations of those who consider a threat, and this type of remote-controlled conventional weapons appears to put an important new tool at their disposal.
Beyond that, this assassination also alerts other technically savvy countries to the possibilities of conducting remote operations over the Internet using a wide variety of robot weapons, of all sizes even down to nano robots.

J NSO GROUP AND CANDIRU BLACKLISTED

In November 2021, it was reported that sophisticated Israeli spyware was employed to cause a variety of problems worldwide. A company called the NSO Group created a spyware program called Pegasus. The company claimed that it sold Pegasus only to government entities in countries with good human rights protections.

But in 2021, NSO was accused of selling the product to dictatorial governments that used it to target citizens that were not criminals or terrorists such as journalists, human rights activists, attorneys and even elected government officials. The danger of Pegasus was that it allowed the operators to implant malware into phones, so they could read all the messages there, access all data stored and even turn on the phones' microphones remotely. It was reported that the US Department of commerce banned NSO and another Israeli spyware company named Candiru:

> The US ban was reportedly based on evidence that these entities developed and supplied spyware to foreign governments that used these tools to maliciously target government officials, journalist, businesspeople, activists, academics and embassy workers.[679]

The unfortunate message in these developments is that the conduct of cyberwar has expanded to the point where not only military assets and infrastructure are attacked but also the data and interaction with the Internet of individual citizens have become targets in international conflicts.

---

678. This account is adapted from an article by Ronen Bergman and Farnaz Fassihi, "The Scientist and the A.I.-Assisted, Remote Control Killing Machine," *The New York Times*, online, September 18, 2021.
679. "NSO Group: Israeli Spyware Company Added to US Trade Blacklist," *BBC News*, online, November 4, 2021.

CHAPTER 21

The Future of Internet Law

Certainly, the nature and variety of the material available on the Internet will change rapidly and dramatically as the future unfolds.

It is probably impossible to imagine all that the future will offer in terms of information, access, and streaming.

This may well raise new challenges for regulators, and they will have to respond with new laws and regulations to control the Internet while making it safely accessible to as wide a population as possible.

It is also probable that the hardware offered to access and use the Internet will also change significantly. We have moved from mainframe computers to minicomputers, to personal computers, to laptops, to tablets, to smartphones, to watches and to eyeglasses.

It is being projected that apps and the Internet will be accessible by even more "wearables" soon. Because of issues having to do with safety and privacy, there will undoubtedly need to be strict regulations governing how these things are made, sold, and used.

A QUANTUM COMPUTING

As has been discussed above in the chapter on cybercrime,[680] until late in 2019, it was thought that quantum computing was still a long way away.

However, when, in October 2019, Google announced that a quantum computing system, named Sycamore, developed by Google had achieved "quantum supremacy," completing calculations much faster than the fastest "supercomputers" existing up until then, the world realized that quantum computing had arrived.

Sycamore, being the first operating quantum computing system, is quantum computing at its most primitive. It is expected that soon quantum computers will be

680. Chapter 19, Cybercrime, above.

much more powerful. Sycamore is a 53-qubit system, but it is believed that future quantum computing systems could operate on billion qubit systems.[681]

The coming of this kind of computing may be happening much more rapidly than had been originally thought. At the end of a October 2021, competition in this area sped forward exponentially. It was reported that China had developed a programmable quantum computer that was a million times more powerful than Google's Sycamore. The light-based Jiuzhang computer can complete in one second, a task that would take a traditional supercomputer thirty trillion years.[682]

Immediately, organizations began to be formed to exploit the commercial potential of such a high-powered new technology.

In early September 2020, *The Times* reported that a Cambridge start-up, Riverlane, was working to create quantum software. There are some scientists that reportedly believe that there is no commercial future in quantum computing, but the founder of Riverlane does not believe that. They have constructed and successfully tested an operating system, Deltaflow.OS, that could serve as the beginning of a software market for quantum computers. The founder and CEO of Riverlane, Steve Brierley, sees the current state of quantum computer development as having parallels to the early days of PC development in the 1970s.[683] As primitive as early PC attempts seem now, the realization of their potential over the last forty years is enough to make one dream of the progress that could be made in quantum computing during the next few decades. Riverlane's efforts are impressive, but it remains to be seen who will take the lead and what the outcome will be.

The impact that such developments will have on the Internet will undoubtedly be huge. The speed and access of computer searches should increase exponentially. This could make vastly more information accessible to users. As stated previously, it will also make it more difficult to protect valuable and personal information from outside hacking. It could indeed be a "new world" for computer users. But whether it will be as satisfying and liberating as the present Internet is unknown.

Will Bitcoins Be Affected?

As noted in the chapter on cybercurrency, bitcoins are produced by computer calculation of complex problems. In the future could the speed of quantum computers make solving such equations so quick that there will be no value in producing cybercurrency this way?

681. Scott Aaronson, "Why Google's Quantum Supremacy Milestone Matters," *The New York Times*, online, October 30, 2019, retrieved September 3, 2020.
682. Stephen Chen, "China Launches World's Fastest Programmable Quantum Computers," *South China Morning Post*, October 26, 2021.
683. James Hurley, "Quantum Computing Is on the Cusp of Commercial Breakthrough," *The Times*, online, September 7, 2020, retrieved September 7, 2020.

Regulation of Quantum Computing

What legal and regulatory guidelines will need to be developed to keep the use of quantum computing within acceptable limits? This will require careful planning.

International and national bodies of regulators responsible for keeping the Internet free and safe will need to be discussing and planning how to put appropriate legislation in place to keep from being outrun by this game-changing new technological development. Regulators should begin talking to the scientists now and arranging for international discussions to exchange ideas and agree on protocols.

Rational control of this kind of computing tool is getting more urgent as the development of quantum computing increases in speed.

It has been reported that a group of scientists working at the Harvard—MIT Center for Ultracold Atoms has developed a new type of quantum computer called "a programmable quantum simulator." This can operate with 256 quantum bits, or "qubits." It is believed that this advance will lead to major breakthroughs in several important fields, including communications finance, material science and many other areas.[684] It would not be unrealistic to expect additional groundbreaking advances in quantum computing to happen rapidly during the next decade or so.

B THE FUTURE OF "PRIVACY"

The issues discussed above raise important questions as to how citizens' rights to privacy will be treated in the future as both computer technology and parallel software technology develop. An important issue in this area is the development and use of AI as a tool for government control.

The President of Microsoft, Brad Smith, recently raised this issue in an interview broadcast on British TV.[685] He said that if AI is not better regulated, the kind of control that was exercised in George Orwell's novel *1984* may be present in many societies within the next five years.

He called for an international effort on the part of governments around the world to put in place stricter laws to control the development and use of AI. His contents were given on this program in the context of how some countries, such as China, were using AI to keep watch on their citizens.

For example, it was claimed that China is using facial recognition and AI to know the emotions of the Muslim Uighurs.

As Smith pointed out, the current state of technology already allows governments to see everyone on the streets, including all political demonstrators in certain countries. Smith's concern about these developments was caused because both Microsoft and Amazon had reportedly started providing law enforcement agencies in the US with facial recognition products.

---

684. Juan Siliezar, "Harvard Led Physicists Take Big Step in Race to Quantum Computing," *The Harvard Gazette*, online, July 7, 2021.
685. Tom Knowles, "Microsoft Boss Warns AI May Mean Orwell's 1984 by 2024," *The Times*, online, May 27, 2021, accessed May 31, 2021.

Some governments have responded positively to these concerns. For example, the city of San Francisco has banned the use of facial recognition technology by government in the city.

In April 2021, the EU issued a report on how the twenty-seven members of the Union would be expected to use and control AI.[686] The EU followed up with a proposal for a regulation mandating harmonized rules on AI.[687]

There remains the issue in all jurisdictions of to what extent the activities of individuals on the Internet should be free of government scrutiny.

Despite the efforts of industry to sell apps and other products to protect a person's communications from being viewed by others, including government and law enforcement organizations, reports in the press have made it clear that the privacy being offered was not always as absolute as the app creators promised.

For example, in June 2021, there was a worldwide roundup of hundreds of international criminals that was made possible by the ability of law enforcement agencies to gain access to a communication that criminals believed to be impenetrably encrypted.

Criminal organizations apparently used the system to plan a variety of crimes relating to drugs, extortion, murder, and other crimes. The app used by the criminals was called ANOM. Unknown to the underworld, this app was created by the FBI and surreptitiously distributed to criminal organizations throughout the world. Criminals enthusiastically used the app leading to their arrest and the seizure of large amounts of weapons and over eight tons of cocaine.[688]

Certainly, most citizens are going to be happy at the damage done to these criminal organizations by this clever law enforcement trick. However, it does graphically demonstrate the ability of government to pry into our "secret" communications if they really want to. This does make the concept of privacy appear to be somewhat limited.

C DIGITALIZATION OF ART

When it comes to the world of electronics, the name Elon Musk keeps turning up. His interests are apparently not limited to electric cars, space exploration and computerization of the brain. Through association with his artist girlfriend, Grimes, his name has also popped up in connection with the digitalization of art.

---

686. European Commission, *A European approach to Artificial Intelligence*, "The European Commission's approach to AI centres on excellence and trust. It aims to boost research and industrial capacity and ensure fundamental rights," April 26, 2021.
687. European Commission, *Proposal for a Regulation laying down harmonized rules on artificial intelligence*, "The Commission is proposing the first ever legal framework on AI, which addresses the risks of AI and positions Europe to play a leading role globally," April 21, 2021 ("*EC, AI Regulation Proposal*").
688. "ANOM: Hundreds Arrested in Massive Global Crime Sting Using Messaging App," *BBC News*, online, June 8, 2021.

In early March 2021, it was reported in the news that Grimes had sold some pieces of her digital "crypto art" for close to $6 million. Crypto art is digital and therefore does not technically exist, at least in a physical sense.[689]

The existence of such a medium raises important questions as to how one can prove ownership of the digital art and protect it from being digitally copied or changed by hackers that may be able to gain access to the work.

The current protection for the medium is something called a "non-fungible token." This is intended to give a buyer confidence that they own the only genuine version of the artwork and identifies that version of the artwork as authentic even though it can be copied online.[690]

It is reported that a digital frame can be arranged for digital artworks so that they can be displayed at digital galleries.[691] There is a digital environment called "crypto-voxels" that purports to allow users to buy space to construct digital art galleries among other things.[692] It may be a way that crypto art will be displayed for public consumption in the future.

If one believes that Grimes was being overpaid for her nonphysical art, it should be noted that on March 11, 2021, *The New York Times* reported the outcome of an auction at Christies where a digital artwork by Mike Winkelmann sold for $69.3 million after spirited bidding in an online auction. The bidding had taken place over two weeks and started at $100. Winkelmann's work entitled "Everydays—The First 5000 Days" comprised a collage of pictures posted online each day by the artist since 2007.[693]

D SELLING OUR CLICKS

In 2020, the video streaming service, Netflix, offered a dramatized documentary entitled "The Social Dilemma," directed by Jeff Orlowski.

It featured interviews with several people who had held responsible positions with major media companies such as Facebook, Twitter and Google.

In addition, there were some dramatized scenes, presented with actors, to emphasize the points about social media the director wished to get across to his audience.

The basic conclusion of the program is that large media companies are making money from selling a new product to their advertisers.

That product is our attention. It includes the content offerings we click on and the length of time that we spend looking at them.

From selling this information, Internet companies can earn many billions of dollars. Capturing this attention from us has become their reason for being because that

689. Tom Knowles, "Buyers Splash out on Art That Doesn't Exist," *The Times*, online, March 3, 2021, accessed March 12, 2021.
690. *Id.*
691. *Id.*
692. Crytovoxels.com.
693. Scott Reyburn, "JPG File Sells for $69 Million, as 'NFT Mania' Gathers Pace," *The New York Times*, online, March 11, 2021, accessed March 12, 2021.

is how they make their money. They do not much care what sites we are clicking or what their content is if we are persuaded to click on them and remain looking at them as long as possible.

This incentive to get clicks and maintain attention on their service causes the major Internet service companies and others to devote their resources to creating algorithms that will tell them which sites or subjects of interest are most likely to cause us to click on them and to hold our attention and to repeat our visits in the future.

The way that these ISPs can accomplish this is by taking information that they collect from our visits to their site and analyzing it to tell them what we have previously used on their site most and often access. With that information, they can create an algorithm to tell them what information we are most likely to want to access and what sites we are most likely to use to provide it.

The result is that to make our use of their site as valuable as possible to their potential advertisers is to provide us with a list of sites or services that they have determined we are most likely to use whenever we come online on their site.

Consequently, although when we visit a social media site, we may think their suggestions to us are drawn from a huge selection of possible choices, in fact they have limited the choices there for us by their analysis, often by their carefully constructed algorithms, of what information we are most likely to want to seek. This is their way of assuring that we will spend the maximum amount of time on sites they have chosen for us and sites which pay them for directing our attention there which maximizes the revenue they can gain from our use of an ISP's site.

This documentary argued that if we believe that our selection of places to visit on the Internet is random or strictly guided by our own wishes, we could not be more wrong.

We are unknowingly directed to places that are carefully chosen for us by the major media companies to maximize their revenue. We are not asked how we would like the selection offered to us to be chosen. That is determined for us, based on their data about our previous usage, by the media services that we regularly use. In other words, the media companies are making every effort to nullify the possibility of our exercising free, which will to maximize their revenue from sites they wish us to visit.

So, the product these media companies are selling to maximize their revenue is us—our attention and our interest. Perhaps more worrying is the fact that, to keep us looking at the sites that are most profitable to them, they use the Internet tools at their disposal to modify our wishes and desires to align most closely with what they want us to look at. The tools they have and the techniques they use are very powerful indeed. The result is that society and human interaction in general are being reshaped by the Internet and will undoubtedly continue to be so for the foreseeable future.

Protecting Freedom of Choice

It seems the case that regulatory intervention is becoming more important to preserve the public's freedom of choice, to protect vulnerable sectors of the public from harmful content and to see that the vast revenue that is being generated from our viewing of Internet media is more fairly and beneficially distributed.

The first two goals are already being addressed by regulation. As discussed in the preceding chapters, many countries and international organizations have introduced laws and regulations to preserve access to the Internet on an equal basis, and to protect vulnerable groups such as children from harmful or unduly influential content. However, it is increasingly clear that the revenue generated from the public's attention to the Internet is being hoarded by increasingly wealthy Internet entrepreneurs.[694]

One solution is for governments to impose a "click tax" on media platforms access by the public within their jurisdiction. That would work as follows. A small amount of money would be collected from the media platform every time someone accessed their site. The basic charge would be multiplied by the amount of time the person accessing the site used that site for viewing. Even if the basic charge was tiny, billions and perhaps trillions of dollars would be earned in tax revenue which could be used to pay for a number of infrastructure, health, education, and other programs to benefit the public who are generating huge amounts of revenue for the media companies.

This tax should be paid by the tech companies from the revenue they collect from public attention to their Internet offerings.

Perhaps most worrying of all is that our dependence on the World Wide Web has become critical. Any major disruption to this form of communication interferes with our lives at nearly every level from family to leisure, to work, to medical care, to shopping. The list goes on and on. This sensitivity to the functioning of the Internet was brought home to us on June 8, 2021, when several important news and information websites went off-line, including those of *The Guardian, Financial Times, Independent* and *The New York Times* news organizations. The websites all displayed the message: "Error 503, service unavailable." It was not immediately understood what caused this disruption. Initially, it was thought that this could be related to a cloud computing provider that served many large websites.[695]

E WORLDWIDE VULNERABILITY

One issue that has come up repeatedly since the web has become such a popular method of communicating is that the worldwide connectivity that the web promotes also makes data systems vulnerable to attacks and technical faults across the world.

A significant example of this vulnerability was an Internet "black out" that occurred in July 2021.

The systems of financial institutions, transportation companies, retailers and government bodies were closed down because of a technical problem resulting from a

694. Erik Sherman, "A New Report Claims Big Tech Companies Used Legal Loopholes to Avoid over $100 Billion in Taxes. What Does That Mean for the Industry's Future?," *Fortune*, online, December 6, 2019, retrieved September 15, 2020.
695. "Major Newspaper and Government Websites Down," *BBC News*, online, June 8, 2021.

software update by a company in Massachusetts that is responsible for helping the web to run quickly and efficiently.

Apparently, the software update caused a fault that prevented important web users from having access to the Internet for approximately an hour. The systems that were affected included those of US and British governments, Amazon, PayPal, and media companies such as *The Guardian* newspaper.

Web shutdowns like this are more than just a matter of frustration with lack of service. Shutdowns on a global scale can cost Internet companies billions of dollars in lost business during the time the interruption is in effect. One reported example was that an outage, that occurred in June 2021, called the "Fastly outage" cost Amazon over $23 million in lost business.[696]

A solution for this may be for countries around the world that are affected by such outages to rise above their political differences and to agree to a covenant to cooperate in order to diminish the negative effects of such an outage as much as possible and to end it as soon as reasonably possible.

It is difficult to see how every country that uses the web could fail to benefit from such an arrangement. However, political differences may make it impossible to achieve such an agreement throughout the world. But it would still be valuable to put one in place by those countries that would agree with it.

Of course, in cases where the disruptions in question are caused by terrorist or criminal activity, it may be more difficult to deal with a major outage. However, it was stated that the July 2021 outage was not a result of terrorist activity.[697]

F FINANCIAL SERVICES LAW

There is a little question that one of the most interesting things about the development of the Internet is the amount of money involved and the fortunes being made by some of the creators of Internet-related products.

Internet users are frequently bombarded with advertisements that claim to have identified or to offer opportunities to make money by investing in "the next big thing."

Internet-related businesses certainly claim this label to include things like various forms of digital currency and Internet developments such as blockchain technology or quantum computing.

As any sophisticated person knows, it is impossible to predict the future with complete accuracy, but millions of people around the world invest money in Internet-related businesses that they hope will provide them with a significant future profit.

696. Nadia Brooks, "Airlines and Banks Hit by Web Blackout," *The Times*, online, July 23, 2021.
697. *Id.*

Regulation of Financial Services

However, it is important to understand that the marketing and sale of opportunities to invest in businesses are highly regulated throughout the world by financial services law.

This is the body of law that governs how, by whom and to whom financial products may be marketed and sold. Failure to comply with these laws and regulations can result in lawsuits, fines, being barred from certain businesses and in some cases, with imprisonment.

As the Internet proceeds into the future and more products related to its operation and use are offered for sale, it is important to understand the relationship between opportunities to make money from these developments and financial services law.

Take, for example, blockchain technology. A "blockchain" is a list of records of Internet-related transactions that are linked by application of a cryptographic code. Each new record is referred to as a "block" because its cryptographic existence prevents that transaction and previous transactions from being changed.

The transactions themselves are in relation to a digital process for "asset" of some kind. The blockchain system can be used for a digital asset that is protected by blockchain such as the bitcoin.

A bitcoin is a statement of financial value that is earned by using computer power to solve complex mathematical transactions. The process of contributing to solving the transactions and earning the statement of value that constitutes a bitcoin is known as "bitcoin mining."

It is notable that the amount of computer power that is necessary to mine a bitcoin uses a huge amount of electricity. As more transactions are conducted with respect to a particular digital asset that conforms to blockchain requirements, they form a list that is called a "blockchain." Because of the number of theoretically unchangeable blockchains that identify a particular asset, its ownership and transfer is supposed to be secure.

The creation of digital currency, the best known of which is bitcoin, and platforms for their exchange and trading was the first permanent and successful use of blockchain technology.

The second most successful, and well known, use of blockchain technology has been the emergence of Ethereum. Although Ethereum does offer a cryptocurrency in competition with bitcoin and others (ETH), it also provides a platform for other applications and services to run using chain technology. Ethereum claims that it is a:

> technology that's home to digital money, global payments and applications. The community has built a booming digital economy of bold new ways for creators to earn online and so much more it's open to everyone, wherever you are in the world—all you need is the Internet.[698]

Ethereum appears to be offering an open, Internet-based operating system on which users can create and use a variety of business platforms and assets.

698. From the Ethereum website at, ethereum.org/en/.

In 2016, another prominent player appeared on the blockchain-centered Internet scene. It is called DFinity. DFinity claimed that it intended to offer an "Internet computer" that would make it less expensive to cloud-based businesses in applications.[699]

However, DFinity did something unusual—it offered coins called "tokens" for investors to buy. Initially, the value of these tokens (known as "ICPs") in the trading market went so high that the total value of ICPs issued by DFinity was, theoretically, tens of billions of dollars. The ICP token was said to be:

> Designed to help operate a de-centralized layer of web infrastructure being built by DFinity that believers say will liberate users from reliance on companies like Amazon and Google. The technically complex network would make it easier for people to build software and publish directly to the Internet without going through the tech giants' platforms.

The market valuation of ICP tokens fell by over 90% by the beginning of September 2021. This caused a great deal of comment in the financial press and could have happened for several reasons. However, it appears that the offering of these tokens may cause DFinity some serious problems because lawsuits have been brought claiming that the offering and sale of such tokens may be in violation of US financial services laws and regulations relating to the sale of securities.

A class-action lawsuit had been filed in California in July 2021, "on behalf of all investors who purchased Internet Computer Project tokens on or after May 10, 2021."[700]

The suit claims that the tokens were sold as unregistered investments in violation of US securities laws and regulations.

Regardless of how this turns out, there was an important lesson to be learned here by Internet and other tech companies—particularly start-ups or those that are looking to raise additional capital to support or expand their business.

One thing that Internet-related businesspeople need to understand is that any financial transactions with other parties might be considered "regulated financial activity" in many jurisdictions around the world.

In fact, regulated financial activity is so heavily regulated and subject to such detailed regulated scrutiny that when an Internet business is considering financial arrangements with third parties, they should seek the advice of qualified financial regulation advisors in all jurisdictions in which they intend to do business.

One should not forget that the international reach of the Internet may involve any business being done over the Internet in financial relationships with parties in a long list of international jurisdictions, each of which will have its own financial regulators and its own set of laws, regulations and customs relating to financial relationships.

699. Gertrude Chavez-Dreyfuss, "Blockchain Project Raises $61 Million from Andreesen Horowitz, U.S. Hedge Fund," *Reuters*, online, July 2, 2018.
700. Tom Hakki, "Dfinity Faces Class-Action Lawsuit Claiming ICP Token Is Unregistered Security: Polychain, Andreesen Horowitz, and Dfinity's Founder Have Also Been Implicated in the Suit," *Decrypt*, online, July 22, 2021.

DFinity now finds itself in the position of being accused of ignoring applicable US laws and regulations with respect to offerings of its tokens. Will there be similar complaints in the many other jurisdictions where DFinity is doing business? That remains to be seen.

It is not within the scope of this book to give a complete overview of what financial regulations might apply to Internet-related business. Because of the extensive and detailed regulation of financial relationships around the world, this is a subject that occupies many entire books and multivolume encyclopedias—and even then, they do not cover all legal jurisdictions.[701]

Here is a non-exhaustive list of the kinds of financial relationships that may be considered regulated activities:

- Soliciting investment of any kind.
- Advising on investments.
- Holding anyone else's assets.
- Managing any third party's assets.
- Dealing in "financial instruments" (shares, bonds, insurance contracts, tradable contracts, options of any kind, etc.).
- Serving as an agent for financial transactions.
- Operating a market or a clearing facility for financial transactions.
- Making a market in financial instruments.
- Dealing in consumer credit.
- Etc.

Generally, throughout the world, no one can engage in "regulated activities" or purport to engage in regulated activities unless one is "authorized."

Usually, one can become an "authorized person" only with the approval of the relevant financial services regulatory authority.

Examples are the Securities and Exchange Commission (SEC) in the US or the FCA in the UK.

However, it is important to note that, because there are many kinds of "regulated activities," some countries and legal jurisdictions may have several financial services regulatory authorities. Just because one is authorized by one financial regulatory authority, that may not entitle one to engage in all regulated activities in all places.

For example, the US has several separate state and federal regulatory agencies for different kinds of regulated activities: banking, insurance, dealing in securities, commodities, derivatives, currencies, and other financial instruments, etc. One approval will not authorize dealing in all types of finance throughout the US.

Such financial regulatory complexity may exist to a greater or lesser degree in other jurisdictions. This is an important reason why any Internet-related business needs to consult competent financial services regulatory advisors in each relevant jurisdiction.

701. For example: *Encyclopedia of Financial Services Law* (London: Thompson Reuters, Sweet and Maxwell).

The necessity for getting proper advice was underlined by a headline in the *Times*, "Wild West" crypto firms told to bow to regulation.[702]

The purpose of this report was to show that there has been an apparent change of policy among the US regulatory community regarding cryptocurrency.

This was indicated by a speech given by the head of the US Securities Exchange Commission, Gary Gensler, at a financial services forum in Colorado in August 2021. He indicated there that he favored toughening up US regulation of cryptocurrency because that field was "rife with fraud, scams and abuse."[703]

His talk was not limited to ICP tokens, but he certainly mentioned them saying that they were not a currency but actually "highly speculative stores of value."

He did not criticize purchases of these tokens for wanting to speculate, but he did indicate that they should not be issued unless there was "rigorous, balanced and complete information" given to potential purchasers.

In effect, he was talking about the kind of thorough information that is required to be given to potential purchasers of regulated securities. This certainly indicates that the SEC is seriously looking at placing issuing requirements on these tokens that will give buyers a level of information reminiscent of that required to be given to securities purchasers.

In summary, it seems fair to say that tech companies that wish to raise capital to support their business will not be able to use innovative financial products, such as "tokens" to avoid regulatory scrutiny in the US, and that will probably be an attitude adopted in other jurisdictions as well.

End-to-End Encryption

Another national regulator that seems to have turned against the tech companies in early September 2021 is the Home Office of the UK, headed by Priti Patel. She reportedly wants to limit the ability of Facebook to offer end-to-end encryption on its platforms such as WhatsApp.[704]

She indicated her views by supporting a series of ads intended to encourage public opinion against Facebook's offering of end-to-end encryption. Her argument is that such encryption prevents law enforcement officials from identifying sexual abusers of children.

The ads themselves are being sponsored by a group of child protection charities. Apparently, they are concerned that Facebook has recently been aggressively promoting its intention to offer end-to-end encryption in several of its platforms. Ms. Patel,

702. *The Times*, online, September 2, 2021, *See also*, "The SEC Sets Its Sights on the Crypto 'Wild West'," *The Economist*, online, August 7, 2021.
703. It may be noted that Mr. Gensler had taught a course at MIT on cryptocurrencies only a few months before his speech in Colorado, *The Economist*, August 7, 2021.
704. Alex Hern, "Priti Patel v Facebook Is the Latest in a 30-Year Fight over Encryption," *The Guardian*, online, April 19, 2021.

along with the head of the UK National Crime Agency, has stated that Facebook's plan will make it harder to catch terrorists as well as pedophiles.[705]

This UK policy raises issues with respect to both freedom of speech and the right to privacy of users of Facebook messaging platforms that are accessible in the UK.

Freedom of speech will always be a key issue for the Internet.

705. *Id.*

Index

B

C

D

E

H

I

J

K

L

M

N

V

W